FUNDAMENTALS OF
GROUP CHILD CARE

FUNDAMENTALS OF GROUP CHILD CARE
A Textbook and Instructional Guide for Child Care Workers

JACK ADLER, ED.D., M.S.W.
Jewish Child Care Association
New York

BALLINGER PUBLISHING COMPANY
Cambridge, Massachusetts
A Subsidiary of Harper & Row, Publishers, Inc.

International Standard Book Number: 0–88410–198–3

Library of Congress Catalog Card Number: 81–3597

Printed in the United States of America

Library of Congress Cataloging in Publication Data

Adler, Jack, 1916–
  Fundamentals of group child care.

  Bibliography: p.
  Includes index.
    1. Handicapped children—Care and treatment.
  2. Handicapped children—Institution care. I. Title.
  HV888.A34 1981   362.2'088054   81–3597
  ISBN 0–88410–198–3   AACR2

DEDICATION

To Jonathan

CONTENTS

PREFACE

As a composite of content and instruction, this book is designed to serve as a basic text for child care workers in group care of children. It evolved during an extensive period of supervising and teaching child care workers in foster care agency programs and academic instruction.[a]

Part I, which deals with content, is an extensive revision and expanded version of a previous book, *The Child Care Worker: Concepts, Tasks, and Relationships* (New York: Brunner Mazel, 1976), now out of print except in a Dutch translation.[b] The sequence has been modified. Each chapter has been updated, revised and enriched with case illustrations. The new topics include: Historical Perspectives, Criteria for Placement, Theoretical Consideration and an Outline of Learning and Psychoanalytic Theories, The Abused Child,

a. Columbia School of Social Work; The Child Care Workers Training Program, School of Social Welfare, State University of New York at Stony Brook; Hawthorne Cedar Knolls of the Jewish Board of Guardians (now the Jewish Board of Family and Children's Services); the group care programs of the Jewish Child Care Association of New York, including residential treatment centers (Childville, for severely disturbed young children; Edenwald Center, for multihandicapped, mildly retarded children; Pleasantville Cottage School, for emotionally disturbed boys and girls; and Youth Residence Center, for young adults); Diagnostic Center at Pleasantville; group homes for adolescent boys and girls; and Vernondale, a community-based group home for physically handicapped children.

b. *DeGroepsopvoeder, Begrippen, Taken en Relaties.* 1980. Deventer: Van Loghum Slaterus, B.V.

Values, Alternate Approaches to Punishment, Leisure Time Activity Profile, Charting and Recording of Crises, Alcohol Abuse, Relationship Networks, Organizational Models of Residential Treatment, Communication Issues in Worker–Child Relationships, Group Cohesiveness, Group Process (in group meetings), Treatment Planning, Community Relationships, Group Homes, Evaluation and an outline for a Child Care Supervision Workshop.

Part II, the Instructional Guide, includes sections on teaching methodology. It focuses on experiential learning, instructional content and practice review exercises, paralleling the content sequence of Part I. Although this section of the book was conceived as a guide for teaching basic child care in in-service training or in academic instructional programs, it may be useful for self-instruction and peer group learning wherever formal in-service seminars or academic courses are not available. Such a course of study could be organized by first reading the topics in Part I, and then following up with the suggested exercises in Part II. Some of the exercises, involving group discussion and role playing, are not feasible for self-instruction, although they can be processed in peer-group study. The Practice Review Exercises may be useful as a study aide and for the purposes of evaluation.

The process of acquiring the necessary knowledge and skills, developing self-awareness, and integrating experience is complex and may be arduous. I hope this book facilitates this process of "becoming."

Jack Adler

ACKNOWLEDGMENTS

I wish to thank the child care workers at the Jewish Child Care Association whose insights and case examples have enriched the content of this book. I am grateful to the numerous reviewers of my first book—*The Child Care Worker: Concepts, Tasks and Relationships*—for the pertinent questions they raised in their critiques. These points served as guidelines in revising a number of the sections in this volume and in adding new topics. Thanks also to Dr. Thomas Gordon for insights on adult–child communication, to Dr. Raoul P. Nadler for the use of his formulations regarding children who become violent, to Dr. Sol Nichtern for some of the material on child and adolescent development, to Charles E. Schaeffer for his guidelines on effective use of punishment, and to Dr. William Goldfarb for his concept of corrective socialization. I reiterate my appreciation to the editors of *Child Welfare, Child Care Quarterly*, and *Journal of Jewish Communal Services* for the use of material which, in modified form, previously appeared in my articles which they published.

Sincere thanks to Barbara Blum, Commissioner, Department of Social Services of New York State, for her encouragement and valuable suggestions regarding the Instructional Guide and the original book.

I also wish to thank Celia Forman, Anita Mirenberg, and Judy Trucios for typing the manuscript.

INTRODUCTION

Group care serves children whose parents are unable to provide them with basic nurturing and developmental needs of childhood, effective controls to prevent destructive and delinquent behavior, and specialized care required by the severely disturbed, physically handicapped, and profoundly retarded. Of these families, there are some who could care for their children if there were adequate community resources to supplement inadequate income, housekeeping, and housing needs. With appropriate supportive services, many parents could also care for a physically, intellectually, or emotionally handicapped child within the family setting.

The lack or inadequacy of community-based preventive services results in inappropriate use both of group care and foster family placement. Such a misuse is costly to the public and personally costly to children and their parents because of the separation and fragmentation of family life. The problem of "too many children in care who do not belong there" will not be resolved by projecting blame on "inadequate" parents or on foster care agencies. The solution lies within the public's acceptance of the need for comprehensive preventive programs and for action by governmental legislative bodies to fund such programs. If accepted and combined with adequate diagnostic and planning services, these programs could substantially reduce placement through community-based treatment programs and family support services, and would therefore eliminate foster care as a last resort option. It would also assure selection of the most suitable type of foster care in cases where the assessment study determines that there is no alternative.

The number of children who require specialized care is increasing. The severely disturbed emotionally, the seriously handicapped physically, and the profoundly disabled developmentally cannot be provided for within a family setting, even under the best of circumstances. Many of them will require lifetime support. Others who are not so severely handicapped may require temporary or extensive residential care.

During the past several decades, children referred for placement are more severely disturbed than in the past. Changing conditions in our society, such as the strains of urban life in deteriorating neighborhoods and higher divorce rates, have contributed to family instability and disorganization. Numbers of working mothers and single-parent families have increased. Advances in medical sciences and broader distribution of medical and social services have resulted in higher survival rates among seriously handicapped children. Recent changes in hospital policies have curtailed long-term hospitalization of emotionally disturbed and mentally ill children, who are now being referred to child welfare agencies for residential treatment. The same applies to the developmentally disabled.

More effectively trained child care workers are needed to serve these severely handicapped children. The universal recognition that the child care worker is a very significant person for children in placement has to be complemented by more extensive provisions for education and in-service training. "Basic training is essential to achieve professional identification, increased resources of staff, transferability of knowledge and skill from one institution to another" (American Association for Children's Residential Centers 1972: 100).

Although advances have been made in developing educational programs for child care workers, their scope is still too modest. The increasing numbers of seriously handicapped children referred for group care require personnel who will maintain a continuous stable relationship with them. This is difficult to achieve because large numbers of workers, especially the college-educated, leave their child care jobs after relatively brief periods of tenure primarily because they view them as "dead end," with no possible realization of professional aspirations. Mattingly (1977: 88–89) points out that if child care as a developing profession "is to survive, the child care worker can no longer be considered expendable. A substantial cadre of mature workers must develop persons who combine knowledge-based practice with the refined clinical skills that come only from experience."

In contrast to a number of western European countries and Canada where professionalization of child care work was achieved decades ago, the United States is still in the thinking and planning stage. There are, however, encouraging developments. Child care diploma programs in junior colleges are increasing, and courses have been introduced on the university level. The high quality of the pioneering Child Care Worker Training Seminar and workshops sponsored by academic institutions like the University of North Carolina at Chapel Hill continue to attract large numbers of child care workers. These courses are now being duplicated in other parts of the country. Federal funds available through Title XX of the Social Security Act are supporting the development of many more educational and training resources. The growing membership of the Associations of Child Care Workers throughout the country is impressive. Their organizational efforts to certify child care workers, the high-quality, professional conferences they sponsor periodically, the literature they disseminate, and the training programs they support all further the effort.[a]

From a modest beginning several decades ago, a body of knowledge has developed and has appeared in print at an increasing rate. Books and articles published in journals such as the *Child Care Quarterly* make available instructional materials for educational and in-service training programs.

During the twenty-five years of our experience in group care and treatment of children and adolescents, we have nurtured the belief that the body of generic knowledge and skills inherent in child care can be conceptualized and, in organized form, taught to child care workers. Supporting this conviction are the writings of such distinguished practitioners, researchers, and educators as Herschel Alt, Jerome Beker, Bruno Bettelheim, Eva Burmeister, Hyman Grossbard, Morris F. Mayer, Howard Polsky, Fritz Redl, Albert Treischman, Karen Vanderven, James Whittaker, and others.

---

a. For a comprehensive statement regarding the professionalization of child care, see Beker (1979).

The role of the child care worker is affected by the dominant treatment philosophy of the institution where he or she[b] is employed. The psychoanalytic model strives for changes in personality within the child; the educative approach utilizes behavior modification techniques and learning reinforcement to achieve changes in specific maladaptive behavior; the existential model relies on group process and student government; the medical model concentrates on medication and psychotherapy; the family model replicates the child's family experience (American Association for Children's Residential Centers 1972). These various approaches may affect the child care worker's "method" of relating to the children but not the "substance" of his tasks, which derive from care of children during the twenty-four hour spectrum of daily living. The tasks include supervising daily activities from waking to bedtime, developing relationships with individual children and groups, recording observations, and consulting with other staff. The knowledge and skills associated with these responsibilities have to be made available to every child care worker through in-service training seminars and supervision.

This book addresses itself directly to child care workers regarding the fundamental issues involved in group care. We believe that with minor adaptations, it can be oriented toward practice in agencies of diverse theoretical and treatment approaches. Although the content reflects the author's orientation toward psychodynamic psychology and social system theories which view the child as the product of biological endowment and environmental nurture, it is not insensitive to the contribution of learning theory and the validity of other methodologies. The child, representing a whole being, is the focus of concern. He must be viewed as an individual, as a member of a peer group, and as part of a family from which he is temporarily separated, and with ties to a community to which he will most likely return. Children's and family needs should take precedence over the prescriptions of a particular theory or treatment methodology.

---

b. *He* rather than *she* or *he/she* throughout the book is used as the generic designation of a person, third person singular, for both female and male workers and children of both genders. This conforms with long established usage and does not imply gender favoritism. Women child care workers have historically made an important contribution to the field of foster care and to children in group care.

REFERENCES

American Association for Children's Residential Centers. 1972. *From Chaos to Order—A Collective View of the Residential Treatment of Children.* New York: Child Welfare League of America.

Beker, J. 1979. "Training and Professional Development in Child Care." In *Caring for Troubled Children,* edited by J.K. Whittaker, pp. 205–230. San Francisco: Jossey–Bass.

Mattingly, M.A. 1977. Symposium: "Stress and Burn-Out in Child Care." *Child Care Quarterly* 6: 88–89.

CONTENT

1 HISTORICAL PERSPECTIVES

Group care of children has a long history. The first shelters for the sick and indigent established by the Catholic Church in the fourth century also cared for abandoned children. Although a small number of children's institutions existed during the Middle Ages, the prevalent pattern of care was within the adult asylums. In England, the Elizabethan Law of 1601 was the first law to assign public responsibility for needy children through placement in alms houses and through indenture. These, respectively, may be considered the precursors of child care institutions and foster family care. Indenture provided for the apprenticing of poor, orphaned, or illegitimate children with master craftsmen. In return for food, board, and training in a craft, these children served the family until they were deemed ready to be independent craftsmen. Child care in mixed almhouses continued in Europe and America until the end of the nineteenth century. Between 1860 and 1900 state laws abolished almhouses in the United States and orphan asylums arose in their stead. Established by private philanthropy, church groups, and local governments, these institutions served orphaned as well as indigent children whose parents could not care for them. The institutional program focused on regimented group living, with emphasis on obedience, learning, and moral and religious training. Daily living was a strict routine. Children's contacts with their families were not encouraged.

In 1923, there were 1,558 orphan asylums in the United States. By this time, the "golden era" of the asylum, with its numerous large buildings and impressive architecture, was on the wane. Asylums were criticized for being authoritarian and impersonal. Some sectors of public opinion advocated their extinction and their replacement by foster family care.

Following the White House Conference of 1909 which recommended foster family care as the most desirable substitute, a number of the large urban orphanages were replaced by "cottage-type" institutions located in suburban communities. The growth of foster family programs was also accelerated. From 1911 to 1942, the number of children in foster home care increased from 8 percent to 49 percent; institutional care decreased from 69 percent to 42 percent.

After World War II, residential treatment centers were developed to care for emotionally disturbed children who could not be adequately served in foster homes or in the large congregate institutions for dependent and neglected children. The growing influence of psychoanalytic theory in the United States and the pioneering work of Bruno Bettelheim and Fritz Redl fostered the growth of residential treatment centers which integrated "milieu therapy" and clinical services for the treatment of the emotionally disturbed and multiply handicapped child. Group residences and group homes were a further refinement, first established to meet after-care needs of children discharged from institutions. During the early 1970s, there was a phenomenal growth of group homes as a consequence of deinstitutionalization in the mental health and child welfare sectors of group care. The most recent development in group care is "part-placement," which makes it possible for children either to remain with their families as in family day care and day treatment or to be closely associated with their families through five-day residential care. These programs also encourage greater family participation in the child's treatment.

According to Keith–Lucas and Sanford, children's institutions, other than residential treatment centers for the severely emotionally disturbed, and in the process of developing into "family-oriented children's homes." Here, "placement . . . is an element of a plan in which the family is given an opportunity to make a new start in its relationships" (Keith–Lucas and Sanford 1977: 13). The agency does not replace the family in caring for the child; instead, both agency and family become "co-planners" to meet the child's needs as well as the needs of the family during the period of separation. The specific goal is reuniting child and family as soon as possible.

As indicated, psychoanalytic theory was the initial influence in residential treatment of emotionally disturbed children. It emphasized the importance of a "therapeutic milieu" based on psychoanalytic concepts and gave primacy to the role of the clinician. This dominance ended in the 1960s with the introduction of behavior modification and educational approaches into group care programs. Among these were Achievement Place, a community-based treatment home for delinquent youth in Kansas (Phillips et al. 1973); The Children's Center in Madison, Wisconsin (Browning and Stower 1971); Project Re-Ed in Tennessee and North Carolina (Hobbs 1974); and Positive Peer Culture (Vorrath and Brendtro 1974). Project Re-Ed, based on learning theory and reinforcement of "normal," socially adaptive behavior, emphasizes the teaching of competence in all aspects of a child's growth and development. Positive Peer Culture is based on modified group guidance interaction techniques which focus on the role of the peer group in affecting positive change in its members' attitudes and behavior.

SCOPE OF GROUP CARE

The scope of group care for children in the United States is not precise because current statistical information is incomplete. The most accurate source—the Pappenfort, Kilpatrick, and Kuby study of children's residential institutions in the U.S.A.—is fourteen years old. According to their census, 155,905 children were living in 2,318 group care facilities in 1966; 60,459 were residents in 955 facilities for neglected and dependent children; 13,876 were in residential treatment centers for emotionally disturbed children (Mayer, Richman, and Balcerzak 1977). Leverington's recent figure of 247,234 children in institutions is quoted by the Child Welfare League of America (1978). A study by The Office of Human Development (1977) estimated that 400,000 children annually require residential care in institutions and group homes. This number is based on the Pappenfort study plus the Children's Bureau estimates of children in non-enumerated institutions (group homes, training schools for delinquents, institutions for mentally retarded, and other psychiatric facilities for children). According to the same document, there are currently 150,000 child care workers.

At the end of March 1977, public agencies were providing social services to 1.8 million children, or 27 of every 1,000 children under 18 years of age in the United States. Two-thirds of these children were living with parents or relatives; over half a million were in foster care. The percentage of children in foster care decreased from 47 percent in 1961 to 28 percent in 1977. The main component of the foster care population—children in foster family homes—dropped from 35 percent to 22 percent. The decline in the institutional segment was even steeper, from 12 percent to 4 percent. This decline in the percentage of children in foster care should not be confused with a decrease in actual numbers. The 28 percent in foster care in 1977 represented 503,000 children, nearly three times the number in foster care under the supervision of public agencies in 1961: 395,000 in foster family homes and 108,000 in group care (group homes, residential treatment centers, and institutions) (Shyne and Schroeder 1978).

REFERENCES

Browning, R.M., and D.O. Stover. 1971. *Behavior Modification in Child Treatment*. Chicago: Aldine.

Child Welfare League of America. 1978. *CWLA Newsletter* 8, no. 4 (July–October): 2.

Hobbs, N. 1974. "Helping Disturbed Children: Psychological and Ecological Strategies," in *Effective Group Care*, edited by M. Wolins. Chicago: Aldine.

Keith-Lucas, A. and C.W. Sanford. 1977. *Group Child Care as a Family Service*. Chapel Hill: University of North Carolina Press.

Mayer, F.M.; L.H. Richman; and E.A. Balcerzak. 1977. *Group Care of Children*. New York: Child Welfare League of America.

Office of Human Development. 1977. *Request for Proposal #105-77-1032*. Washington, D.C.: Dept. of Health, Education and Welfare.

Phillips, E.L., et al. 1973. "Achievement Place Behavior Shaping Works for Delinquents." *Psychology Today* 1: 74-80.

Shyne, A.W., and A.G. Schroeder. 1978. *National Study of Social Services to Children and Their Families: Overview*, pp. 1 and 8. Washington, D.C.: U.S. Children's Bureau.

Vorrath, H.H., and L.K. Brendtro. 1974. *Positive Peer Culture*. Chicago: Aldine.

2 CRITERIA FOR PLACEMENT IN GROUP CARE FACILITIES

Children are placed because of parental incapacities or child-related problems, including parent–child conflicts which cannot be resolved by out-patient, community-based services. Relatively few children are in placement because of the death of both parents. Parent-related problems include physical or emotional illness, drug/alcohol addiction, child neglect and abuse, parental unwillingness to care for a child, abandonment, or desertion. Child-centered problems include severe emotional difficulties, mental retardation, physical handicap, "incorrigible" behavior beyond control by parents, and delinquency. The majority of children are placed because of parental problems. For example, during 1976, 80 percent of almost 30,000 children in foster care in New York City were placed because of parent-related difficulties (Bernstein 1975).

The decision to place a child should not be made without a thorough study of alternatives. Yet children are in placement because of "predilections of individual workers and agencies" (Phillips, Haring, and Shyne 1972) or because there are insufficient supportive community services to enable parents to maintain their families intact. It has been estimated, for example, that about 4,000 children in placement in New York City in 1975 could have been maintained in their own homes if supportive services had been available: for example, homemaker services, housing assistance, caseworkers, and services involving child guidance, day care, day treatment, special education, and drug rehabilitation (Bernstein 1975).

Once a decision to place has been made, the appropriate type of foster care should be considered. Temporary placement may be a prior step because of a family emergency, child abuse, or severe neglect, and where there is need for observation and assessment in a diagnostic or other type of temporary group facility.

Criteria

There are two types of group care facilities—the group home and the institution (Mayer et al. 1977).

Group homes include the following:

1. **Family group home** (or agency-operated boarding home). This is basically an extended foster home where the foster parents are employees of an agency caring for a group of four to six children on a board rate or service-fee basis in a home owned or rented by the agency. It is appropriate for a child who can profit from living in a family-type atmosphere but rejects living with a substitute (foster) family, and who is capable of attending a community school and utilizing community resources.

2. **(Peer) group home.** This home is owned or rented by an agency and staffed by child care workers, serving a group of seven to twelve children. It is appropriate for children of school age or older who can be maintained in the community with access to schools, recreation, neighborhood, and relatives; for children with intense emotional ties to their own parents which preclude their acceptance or adjustment in a foster family; and for children with emotional, intellectual, and physical handicaps which require specialized professional help not available in a foster home.

3. **Group residences.** These care for larger numbers of children than group homes. Anywhere from thirteen to twenty-five adolescents are served who can attend community schools or who are able to work, but require a supervised living situation and specialized professional services. They may also serve younger children who require greater specialized care and clinical services than are possible in group homes.

Institutions consist of one or more buildings, especially constructed to care for groups of children who cannot live with their families or adapt to the requirements of community living. There are three types of institutions:

1. The **General institution** (Sister Mary Paul 1975) or the **Child care center** (classified by Mayer et al. 1977: 53). This type serves twenty-five or more children whose homes are unavailable because of parental problems and who are considered "dependent or neglected." They live in cottage or dormitory groups under the supervision of child care workers, and attend community schools. A professional staff of caseworkers and part-time psychologists and psychiatrists are available to serve the children and their parents. Currently there is a trend to replace these centers with smaller group care units, including group homes, group residences, or specialized residential treatment centers.

2. **Residential treatment center.** Two types are distinguished, which Sister Mary Paul classifies as "Type A" and "B" and which Mayer and others call the "Children's Service Center" and "Child Therapy Centers," respectively.

The Children's Service Center addresses serious behavior problems, manifested by the child's impulsivity, impaired socialization, and deviant behavior; such children require strong patterning of behavior and relationships. Group living is structured; corrective socialization is stressed in cottage living, school, and recreation programs. Service is provided by multidisciplinary teams consisting of child care, clinical, educational, medical, recreational, and social work staffs. Children are expected to take care of their personal hygiene, grooming, and chores, and to participate in group activities. These expectations help the children view themselves in relation to reality. According to Mayer and others (1977: 60), disturbed children who cannot cope with the expectations of this type of program are at a disadvantage because their failure to live up to the expected behavior may reinforce their sense of inadequacy.

The Child Therapy Center (or Type B residence) serves severely disturbed children who require twenty-four-hour supervision and a high child–staff ratio. Unlike the Children's Service Center, the Child Therapy Center does not have the initial expectation that the children function within a framework of "normal" behavior. This is a goal to be achieved. Clinical services play an important role in the treatment program, with individual and group therapy for the children and their parents generally playing a part. Although the program is highly individualized, group living is the major form of social interaction, with emphasis on corrective socialization.

REFERENCES

Bernstein, B., et al. 1975. *A Preliminary Report—Foster Care Needs and Alternatives to Placement. A Projection 1975–85.* New York: State Dept. of Social Welfare.

Mayer, F.M.; L.H. Richman; and E.A. Balcerzak. 1977. *Group Care of Children.* New York: Child Welfare League of America.

Philips, M.H.; B.L. Haring; and A.W. Shyne. 1972. *A Model for Intake Decisions.* New York: Child Welfare League of America.

Sister Mary Paul. 1975. *Criteria for Foster Placement and Alternatives to Foster Care.* New York: State Board of Social Welfare.

3 THEORETICAL CONSIDERATIONS

There is as yet no unified theory of group care. Furthermore, it is doubtful whether there will be one in the foreseeable future. Whittaker's point of view seems realistic and constructive:

> Rather than continuing a search for an encompassing theory of milieu treatment, we should accept the fact that theory development will proceed slowly through a series of experiments and program demonstrations in which the wisdom of clinical practice and the knowledge from clinical research and theory are tested against the real-life problems of children and families in need of care. We must therefore guard against overreliance on a single body of theory, even though there is a need for coherence and a value in commonly held precepts. [Whittaker 1979: 13).

No single theory dominates the field of residential treatment today. Although psychoanalytic theory was the initial influence, learning theory and other educational approaches have assumed a significant role in recent years. These two theories and the treatment modalities they represent—psychotherapy and behavior modification—continue to exert a predominant influence in current group care programs; therefore, child care workers should be familiar with their concepts and terminology.

LEARNING THEORY AND
BEHAVIOR MODIFICATION

Behavior modification, based on principles of learning theory, has as its basic tenet that most behavior—adaptive as well as maladaptive patterns—is learned. Undesirable behavior can be unlearned, and more acceptable new patterns of behavior, learned. Behavior modification includes a number of techniques based on operant conditioning principles. Among these are:

1. **Positive Reinforcement.** The individual learns to react in a certain way if he finds that his response is followed by a gratifying consequence or a reward. Positive reinforcement increases the probability that the rewarded behavior will be repeated. When a particular behavior is followed by a painful or unpleasant consequence, that behavior will tend not to be repeated. There are two major categories of reinforcers: (a) *social reinforcers*, personal responses of other people to a behavior, which may range from praise, approval, and rewards to deprivation, scolding, or other types of punishments; and (b) *Artificial reinforcers*, which include gifts, food, cigarettes, tokens, or money.

In a positive reinforcement program, rewards are given consistently. They may be given immediately after the desired behavior has been performed or at specified times. These procedures are called *schedules of reinforcement.* Thus, in training a child to use a fork rather than his fingers while eating, he is praised or given a material reward every time he uses a fork instead of his fingers. Once he begins to use it without being reminded, the reward is given every second or third time. When the desired change is maintained without having to remind the child, he is given rewards occasionally, then not at all when the desired behavior has been thoroughly learned. Initially, the child is on a continuous schedule of reinforcement; later, on what is called an intermittent schedule of reinforcement.

In some residential settings, "token economy" programs are in use for cottage groups or group homes or the institution as a whole (Pizzat 1973). Every child is given a card listing behaviors to be modified. Throughout the day, staff members mark the cards with a plus (+) if a designated (target) behavior was satisfactorily completed or a zero (0) when the child did not comply or "weakened" the target behavior. At the end of each day, a child care worker acting as the "banker" adds up the pluses and zeros and gives each child a receipt for the total number of pluses earned. The pluses can be exchanged for candy, toys, grooming items, etc. The child who gets zeros must explain the reason to his child care worker. An alternative format involves the giving of chips for conformity to expected or desirable behavior (Klein 1975).

In some behavior modification programs, a child is expected to move through several levels of increasing expectations. On admission, a child starts on Level I which involves adherence to minimal responsibilities. Throughout designated periods of the day (in group living, school, or recreation), various staff members observe him and award points for meeting expected behavior in relation to self-care, group chores, cooperativeness, classroom activity, etc. Points earned are posted enabling staff and children to chart performance. The total scores earned by each child in the group are announced and discussed in weekly group meetings. Generally, points earned are not rewarded materially as in a token economy program. Instead, a child who has satisfactorily earned a specified number of points is moved to the next level of achievement.

Level II extends responsibilities as well as privileges. These may include off-grounds trips, participation in paid work programs, a later bedtime, or additional free time. When the child moves on to Level III, the range of privileges is increased. He is considered to be more responsible and capable of greater self-direction. When the child satisfactorily completes Level III, he is promoted to Level IV which represents completion of the behavior modification program. He is considered capable of functioning independently with only minor supervision and guidance by staff.

The following steps are involved in the application of positive reinforcement:

- *Definition of the "target" behavior.* The behavior to be developed must be precisely defined so that the occasion for reinforcement is clear to everyone involved in the procedure, and changes in the frequency of the occurrence can be monitored. Ongoing observation and recording of the behavior are an integral part of the process. Initially, *baseline data* are collected. This involves counting how frequently the behavior in question occurs under ordinary conditions in a given period of time.

- *Designation of the positive reinforcers.* These may be material objects, praise, or granting of specific privileges which will be utilized to bring about change in the target behavior.

- *Arrangement of conditions.* The purpose of this step would be to enhance the tendency to bring about the desired change in the target behavior. Giving instructions, demonstrations, and employing other types of behavior modification procedures are included here.

- *Establishment of schedules.* When the desired behavior occurs, it has to be strengthened through appropriate reinforcement schedules. The behavior is likely to occur more frequently when followed immediately by a reinforcer. Later on the intermittent use of reinforcers should reduce the likelihood of the disappearance of the behavior when the controls maintained during the behavior modification period are removed.

- *Evaluation.* By means of charting procedures, the changes that have occurred in the (child's) behavior can be plotted.

2. **Shaping.** This is a process used in establishing more complex behavior patterns by breaking a behavior pattern into smaller units and reinforcing each unit in turn until the desired pattern is established.

3. **Modeling.** This is the process by which the child or person imitates a model who is displaying the desired behavior pattern. For example, a child care worker may demonstrate to a hypersensitive child through role-playing exercises how to cope with provocations from other children in order to avoid triggering a temper outburst.

4. **Other forms.** There are other forms of behavior modification therapies generally not practiced in residential programs for children. These include *aversive procedures* utilizing negative or punitive reinforcements such as *implosion* or *flooding* which involves a number of procedures to expose a person to a feared or phobic situation. "Emotional flooding" is when the implosion consists of exposing the person in imagined phobic situations. "Flooding in reality" is when the person is helped to confront the actual feared situation. *Systematic desensitization* is the most gradual method.

According to Agras (1972: 11), the major difference between insight-oriented psychotherapies and behavior modification therapies "is that the former aims first to change attitudes and feelings as expressed in a verabal interchange, expecting like behavior to change later, while the latter first changes behavior expecting the attitudes and feelings to follow." A controversial issue between proponents of behavior modification therapy and psychoanalytic psychotherapies is the importance of the relationship between therapist and patient. The clinical groups view it as essential in effecting outcome. The extremes among behavior modification practitioners minimize its importance. Their primary concern is with observable behavior and techniques aimed at modifying or eliminating this maladaptive behavior. However, other learning theorists and practitioners like Agras consider the relationship variable important. Schwartz and Goldiamond maintain that behavior modification therapy approaches "take place within the context of interpersonal relationships" (Schwartz and Goldiamond 1975: 15).

PSYCHOANALYTIC THEORY

In contrast to behavior modification methods which aim at elimination of deviant behavior directly, the psychotherapies focus on achievement of "insight" or intellectual and emotional understanding of deviant or symptomatic behavior. Once this is achieved, the symptoms or maladaptive behavior would be controlled, if not eliminated altogether. Behavior is viewed as more complex than it appears and motivated by unconscious forces. It comes to expression through the impact of unconscious wishes on a given reality. Psychoanalytic-oriented psychotherapies are based on Freudian psychoanalytic principles.

According to Freud, the personality is made up of three major interacting systems—the id, the ego, and the superego. The *id* represents the inner world of subjective experience and has no knowledge of objective reality. It derives its energy from bodily processes. It cannot tolerate states of tension produced by external or internal stimuli. The *id* has two processes at its command to reduce tension: the *reflex actions* which are inborn, and the *primary thought process* which discharges tension by forming an image of an object that will remove the tension. Early childhood thought processes, dreams, and hallucinations are examples of the latter process.

Since the primary process by itself cannot reduce the pain caused by the accumulated tension, a new or secondary psychological process develops. This becomes the second system of the personality organization known as the *ego*. The ego becomes the intermediary between inner needs and outer reality—the mediator between instinct and environment. It follows the "reality principle" and operates by means of the *secondary thought process*, or realistic thinking. The aim of the reality principle is to prevent the discharge of tension until an object which is appropriate for the satisfaction of the need has been identified.

The third system of the personality is the *superego*, the internal representative of the values and ideals of society which the child learns from the adults around him, especially his parents. Violation of superego or "conscience" requirements is experienced as guilt and anxiety.

The personality is formed during the psychosexual stages of development, designated in terms of erogenous body zones (mouth, anus, and genitals) which are responsive to erotic, pleasurable arousal when stimulated. The first is the *oral* stage (first year), the *anal* (second to fourth year), and the *phallic* or genital (fourth to fifth year). The auto-erotic activity involving the genitals results in the appearance of the oedipus complex. This implies a sexual attachment to the parent of the opposite sex, and a sense of hostility for the parent of the same sex, who is considered a competitor. Thus, the boy wants to possess his mother and get rid of his father, and the girl wants to possess her father and displace her mother. The fear of parental retaliation gives rise to "castration" anxiety which induces repression of the sexual desire toward the parent of the opposite sex and (normally) the resolution of the conflict through identification with the parent of the same sex. This continues to be a controversial concept within the psychoanalytic movement itself. During the pregenital stages, the individual obtains gratification primarily from stimulation of his own body. In the ensuing genital stage, this self-love or narcissism becomes channelled to objects outside the self.

If a child's physical and emotional needs are inadequately met during the various stages of development, there may be partial or permanent fixation of the energy associated with that phase of development. These become part of the developing personality, interfering with mature functioning. As an adult, the person may show vestiges of the oral period such as passive dependent traits, overeating, greediness, and excessive argumentativeness. In relation to the anal period, there may be development of obsessive compulsive characteristics such as obstinacy, withholding, stinginess, and excessive cleanliness and orderliness.

Freud described three types of anxiety: *reality* anxiety, which represents a fear of real danger in the external world; *neurotic* anxiety, which is the fear that the instincts will get out of control and cause the person to do something for which he will be punished; and *moral* anxiety associated with fear of the conscience and experienced as *guilt.* Under the pressure of excessive anxiety, the ego develops *defense mechanisms* which operate unconsciously so that the person is not aware of what is taking place. They tend to deny, falsify, or distort reality. Personality disorders can develop because of misuse of defense mechanisms.

The child care worker in psychoanalytically oriented settings should be acquainted with commonly used terminology. Among these are:

- *The unconscious*—Defined as that part of the psyche or mental functioning, the content of which is not, or is very rarely, subject to awareness.

- *Dynamics*—Human needs expressed through behavior that is purposive and motivated by conscious and unconscious factors.

- *Psychic determinism*—Every mental event, like every physical event, has determinant causes even though at a particular point we may not be in a position to explain them. Behavior is not simply spontaneous but has a cause and an origin which we must strive to discover.

- *Genetics*—Behavior has a history. The importance of the early years in the development of the personality is the essence of this concept. To understand the individual and what he is at the moment, one must have an understanding of his life's experiences.

- *Ambivalence*—The coexistence of opposite emotions, attitudes, or wishes toward the same person or situation: for example, love and hate.

- *Transference*—The unconscious transfer to others of feelings and attitudes which were originally experienced in relation to significant persons in one's early life such as parents and siblings.

- *Defense mechanisms*—These unconscious processes which are employed as protection from excessive anxiety generated by emotional conflict may be classified into three broad categories: (a) *aggressive reactions* such as displacements; (b) *withdrawal reactions* such as regression, repression, and denial; and (c) *comprom-*

ise reactions which include compensation, intellectualization, isolation, projection, rationalization, sublimation, and undoing.

The defense mechanisms are defined as follows:

- *Compensation*—the individual attempts to make up for real or fancied deficiencies.
- *Denial*—exclusion from consciousness of a feeling, thought, wish, need, or external reality which is consciously intolerable.
- *Displacement*—an emotion transferred from its original object to a more acceptable substitute. For example, if a child is angry with a parent, he'll strike another child because it is safer to do so.
- *Intellectualization*—reasoning used as a defense against the confrontation with an unconscious conflict. There is overemphasis on ideational content, often unrelated to the impulse.
- *Isolation*—an unacceptable impulse, idea, thought, or act separated from its original memory source, removing the emotion associated with the original memory from consciousness.
- *Projection*—a personal wish or impulse attributed to some other person or object because it is emotionally unacceptable to the self.
- *Rationalization*—a tendency to explain away impulses. A particular act or thought is attributed to a motive different from the one which is actually responsible for the act.
- *Regression*—a partial symbolic return to more infantile patterns of reacting.
- *Repression*—unacceptable ideas or wishes, memories, feelings, or impulses barred from consciousness. Repressed material may emerge in a disguised form. It reduces the effectiveness of the ego because it requires expenditures of psychic energy to keep the repressed from entering consciousness.
- *Sublimation*—instinctual drives unconsciously unacceptable, diverted into personally satisfying, socially acceptable channels of expression.
- *Undoing*—striving to disprove or undo harm which the individual unconsciously imagines or consciously perceives. It may be expressed in ritualistic behavior.

Among the other terms which should also be assimilated are: *acting-out*, defined as "inappropriate" activity which "results when impulses, wishes and fantasies which strive for expression are frustrated and cannot work their way through the usual channels— namely reflective thought, speech, judgment or goal directed constructive activity" (Frosch 1977). Acting-out is basically a "substitute" action and an immature attempt at resolving a conflict. It should not be confused with *antisocial* behavior which is delinquent or socially unacceptable nor with *impulsive* behavior which is "generally unpremeditated welling up of a drive toward some action that usually has the qualities of hastiness, lack of deliberation and impetuosity" (Frosch 1977).

Impulsive acts are direct expressions of a particular drive or inner urge. If anger results in aggressive urges and if the tension is great enough, it may result in a violent outburst; if the drive is sexual, it results in sexual activity. When expressed, the action is experienced as pleasurable, even though afterwards it may be regretted because it hurt someone.

Disorders associated with lack of impulse control include *symptom disorders* and *impulse-ridden character disorders*. Thus a person in the first group (symptom disorders) gets angry because he cannot control his impulse to express his anger in a direct aggressive action. When he has an impulse to steal or set fires, he will do so; when sexually aroused, he will act to satisfy the urge. In the case of the character disorder, the impulsiveness permeates the total personality. Such people are generally immature, have a low frustration tolerance, and tend to react explosively when frustrated or deprived.

REFERENCES

Agras, S.W., ed. 1972. *Behavior Modification: Principals and Clinical Applications.* Boston: Little Brown and Co.

Frosch, J. 1977. "Relation Between Acting Out and Disorders of Impulse Control." *Psychiatry* 40 (November): 295–296.

Klein, A.F. 1975. *The Professional Child Care Worker.* New York: Association Press.

Pizzat, F.J. 1973. *Behavior Modification in Residential Treatment for Children.* New York: Behavioral Publications.

Schwartz, A., and I. Goldiamond. 1975. *Social Casework: A Behavioral Approach.* New York: Columbia University Press.

Whittaker, J.K. 1979. *Caring for Troubled Children.* San Francisco: Jossey-Bass.

4 CHILD DEVELOPMENT

Being knowledgeable about normal child development is helpful to child care workers because it provides a point of reference to judge deviations from what is, in our society, considered as "normal" and "healthy." The term normal does not mean average or sameness since the developmental stages of childhood involve innumerable nuances and combinations of biological, cultural, and social variables. Normal does imply growth unhampered by physical, emotional, and cognitive handicaps.

From the moment of birth, the human organism with its innate genetic endowment and physiological structure, begins a lifelong interaction with environmental forces that affect it. According to Nichtern (1974: 87).

> All behavior is developmentally determined so that it is sequential and identifiable with the stages of life. The early reflex movements become the exploratory movements of the infant, become the purposeful movements of the young child, become the play movements of the older child, become the expressive movements of the adolescent, become the work movements of the adult. Stages of life are established arbitrarily by the process of selection and grouping of behavioral characteristics, and by the dominance of some features over others . . . each of these stages has behavior and communication that distinguishes it from others.

The unfolding of the child's biological potential is determined by the quality of the nurture he is given and the persons who provide it. In our culture, a loving, secure family environment seems to be the most desirable setting. However, even in our materially affluent society, there are many children who have not had the benefit of growing up in physically comfortable, economically secure homes. There are parents so harassed by environmental pressures that they are unable to provide the nurture and supports their children require for healthy, mature development. Many children are being reared in single-parent families whose mothers have to work; others live in pathologically disorganized families. There are a large number of children of economically poor families who cannot enjoy opportunities for extended play and education because they have had to assume adult responsibilities when still young. Because their mothers had to work, they had to care for themselves or for younger siblings at an early age. To supplement family income, many had to work at a time when their more affluent peers enjoyed the luxury of extended economic dependency. Historically, this has been the prevalent condition of minority group children in America, especially among the black and Hispanic population. Comer and Poussaint (1975: 20) state:

> Black children . . . have often assumed the burdens of adulthood at a far too early age. Many have had little of what we call a childhood. In the black world, adolescence starts early in life, and unlike most white youngsters, many black children do not enjoy the luxury of playtime and learning which extends into their late teens.

These children have carried the burden of growing up poor as well as black.

These factors must be taken into consideration in evaluating a child's development from infancy through adolescence. Deviations from societal norms as represented by the following outline of so-called normal child development may be due to these external, societal conditions. This should not detract from the efficacy of a standard predicated on the existence of a family environment in which sound nature (the child's innate endowments) interacts with sustaining nurture of parenting. Since the outline describes physical, social, and psychological characteristics during the various stages of childhood, it provides a structure for judging maturational levels.

A framework of developmental theory is also important because it may be helpful in clarifying why a child may not function at an age-appropriate level.

The objectives of this book limit exposition of the wide scope of developmental theories formulated by Freud, Piaget, Erikson, Maslow, and other investigators. We shall limit ourselves to a summation of Erik Erikson's theory of developmental stages which focuses on basic human needs during the life span (1956). Only the first five of the eight stages will be referred to since our concern is with infancy, childhood, and adolescence. Each stage has a theme or a critical set of tasks to be resolved by the child to enable him to move successfully to the next stage of development. If certain of his needs are met by his environment, he can develop successfully. If not adequately met, his capacity to cope with the developmental tasks of the subsequent stage(s) of growth is affected.

INFANCY

During the first half year of life, the infant's muscular, neurological, and sensory development accelerates his capacities to move his body, to sharpen his senses, and to react emotionally. He is able to turn his body, to sit and stand up when held, to see, hear, smell, touch, and express anxiety when separated from his mother. He begins to experiment with people and objects so that by nine months, he is responsive to being left alone or to the absence of a familiar toy. He seems to find comfort in the familiar, clings to his mother, and is shy with strangers.

The infant is totally dependent on others to meet his physical needs of nurture, warmth, and body care. He experiences discomfort when he is hungry, wet, or in pain. He voices his demands by crying. His first and primary social contact is his mother (or a substitute mothering person) who satisfies his basic needs. When these are provided in a way that makes the child comfortable and secure, he begins to develop a sense of trust in the giving person. Erik Erikson named this phase of life as *Trust vs. Mistrust.* Its theme or main task relates to the infant's establishment of a sense of basic trust in the world around him. Erikson maintains that the successful resolution of this fundamental crisis depends on consistent and loving care by a mother. This enables the infant to face his need sensations with a feeling of comfort and security and assurance that they will be provided as needed. If these needs are not satisfied, are partially or inadequately met, or are offered hastily or angrily, the infant begins to feel anxious and fearful of new experiences and develops a sense of mistrust. This process does not occur consciously. According to Erikson, this initial period of life determines whether an individual's basic feelings toward himself and others will be characterized by basic trust or basic mistrust.

By the end of the first year, the infant has begun to crawl or creep about, can stand alone, and perhaps take a few steps. He likes to manipulate toys and utensils. Speech begins to emerge, and he seems to respond to words like "yes" and "no." Eating and elimination as well as waking and sleeping become regulated. Between eighteen and twenty-four months, the infant may walk by himself and push moveable objects. He intensifies his explorations, understands verbal instructions, begins to use a few words, and responds cooperatively to the routines of eating, dressing, and toilet training. His behavior reflects his self-awareness, his need for his parents, and increasing curiosity which is satisfied through his explorations.

During the second year, as the child begins to show independence and initiative, he confronts adult controls and demands. Erikson refers to this phase of development as *Autonomy vs. Shame.* The critical task for the child is to develop a sense of autonomy and willpower. As a consequence of physiological growth, he is now capable of doing things for himself—to experiment, to explore, and to make choices. When he exercises these capacities, he discovers the word "no" or the phrase "you must not." Thus, he becomes conscious of the will of others. In such areas as feeding or bowel control, the child becomes aware of his own power to eat or not to eat, to determine whether he will hold on to his stools or not. This may bring him into conflict with his mother. Depending on his feelings toward her, he may refuse to eat or spit out the food she forces on him. He may time his bowel movements to please her or withhold them to punish her. He must learn to make choices. During this process, which for some children may be a painful experience when it involves a power struggle between child and parent, the child becomes aware of his limitations and weaknesses and the power of adults. Thus, he may be caught in a conflict between his self-assertion as an independent being, and compliance to adults on whom he depends to meet his emotional and physical needs. During this period, the child needs loving support and acceptance, as well as guidance. If his efforts toward independent action are met with ridicule, shaming, or abuse, his inner drive for autonomy may be stifled and replaced by a sense of doubt regarding himself and others. If he isn't given adult direction and control, he is unable to develop inner controls essential for socialization.

EARLY CHILDHOOD (TWO TO FIVE YEARS)

The two- to three-year-old can walk, run, and use objects appropriately. Most children of this age are toilet trained. The child likes to feed himself and to play near other children, but he is not yet ready for collective play. He begins to express himself in sentences, asks questions, and likes to listen to stories. His emotional responses become more varied, including expressions of affection, joy, sadness, and concern. At four, he is active and lively, plays imaginatively, and has fine motor coordination. He can take care of his dressing and grooming needs. He enjoys playing in a peer group and may attach himself to an individual child as his friend. He is more aggressive, assertive, and, at times, negative toward adult authority, which indicates his growing sense of independence. Speech is more extensive and appropriate; he tends to ask innumerable questions.

By five years of age, his behavior is well controlled and goal-oriented. He accepts rules in games and routines at home. He continues to demonstrate his growing independence by wanting to assume responsibility for personal care and he does not hesitate to venture outside the home to visit with relatives and neighborhood friends. He becomes more aware of differences in size, age, time, strength, and sex. He shows an interest in the written word and in expressive arts such as singing, dancing, and acting. He becomes preoccupied with family. Boys and girls play games using the father and mother roles; they enjoy keeping house. The range of emotional reaction expands, displaying a diversity of feelings and attitudes.

This early childhood phase, termed *Initiative vs. Guilt*, is a time for testing skills. The child now plays with other children his age and tests his capabilities against them. If, in relationship with his peers, he finds that he is competent and is accepted, and if he experiences support and encouragement from significant adults, he will most likely develop a sense of confidence and optimism about himself. If he experiences failure, criticism, or shaming, he may develop a sense of inferiority and insecurity. As a consequence, he may hesitate or give up trying anything new. This will stifle his initiative and tend to make him feel inadequate.

This stage, which extends into the sixth year, involves the resolution of the conflict between a child's developing initiative and developing sense of guilt. As his awareness of himself and others increases, he learns that other people have needs similar to his own. He also has to learn to conform to parental values and expectations which also represent the broader values of society. Through identification with his parents, he incorporates these values and develops a sense of conscience. Successful resolution of the conflict of this phase marks the beginnings of a developing sense of purpose and goal directedness.

LATE CHILDHOOD (SIX TO ELEVEN YEARS)

This stage of development involves children in testing, strengthening, and expanding their physical, social, intellectual, and emotional capabilities outside their immediate families. The child moves out from the family to peer, school, and neighborhood. He has to cope with adult authority other than his parents and success and failure in areas of learning, play, and work; he must develop a sense of commitment and expand his interests and social relationships.

The overall rate of growth and development slows down, ushering in a seemingly latent quiescent phase in preparation for the dramatic developments of puberty and adolescence that follow. However, children's intellectual, social, and emotional development is substantially greater than their physical growth. At this time, boys and girls enjoy creative activities, hobbies, and sports. They readily accept adult authority, rules, and routines at home and at school. They find emotional gratification in a diversity of relationships with peer friendships and attachment to adults other than their parents. They enjoy group activities. The characteristic concreteness of early thought is gradually replaced by a capacity for abstract thinking which facilitates learning. Sexual identification becomes strengthened, with boys preferring the company of their fathers and other boys, and girls, the company of their mothers and peers of the same sex. Their main investment is in peer relationships. They become involved competitively in activities and strive to become popular and admired by their friends for achievements in sports, games, and learning.

At the same time, school provides the child with a new set of authority figures, the teachers. School makes demands for self-control and productivity. The child now has a basis for comparing his teachers with his parents, and he has a choice of additional models with whom to identify. He needs understanding, encouragement, and support from both adult groups to resolve successfully the crisis of this fourth stage of development, *Industry vs. Authority.*

PUBERTY AND ADOLESCENCE
(ELEVEN TO TWENTY YEARS)

Puberty (age eleven to thirteen) marks the onset of biological maturation. Hormonal activity results in dramatic changes in physical development. Secondary sexual characteristics include breast development and menstruation in girls; increase in size of penis and testicles, deepening of the voice, and appearance of facial hair in boys; and the growth of pubic and underarm hair in both sexes. On the average, girls reach puberty about two years earlier than boys, although there is a great deal of individual variation. The physical changes are accompanied by emotional and social components which are expressed behaviorally.

Psychologically, the adolescent is affected by his evolving capacity for abstract thought, the intensification of sexual urges, and his identity needs. The horizons of his knowledge expand, sharpening his critical judgment of his immediate surroundings and the greater society, both of which affect his life. His developing sexuality may produce inner tensions experienced as anxiety and guilt because of his emerging sexual feelings. Boys and girls wish for close relationships with members of the other sex, but are fearful of them. Romantic fantasies and "crushes" develop on teachers, star athletes, and movie and popular singer idols. The adolescent's search for identity is influenced by family peers and significant (to him) adults other than his parents. It is reflected in hairstyles and clothes, fads he perpetuates, heroes he worships, enemies he hates, and political and religious causes he follows.

Adolescence represents a state of fluidity in all aspects of development. It is characterized by emotional turbulence, ambivalence, impulsivity, search, and experimentation. According to Nichtern (1974: 109),

Function, behavior and communication are combined and recombined in many different ways, making the adolescent unpredictable. . . . Their experimentation is physical, social, emotional and intellectual. Their sexual explorations with each other help refine their identity to themselves while preparing them for the adult roles of marriage partners and parents. Their strong involvement with social groupings and causes serves again to refine their identities to themselves while preparing them to accept the rules and order of the society in which they must live. Their emotionality exposes them to all nuances of feelings, bringing them to a better awareness of their own needs and those of others. Their intellectual explorations help them toward a selection of a model of work designed to sustain them through later years.

The adolescent's goals are affected by his family and peer values, his self-concept, socioeconomic circumstances, and the educational-vocational opportunities available to him. Erik Erikson characterized this phase as *Identity vs. Identity Diffusion.* It represents a search for self which involves a number of crucial questions: Who am I? What do I believe in? Where am I going? How will I get there? What shall I be doing? The adolescent is confronted with many conflicts which he must resolve, including sexuality, work, and dependence-independence. His uncertainties may get him involved in instabilities and difficulties. Here the problem is to establish a sound identity, a sense of constructive self. Otherwise, he faces an uncertain, insecure, "diffuse" sense of himself and the world around him. The result is identity confusion. The successful resolution of the conflicts of this stage is the development of a sense of faithfulness and security with oneself, connectedness with a group, and the ability to be committed to some ideological view of life. The first, which refers to a personal identity, implies a positive sense of oneself as a separate, positive functioning person who knows who he is, where he is at, where he wants to go, and how he is going to get there. The second, involving group identity, implies the capacity for developing peer-group affiliation. The third, referring to philosophical identity, involves the process of finding a meaning to one's life and one's place in society.

According to Erikson's developmental theory, a child moves from complete dependence during early infancy toward independence and individuation in adolescence. This maturation process is determined by the individual's innate attributes and their fruition within the environment in which he is reared. Chronological age cannot be considered the sole index for judging a child's maturational level. This is particularly applicable to children in group care. Emotional stresses experienced by them may deter movement from one stage of development to the other and, in some cases, may reverse the process, resulting in regression to an earlier maturational level. In most cases, regression is only temporary. Through sensitive intervention and supportive, encouraging guidance, the child care worker can be helpful in enhancing such children's development. Erikson's theoretical model provides a useful framework for assessing a child's level of development. Such assessment is essential for setting goals, and planning for needed services and individualized programs. If the assessment is not available at a child's admission, it should be completed as soon as possible. In addition to family, developmental, educational, and clinical data, it should include observations of the child's functioning in group living situations.

Children will respond more readily to demands and expectations if the approch is geared to their level of comprehension and capabilities. Thus, two children of similar age, I.Q., and socioeconomic family background, living in the same cottage group, have to be dealt with differently by their workers, as these examples illustrate.

1. Johnny, age 10, acts on impulse, demands immediate gratification, and cannot tolerate frustration. He has difficulty in following group routines, prefers individual play to group games, has poor grooming and eating habits, and at times is disoriented in relation to time and space. Reasoning and explanation seem to be ineffective because most of the time he does not seem to comprehend what the workers are talking about. Disciplinary actions evoke tears and complaints instead of modification in behavior. Johnny will require a great deal of individual attention, guidance, precise and simple directions, patience, and firmness if he is to learn to cope with reality and to give up immature patterns of relating to others. In a group game which requires conformity to rules, Johnny has difficulties. He becomes impatient, cries, or withdraws if he performs poorly. He has gradually responded to his worker's direct approach which includes statements like "That's not the way to behave!" followed by an explanation and demonstration of appropriate modes of behavior.

2. Billy, Johnny's roommate, functions on a higher maturational level. He has greater control over impulsive urges and postpones gratification for a limited period of time. He can describe feelings he experiences, has some understanding of cause and effect, is more sensitive than Johnny to other people's feelings, and has more respect for their needs. He prefers peer activity to individual fantasy play. When he does something wrong, he seems to understand when told, "That is not the way to get what you want." When asked, he can also talk about the

feelings he has that trigger a hostile or aggressive action. He also responds more readily than Johnny to suggestions of alternative, more acceptable ways of reacting to frustrations. In competitive group games, he is more capable of understanding the rationale for rules. When he breaks a rule, he is told, "To make the game possible, rules must be followed. If you can't play by the rules, you can't be in the game." Unlike Johnny, Billy wants to be in the game and conforms to requirements.

In both cases, the workers adopt an approach relative to each child's level of maturation. They start "where the child is at" and aim toward strengthening his capacity for adapting to realistic requirements of group living. This method serves to reinforce already existing capabilities and stimulates the development of additional controls and skills which he does not yet possess.

REFERENCES

Comer, J.P., and A.F. Poussaint. 1975. *Black Child Care.* New York: Simon and Schuster.

Erikson, E.H. 1956. *Childhood and Society.* New York: Norton.

Nichtern, S. 1974. *Helping the Retarded Child.* New York: Grosset & Dunlap.

5 DISTURBANCE IN CHILDHOOD

Children in group care, whether they are classified as abused, dependent, neglected, emotionally disturbed, or multiply handicapped, have experienced varying degrees of emotional deprivation. By this we mean a lack of appropriate and adequate environmental and interpersonal experience. The greater the deprivation, the greater the likelihood that the child will be unable to function in accordance with requirements of group living. The primary reason for this is because he is not fully in control of his behavior. Many emotionally deprived children manifest disturbance in relation to reality, impulse control, relatedness to others, and thinking. They also manifest extremes in anxiety, anger, aggression, and guilt.

RELATION TO REALITY

A child's relation to reality involves the ability to perceive accurately the external world and the self. The child or person whose perception of reality is impaired believes that his view correctly represents reality. Delusions are an extreme form of misconceiving reality; hallucinations, the extreme in misperceiving it. Severely disturbed children may also be disoriented in time and space. Without supervision and direction, they tend to wander off, may not get to class or to appointments on time, may be confused about following routines, and have difficulty in completing the simplest tasks.

RELATEDNESS

The healthy child reaches out for relationships with others, is able to experience relatedness even in the physical absence of the other person, and does not exhibit severe ambivalence. Disturbances in this capacity are expressed in withdrawal from others, instability to maintain interest in people, or in extreme expression of ambivalence (of love and hate) to the same person within a very brief interval. Children who have difficulty in relating to others seem to lack the sense of basic trust. "The amount of trust derived from earliest infantile experience depends on the quality of maternal relationship rather than the quantity of goods or demonstration of love" (Erikson 1956: 220).

Many children in group care have difficulties in establishing close mutual relationships with others. They express it in a variety of ways, ranging from the autistic child who is totally isolated from interpersonal relationships and the schizophrenic child who is immersed in his fantasy world to a broad range of behaviors which are not generally viewed as expressing relationship deficits. For example, the overtly aggressive, intimidating youngster may utilize these methods to keep others at a distance because closeness with others is viewed as dangerous. The manipulator views others as objects to be exploited for one's pleasurable needs. He does not trust closeness and mutuality. The child who provokes others to keep him in a scapegoat role may be encouraging others to deny him acceptance and closeness which he feels are threatening. These illustrate defensive behaviors against relatedness. There are also children who, for a variety of reasons, lack social and play skills that enhance relationships. They have to be helped to acquire them through teaching, demonstration, and encouragement (Whittaker 1979).

IMPULSIVITY

The healthy child develops increasing control of his inner impulses. He is able to tolerate frustration and postpone gratification. The disturbed child is not capable of doing so. His behavior may range from an inability to sit still for any length of time to destructive outbursts, attacks on others, or temper tantrums; or he may be self-destructive. There may also be emotional expressions and thinking that are inappropriate. Since such children are readily influenced, they may be easily led into mischievous or disruptive acts and be exploited by their peer group to act destructively.

THINKING DISORDER

The thought patterns of many disturbed children and the intellectually handicapped show a tendency to concreteness which represents lack of development in thought organization. This calls for an approach (by the workers) which will facilitate communication through simple and, if necessary, repeated instructions, and by breaking down a complex task into its constituent parts.

ANXIETY

Anxiety expresses itself in an excess of tension, restlessness, and undirected movements. It is a state of feeling generated by instinctual urges when they are not satisfied by the environment. When this occurs in infancy, the child reacts with crying and bodily dysfunction. Years later, if anxiety develops into a state designated as neurotic anxiety, the extreme emotional and physical reaction to the disturbing stimuli may have little connection to the actual objects or situations that evoke it. It is no longer a fear reaction to a real danger but a state of fear of the unknown. Normally, children either cope with threatening circumstances by learning to overcome the danger, sometimes asking for help, or avoid it by seeking satisfaction elsewhere. They cope with inner anxiety by developing defense mechanisms, reenacting it in play activities and fantasy. Some children may develop phobias or compulsions. There may also be regression and denial.

In children whose ego development[a] is highly impoverished, anxiety leads to a breakdown of inner controls, resulting in panic, flight, or uncontrollable aggression. Redl and Wineman (1951: 96) describe the panic state as "total flight and avoidance, in which an otherwise pleasure-promising activity is abandoned in panic or avoided in the future, if even mild anxiety or fear elements are present." They describe the aggression phase as "ferocious attack and diffuse destruc-

a. According to psychoanalytic theory, the ego, whose prime function is the perception of and adaptation to the physical and social environment, inhibits the expression of instinctual drives.

tion, when whatever is in reach, or whoever is near becomes the immediate object of attack, as where the children tear off on a binge of general wild behavior and destruction in a more diffuse way." Such children do not respond easily, if at all, to residential treatment in large settings. They require a great deal of individual attention and highly skilled staff. For example, Ronnie was a boy who could not involve himself in a closely significant relationship with any staff member. At the age of nine, when he was admitted to the residential treatment center, he had already failed in thirty-two foster homes. He repulsed all who attempted to work with him. He threw stones at staff, fought with his peers, and ran away. The slightest frustration set off wild rage and assertive behavior. He had to be transferred to a hospital.

ANGER AND AGGRESSION

Anger and aggression have positive as well as negative connotations. Anger has value in mobilizing a person to act against a realistic danger, hurt, or injustice. Aggressiveness is valued in our culture as assertiveness, determination, and ambition.

As a consequence of severe or chronic frustration, however, anger may lead to hostile feelings and to aggressive and destructive actions against the object or situation that evokes the painful feelings. It may be turned against the self, producing depression, proneness to accidents, physical illness, and, in extreme cases, destruction of the self through suicide. It may be displaced onto weaker or more vulnerable persons. A child growing up in a family atmosphere where anger and aggression are common modes of expression and interaction will most likely identify with such patterns and reenact them wherever he may be.

In disadvantaged, poverty-ridden families, the consequences of prejudice and discrimination are experienced as deprivation of basic necessities, low social status, feelings of inadequacy and low esteem, helplessness, and hopelessness. Under the burden of extreme frustration which cannot successfully be expressed against the environmental forces which produce it, adults in a family may displace their anger and hostile feelings onto each other and their children. Many troubled parents, especially fathers, may have little love and tender sentiments left to convey to their children. As a result of tension and impatience, they resort to controlling their children through physical punishment. This tends to weaken emotional bonds, hinders positive identification within the family, and affects superego or conscience development in their children. The result is weak controls against impulse expression (McKinley 1964). Many such children become delinquent. Some may even become "children who hate." As a consequence of their destructive aggression they soon become "children nobody wants." Their rehabilitation is extremely difficult because they have severe disturbance of their control system (Redl and Wineman 1951: 21–28).

GUILT

Guilt is associated with conscience or (in psychoanalytic terminology) the superego. "Conscience represents the mental mechanisms that guide and assist the individual in inhibiting himself from performing acts that are unacceptable to significant figures in his environment. The feelings an individual experiences when he performs, or is tempted to perform, such unacceptable acts is guilt" (Gardner 1973: 125). Conscience develops through the internalization of parental prohibitions which ultimately become the unconscious censors of unacceptable thoughts or acts, as well as through identifications with parents and other significant persons in one's life. Their characteristics, standards, and values are also internalized and guide future attitudes and behavior.

Guilt has a positive value in regulating social living. When it is excessive or insufficient, it results in maladaptive behavior. Both are evidenced among children in residential treatment. In cases where the child's sense of guilt is excessive, he may suffer from anxiety because he may anticipate retaliation or retribution for angry thoughts or hostile feelings. He may blame himself for misfortunes, accidents, illness, or death of loved ones with no basis in reality. He may seek relief by repressing his feelings, by displacing his anger, by developing phobias or compulsions which in symbolic form represent his inner conflicts. He may become depressed or seek punishment for his imagined sins or misdeeds by provoking others to anger and even physical attack or abuse.

An underdeveloped conscience results in lack or deficiency of guilt feelings. It may be a consequence of impairment in ego development or a result of faulty identifications. When inner urges are not adequately controlled, a child is driven to behave in ways which are unacceptable to others or contrary to established norms or expectations. He may strike out physically, destroy others' belongings, steal, set fires, etc. When lack of guilt is due to identification with antisocial values, the child, acting in conformity with his life experience and family or peer expectation, does not feel he is doing anything wrong. He is behaving in accordance with an acceptable lifestyle which profits from antisocial activity.

Ben exemplified this type of youngster. He was an only child who was reared by a delinquent mother. His father, who was deceased, had died in prison. His was not a poor or disadvantaged family; its lifestyle was delinquent. During the two years of attempted treatment, Ben's mother was uncooperative and encouraged the boy's delinquencies both in the institution and during home visits. He conformed superficially and after his discharge he, in partnership with his mother, became a dealer in drugs. They became affluent, but ended up in prison.

Antisocial behavior may also be a consequence of growing up in disadvantaged, economically and socially deprived families and neighborhoods. Many react by rejecting prevailing social norms and moral values, are antagonistic to them, and feel no sense of guilt when they violate them. This was true of Jim during his first year in residential treatment. From the moment of his admission, he made life difficult for his cottage staff and teachers. He talked back and was insulting to his child care workers, ignored his teachers, and bullied the other children in his cottage and classes. "We can't get through to him! We don't understand him! He is getting us angry!" were frequently heard complaints.

When one considered Jim's background, his behavior was not surprising. Jim was only twelve years old, but he had been involved in aggressive and antisocial behavior for years. He had been expelled from school, roamed the streets, and was a leader of a delinquent gang. He distrusted adults and felt comfortable with peers only when he could dominate and control them. He seemed to have adopted a style of life characterized by antisocial values and defiance of authority. Jim seemed to behave as if he had brought his previous environment with him. This was a distortion of reality because Jim's cottage living situation was entirely different from his conflict-ridden, disorganized home, broken by his father's desertion. Neither was his cottage peer group equivalent to his neighborhood delinquent gang. Jim's current situation, however, was his "psychological" reality based on pathological family experiences and deprivation. It seemed that Jim could not be expected to readily give up his characteristic pattern of relating to others and that he would probably resist the institution's encroachment on his accustomed way of life. An essential and initial task was to help the adults who lived and worked with him anticipate, understand, and not be provoked by his behavior. This effort was successful, and Jim eventually gave up his delinquent lifestyle.

SEVERE CHILDHOOD DISTURBANCE

The highly disturbed children referred for residential treatment represent a wide range of disorders. The extremely disturbed exhibit highly atypical behavior including a wide variety of psychotic-like manifestations. They have been classified in broad terms as "atypical" or, until very recently, "schizophrenic." The psychiatric classification of "childhood schizophrenia" has been excluded from the 1980 revision of the *Diagnostic and Statistical Manual of Mental Disorders* (DSM III) published by the American Psychiatric Association. These children suffer from pervasive anxiety. Their perception and cognition of inner as well as outer stimuli is distorted; their impulse control, severely impaired; and they have developed protective defenses of withdrawal from contact with others. Consequently, they have difficulty in assessing reality and adapting to changing situations. In addition to chronic anxiety, they also manifest a wide range of behavior, characteristic of neurotic symptomatology—phobias, obsessive-compulsive traits, bizarre behavior, hysterical reactions, depression, and intense suspiciousness. Unlike normal or neurotic children, they do not have the capacity to communicate to others the nature of the anxiety they experience, or to repress or sublimate it.

The unique dilemma of such a child is: "He faces an insoluble situation of irreconcilable extremes against which he protects himself primitively by relinquishing feeling and interest, thereby foregoing responsibility for his own actions. Since all solutions are unbearable, his primary motivation is to avoid all solutions" (Goldfarb, Mintz, and Strook 1969: 121). Thus, he may want close personal contact, to be loved and nurtured, but is afraid of being overwhelmed—literally swallowed up. On the other hand, if he moves away from close relationships, he fears abandonment and aloneness.

In his confusion, he may react with fury against others or himself. If his actions frighten or confuse others, if the persons who become targets of his projection react with anger or rejection, a vicious cycle of hostile, aggressive actions and counterreactions may be set in motion which then reinforces in the child's mind his sense of rejection, violent fantasies, and paranoid projections.

One must first focus on helping such a child overcome his psychotic modes of dealing with demands of reality. By sympathetic but firm handling of his reaction to the environmental demands of the residential treatment program, bizarre and regressive behavior is discouraged and appropriate responses encouraged and rewarded. This treatment approach, termed "corrective socialization" by Goldfarb, Mintz, and Strook (1969) involves a sharply defined reality and the in-depth exploration with each child of what his inner meaning of that reality is. First, the "structuring of time and place, the fostering of a complete use of all five senses and of physical and intellectual abilities, the nurturing of social relationships and of their normal expression, the encouragement and appreciation of reward and punishment" is the function of the child care worker in the living situation and of the teacher in the classroom. Second, it is the psychotherapist's role to explore with the child his feelings and thoughts about the reality which is defined for him by the therapeutic environment (Goldfarb, Mintz, and Strook 1969: 123).

The following paraphrased vignette (Goldfarb, Mintz, and Strook) 1969: 75-76) is illustrative of the corrective socialization approach:

> When Joseph, age ten, was asked by his worker to wash up for dinner, he began to whine, "Why do I have to wash up all the time and why do I have to eat, dress, and sleep at regularly set times?" When the child care worker explained that everyone has to do certain things at certain times, like getting up, dressing, working, going to bed, in order to be "well and happy," Joseph cried, "Why can't I make things happier the way I want it? Why can't I make the rain stop? Why does nighttime always have to come?" The worker explained that "no one can change certain things; one has to learn to live with them." Joseph said, "I'll try, but I don't know if it will make me happier."

A child like Joseph has an exaggerated sense of personal omnipotence. He has to feel in control of everyone and everything. Otherwise, he feels vulnerable and extremely anxious. He has to be helped to develop the capacity to perceive reality correctly and to live within its demands. Some children have difficulty in expressing themselves verbally. Because their words do not always represent what they intend to convey, they appear to others confused and inconsistent. They require patience and understanding of the mood and gestures accompanying their words, and coaching in making their intended meaning clear.

Corrective socialization can also serve as an effective treatment method for other types of ego-deficiency disorders due to a child's sensory impairment, extreme emotional deprivation, neurological dysfunction, and mental retardation.

THE ABUSED CHILD

Research studies (Kinard 1980) on the personality characteristics of abused children confirm that they have serious emotional problems. They are distrustful, have difficulties in establishing relationships, cope inappropriately with aggressive impulses, and have a low sense of self-esteem. They view themselves as unhappy, willful, "doing bad things," and unpopular with peers. When such children are removed from their abusing parents for placement and treatment, these characteristics quickly become evident in the daily living situations. Their inability to trust others may seriously impair their capacity to form relationships with staff and peers. They have difficulties in socializing within the peer group. More frequently than non-abused children, they are likely to direct their aggression against other children. This tendency interferes with being accepted by members of their groups and frequently precipitates crisis situations which require intervention by child care staff.

Such a child will require special sensitivity and understanding in order to modify his negative perception of others and his own low sense of self-esteem. He will need help to explore his feelings about having been abused by his parent(s), and assurance that he will not be abused there and will be treated as a valued person.

There is clinical as well as research evidence that battering parents were themselves physically abused children, that they tend to be impaired in controlling aggressive impulses, and tend to have negative feelings about themselves. Abused children, when untreated for their traumatic experiences, may grow into adults who as parents may become abusive toward their own children, thus perpetuating generations of battering parents.

MILDLY RETARDED

Intellectually retarded children have multiple handicaps, including a combination of mental retardation, neurological deficits, and emotional disturbance. They all lack elementary knowledge and skills, are anxious, suspicious, and defensive. Throughout their lives, they may have been told by their families, teachers, and peers that they were inept, "dumb," and lazy. If they evoked impatience and low expectations in learning, self-care and social relationships, they may have been neglected. Others may have been overprotected and given little incentive to learn.

Communication with these children may pose problems for child care workers. Their cognitive deficits, expressed in the form of perceptual and language disorders, affect their capacity both to comprehend and to respond appropriately. This tends to evoke negative responses from others. For example, child care workers may interpret the behavior of a child with a language disability as evidence of negativism or laziness whenever he does not respond in accordance with expectations. Parents and teachers may have done the same prior to the child's placement. His perceptual problems are not readily recognized as responsible for his clumsiness or lack of responsiveness. He may be criticized as "stupid," or even punished for being willfully noncompliant. Adult feelings of hopelessness and helplessness are communicated, reinforcing the child's sense of inadequacy and worthlessness.

The mentally retarded child is a traumatized child because of the chronic rejection he has experienced as a consequence of negative and hostile adult and peer reactions to his inability to meet performance expectation. He is distrustful because he has not experienced a sense of basic trust in his relationships with others. Acceptance of him as a whole child with handicaps conveys a positive attitude that he is worthy of help and that he is likeable. This helps him develop a sense of confidence to master required tasks (Adler and Finkel 1976).

THE AGGRESSIVE ADOLESCENT

Disturbed, aggressive, violence-prone, delinquent-oriented adolescents present special problems for child care workers. As a group they are difficult to live with, work with, and rehabilitate. Most are in placement as a consequence of antisocial acts which brought them to the attention of family courts. They are adjucated as either "juvenile delinquents" or "persons in need of supervision." The former refers to offenses by children under sixteen years of age which would be considered crimes if committed by adults; the latter refers to boys under sixteen and girls under eighteen, who are beyond the control of their parents or some other authority because they are incorrigible, ungovernable, habitually delinquent, or truant from school. These are legal designations. The label "delinquent," which by definition is "guilty of a fault or misdeed," implies an accusation rather than a description. Such children and youths generally evoke adult anger and hostility rather than concern and sympathy. The fact that society fosters delinquency, indirectly or unintentionally, by doing very little about conditions such as slums, poverty, discrimination, and family disorganization which bred delinquency is frequently disregarded.

Children's antisocial and destructive acts may indicate that something is wrong in their lives. It is often their cry for help and rescue from intolerable life situations. If society does not respond with understanding and constructive efforts to ameliorate conditions which generate their frustrations, delinquency will flourish (Adler 1969). The categorization of juvenile delinquent tends to stereotype large numbers of children and youth, de-emphasizing that each is an individual with a life experience of his own. As a group they represent a wide range of disturbances.

The principal characteristic that juvenile delinquents seem to have in common is lack of a wholesome family environment. In the physically deteriorated neighborhoods where the economically and socially disadvantaged reside, harsh conditions of family life contribute to increased family disorganization, interpersonal conflict, and development of emotional difficulties. Destructive parental attitudes and behavior—whether expressed in direct, overt rejection through abuse and hostile attitudes or in the form of inconsistent, confused parenting, lack of adult direction, or overindulgence—contribute to childhood confusion, mistrust, conflicts, rejection of society's ethics and values, and the development of antisocial traits and delinquent behavior.

In relatively affluent communities, the emotionally disturbed child or youth may act out his disturbance in destructive ways. Groups of these boys and girls constitute the disruptive, destructive, vandalizing groups present in every suburban community.

This has been an increasing phenomenon in so-called middle-class and wealthy neighborhoods and in the suburbs of our cities. Although the official statistics indicate a much bigger delinquency rate among the underprivileged and the low-status families who populate marginal and deteriorated neighborhoods and city slums, juvenile delinquency is not the monopoly of the lower socioeconomic classes of our society.

Another neglected element in evaluating the aggressive and disturbed adolescent is his underlying insecurity in forming close relationships with others. Aggression, impulsivity, hostility, and destructiveness may be distinguishing traits of delinquent adolescents as a group, but these are not categorically their all-encompassing or exclusive characteristics. Rorschach examinations of the boys in the Glueck studies (Glueck and Glueck 1950) indicated that the delinquent boys as a group showed a higher incidence of feelings of isolation than the nondelinquent boys. Thus, the individual delinquent's extroverted, aggressive acts may, figuratively speaking, represent only the exposed parts of the iceberg of his personality. The individual may camouflage emotional factors such as insecurities and inhibitions in interpersonal relations by behaving aggressively and destructively and by being defiant of adult authority. A study of an adolescent boys' group at the Hawthorne Cedar Knolls School (Adler 1965), a residential treatment center for emotionally disturbed children, resulted in similar findings, indicating that these emotionally disturbed and, for the most part, delinquent-oriented boys had experienced extensive difficulties within their homes, schools, and communities. As a group, they tended to be isolated and inhibited in their capacity for close personal relationships.

From the point of view of rehabilitation objectives, a residential facility should provide children with opportunities for social relationships which would serve to counteract previous destructive interpersonal experiences, and make available the social and psychological nurture necessary for mature personality development. Regrettably, there are youngsters who are so extensively damaged in their capacity to trust that it is unlikely they will be able to respond to efforts by the staff to involve them in positive relationships. Perhaps because of a lack in the current state of knowledge, even the most sophisticated residential treatment center cannot undo or repair the emotional damage some of these children have suffered. For this task, additional research and development of more effective treatment methods will be required.

Child care workers are aware of the difficulties these violence-prone children represent in group living. The frustrations they impose on other children and on staff can be extreme and at times unbearable. They can develop a sense of hopelessness about their potential for change and a sense of helplessness about one's capacity to be of aid. The child care worker should not expect of himself more than he can possibly give. If there is lack of success, he is not to blame. If there is a burden of guilt, it is not his own. It belongs among the social forces and circumstances of life which contributed to the development of such severely damaged personalities. A collective communal effort is required to prevent the perpetuation of conditions that produce such children and to protect society from their violence while developing more effective rehabilitation programs.

VIOLENCE-PRONE YOUTH

The extremely violent adolescent is relatively rare in current residential treatment programs. However, such youths, including those committing homicide, appear to be increasing in number. They are mentioned here because their background, attitudes, and behavior are similar in some respects to the violent-prone youth referred to group care programs who present serious management problems for child care workers. In a recent study (Lewis et al. 1979) comparing extremely violent and less violent incarcerated juvenile offenders, the former were found to have paranoid symptoms, and major and minor neurological abnormalities. In contrast to the less violent group, they had been severely abused and had witnessed extreme violence in their homes. Their family experiences may have provided a model with which to identify. The rage generated toward an abusing parent may have been displaced unto others. Their paranoid orientation and impulsivity seemed to contribute to their tendency to attack, sometimes brutally, for either imagined or real threats. This study confirmed King's (1975) description and findings. The family circumstances of this homicidal group of youngsters were marked by turmoil, instability, and a state of fear. They were witness to violence between parents and were frequent objects of parental abuse. Their parents were inconsistent and ineffective. All of these youths were distrustful, expecting insult and injury from everyone. To counteract a sense of vulnerability in social situations, they were ready to attack first. Their primary concern was the satisfaction of their needs without any consideration for others. Anyone who did not give in to their wishes was viewed as a depriving and hostile object that had to be demolished.

They were all severely retarded in reading and language skills. This handicapped their thinking, comprehension, and verbal communication. Their educational deprivation made them defensive about learning. Their capacity to think abstractly and to understand social concepts was very limited. Their total reliance on subjective feelings in coping with their environment resulted in impulsive acts and misperception of other people's feelings, behavior, and motives. Their reactions, hostile and aggressive in nature, were a prevalent mode of behavior in social situations. If their behavior was questioned, they tended to react with provocative terseness such as "Who, me?" "Get off me!" "Fuck you!" "Make me!" "I dare you!" Their manner provoked anxiety, anger, and rejection; the violence they emanated generated feelings of counterviolence.

This profile is familiar to child care workers responsible for the care of violence-prone (but not necessarily homicidal) youth. The frustration they impose on peers and staff can be extreme. The presence of one or more such youngsters in a group may at times become unbearable because of the fear they generate and the disruption they are capable of creating. They seem to cling desperately and stubbornly to accustomed patterns of behavior, resisting staff efforts to involve them in relationships and in education. They frustrate attempts to help them overcome distrust of social relationships, to develop mastery skills, to enhance a sense of confidence they lack, to sublimate destructive energies into constructive endeavor, and to experience a sense of success in achievement rather than failure.

It is, therefore, not surprising that many child care workers develop a sense of hopelessness about such youngsters. What is more difficult to bear is the feeling of helplessness, of not being effective in helping them change. Some workers question their capacities; others may even blame themselves. This is unrealistic. These adolescents apparently require more than is available today in community-based group care programs and residential treatment centers.[b] Addi-

---

b. The Closed Adolescent Treatment Center in Colorado has developed an effective program for treating violent and resistive youth. For a description of the program, see Agee (1979).

tional funding is essential to provide existing residential treatment programs with a higher ratio of well-trained child care and clinical personnel, special education, vocational training, intensive aftercare services, and research potential.

PSYCHIATRIC DIAGNOSES

Generally, children in residential treatment centers have been examined psychiatrically and their disturbance diagnosed. The diagnosis represents a description of a specific configuration of mental disorders within the general system of psychiatric classification. There are recognizable risks in diagnostic "labeling" because of the fluidity of the child's personality. However, a clinical diagnosis facilitates understanding and formulation of treatment plans. For example, whereas "psychoneurosis" implies the need for resolution of internalized conflicts through acquisition of insight by means of psychotherapy, a schizophrenic patient requires therapeutic support in daily living based on reality rather than evocation of psychological insights. When classifying children as "schizophrenic," "character disorder," "neurotic," and so on, we should keep in mind that "each child whatever his symptom is a distinct individual with his own . . . pattern and range of potentialities" (Murphy 1974: 14).

In child care work there are innumerable situations where differential approaches are indicated based on a diagnostic understanding of the children involved. For example, four children during a meal may refuse to eat vegetables. When the worker insists, they all get upset but express it differently. The psychotic child may become extremely anxious and, if forced, may be propelled into a psychotic episode. This is because he may view this type of food as a harmful substance which will poison him if he eats it. The worker who insists on it may then be viewed as a poisoner, and the possibility of continued trusting relationships with him is destroyed. The second child, with a history of mother–child conflict, may associate vegetables with traumatic experiences related to forced feeding by his mother. If pressured, he may have a temper tantrum, repeating previous reactions to his mother. The third child, who does not like vegetables because he doesn't like their taste, may ask to be excused from eating them. The fourth child, with manipulative tendencies, will want to skip vegetables in order to get to the dessert. He will attempt either to trade off to another child or to manipulate the worker out of pressuring him to eat them. Diagnostic understanding will suggest that the first child cannot be forced; it will take a long time before he feels secure enough to trust an adult's offer and eat this food. The second child will need time to dissociate the worker's behavior from emotions associated with early feeding experiences. The value of vegetables can be discussed with the third child, possibly to the point of convincing him he should try them even though at this time he doesn't like the taste. Manipulative behavior by the fourth child should not be permitted. The dessert could be withheld without inordinate emotional or physical harm to him since other food is still available.

Routines of daily living need not be changed for each child on the basis of his diagnosis; however, children require some degree of individualization. A child care worker should not hesitate to ask for clarification by clinical personnel if a diagnostic statement is unclear and if he is not sure of its implications in dealing with a particular child.

SUMMATION

Children in group care present multiple problems as a consequence of negative life experiences. Developmental difficulties and unwholesome environmental factors have affected their maturational growth.[c] These deficits expressed in cognitive, emotional, physical, and social functioning affect a child's sense of security in himself and with other people. The handicapped child may be mistreated, ridiculed, or rebuffed by peers and family members. As a consequence, he may withdraw from relationships or he may defend himself by developing learning and behavior difficulties. The result may be placement. Many children in care resist growth even when encouragement and support is offered them because they expect to fail. They cling to maladaptive patterns of behavior as protection against the uncertainty of change and because they have not experienced a sense of trust. Group care provides opportunities for (positive) change, for learning, and for relationships. Through appropriate assessment of strengths and weaknesses, planned intervention strategies are developed to help each child advance to a higher level of

c. *Therapies for Children* by Schaeffer and Millman (1978) covers a broad range of children's behavior problems and presents summarized clinical reports illustrating a diversity of therapeutic procedures for dealing with specific disorders.

functioning. This involves a flexible set of expectations geared to his developing capabilities and potential, an environment conducive to growth, and adult supports and encouragement to help him achieve realistic goals. Child care workers are the crucial contributors to this interdisciplinary endeavor.

REFERENCES

Adler, J. 1969. "The Aggressive Delinquent Oriented Adolescent in Residential Treatment." *Child Welfare* 48, no. 3: 142–147.

_____. 1965. "Transfer of Interpersonal Behavior Among Emotionally Disturbed Adolescents in Residential Treatment." Unpublished. Ed.D. thesis, Teachers College, Columbia University.

Adler, J., and W. Finkel. 1976. "Integrating Remedial Methods into Child Care Practice." *Child Care Quarterly* 5, no. 1: 53–62.

Agee, V.L. 1979. *Treatment of the Violent Incorrigible Adolescent.* Lexington, Mass.: D.C. Heath.

Erikson, E.H. 1956. *Childhood and Society.* New York: Norton.

Gardner, R.A. 1973. *Understanding Children.* New York: Jason Aronson.

Glueck, S., and E. Glueck. 1950. *Unravelling Juvenile Delinquency.* Cambridge, Mass.: Harvard University Press.

Goldfarb, W; I. Mintz; and C.W. Stroock. 1969. *A Time to Heal: Corrective Socialization, a Treatment Approach to Childhood Schizophrenia.* New York: International Universities Press.

Kinard, M.A. 1980. "Mental Health Needs of Abused Children." *Child Welfare* 59, no. 8 (Sept.–Oct): 451–462.

King, C.H. 1975. "The Ego and the Integration of Violence in Homicidal Youth." *American Journal of Orthopsychiatry* 45, no. 1 (January): 134–145.

McKinley, G.D. 1964. *Social Class and Family Life.* New York: Free Press.

Murphy, B.L. 1974. *Growing Up in Garden Court.* New York: Child Welfare League of America.

Redl, F., and D. Wineman. 1951. *Children Who Hate.* New York: Free Press.

Lewis, D.O.; S.S. Shanok; J.H. Pincus; and G.H. Glaser. 1979. "Violent Juvenile Delinquents." *Journal of Child Psychiatry* 18, no. 2: 307–319.

Schaefer, C.E., and H.L. Millman. 1978. *Therapies for Children.* San Francisco: Jossey–Bass.

Whittaker, J.K. 1979. *Caring for Troubled Children.* San Francisco: Jossey–Bass.

6 CONCEPTS

A group care facility provides children with corrective experiences through a framework of planned and structured activities, education, socialization, and identification with positive adult models. This is achieved through the therapeutic milieu defined by Whittaker (1979: 36) as "a specially designed environment in which the events of daily living are used as formats for teaching competence in basic life skills. The living environment becomes both a means and a context for growth and change, informed by a culture that stresses learning through living." It also makes available casework and clinical services for diagnostic and treatment purposes. The scope of the clinical input depends on a child's developmental level, motivation, and need. Casework and psychotherapy can help him evaluate his reactions to the planned and controlled environment in which he lives, his feelings about himself and others, his reality functioning, and his perceptions and distortions of past and current experiences. The differential use of psychotherapy should be taken into consideration since not all children in placement are in need of intensive psychotherapy.

The child's family is also served through casework contacts on the basis of assessed needs. They are involved in the child's care through visits, through contacts with staff, and as participants in defining goals, and planning and implementing services tasks.

There are a number of concepts basic to group care of children. The following list is based on psychological and sociological theories including group dynamics and role theory as well as pragmatic experience in group care of children.

RELATIONSHIPS

Human beings grow through the nurture of relationship. Perlman defines it as "a human being's feeling or sense of emotional bonding with another" (Perlman 1979: 23) and elaborates upon this in very human and poetic terms:

> Love and caring and the compassionate responsiveness and steadfastness from other human beings are the essential nourishment for our emotional and spiritual development. When these are missing or scant, or when their opposite predominate — indifference, aggression, rejection, inconsistency — the humanizing of the unfolding person is dwarfed or malformed just as surely as physical mal- or under-nutrition will stunt or deform bones, muscles and nerve development (31).

Children in group care have experienced difficulties if not trauma in their interpersonal relationships. Upon admission, many feel rejected and abandoned because of separation from their families. As a consequence, they approach the prospect of relating significantly with peers and staff with caution. Initially, they may feel anxious in the group, suspicious of their child care workers. Overtly, they may be defensive, hostile, unresponsive, or withdrawn. There are few if any children, however, who give up on relationships with others. They will need time as well as patience and understanding from others to enable them to reach out again for the emotional bonding they crave.

The child care workers' role in establishing and maintaining a meaningful, helping relationship with the children in care is fundamental in the overall therapeutic program. It begins with the first personal contact between child and worker, and evolves through the mutual experiences of working and living together. The child's misconceived and misperceived view of adults will initially guide his responses and color his reactions to the worker's efforts to establish a relationship through which he can, in a "compassionate, working alliance" (Perlman 1979, p. 54) with the child help him cope and hopefully overcome handicaps which deter his growth and interfere with the realization of his potential. The burden of responsibility will initially rest on the worker. He is more likely to succeed if he approaches the child with "warmth," "acceptance," "empathy," "caring-concern," and "genuineness" (Perlman 1979: 55–63). *Warmth* connotes a reaching out with interest and compassion. *Acceptance* is not only viewing the child as he is in terms of his level of development, past experience with others, and degree of his handicaps but also with a degree of expectation of his potential for growth for "becoming." *Empathy* is the quality of *feeling with* another. For the worker, it means literally to "get into the child's shoes" to feel how he feels so that he can understand what the child is experiencing at the moment. An essential condition is to do so without losing one's objectivity, through a sense of awareness of one's emotional response to that particular situation. *Caring-concern* for the child's problems and hurts is part of one's concern for the consequences of his behavior which may be harmful to himself and others. *Genuineness* means to come across as "real" without pretensions or sentimentality or superficiality, with a readiness to admit (to the child) that one may not know, or that one may be wrong or err.

The subject of relationship is elaborated on in the section on relationships with individual children and groups.

SEPARATION

The infant is totally dependent on others. Without parental (or substitute family) care for his physical and emotional needs, his life would be endangered. This dependency, which is biologically determined and reinforced by experience, strengthens the child–parent attachment bonds. The facts of earliest years may not be remembered but the emotions associated with those experiences are not lost. The deeply ingrained feelings associated with fundamental relationships persist despite frustration, deprivation, and disappointments (in parents) during later years. There is one possession, one constant in a child's life he cannot be emotionally deprived of—his biological family. This may explain why relatively long-term separation associated with placement is experienced as traumatic.

One must differentiate between the processes of separation inherent in normal development and the emotional shock of forced separation. During the course of a child's growth, separation experiences are inevitable and necessary for maturation and individuation. Although each new step of separate functioning entails anxiety for the very young child, the mother's availability, love, and support minimize anxiety and make the process of achieving individuation pleasurable. Under these circumstances, separation experiences are viewed as essential and constructive (Mahler and La Perriere 1965). Precipitous, long-term, or repeated separations have been found to be destrictive. The emotional implications of such separations permeate placement from its beginning through termination. Separation affects both the child who is placed and his family. Child care workers inevitably become involved with children's and parents' reactions to separation and its manifestations during placement.

Children's Reactions

Children's reactions to separation vary (Littner 1956). Most children experience a sense of abandonment. They may feel helpless because they have no control over what is happening to them, and "worthless" because of feeling that if they were worthy, their parents would not have placed them. They may blame themselves for offenses which have no basis in reality. They may not only consider themselves "bad" but also view placement as punishment for their behavior. Their feelings of guilt and anger may be repressed, with resulting anxieties and emergence of neurotic symptoms.

The placed child may react with displacement of emotions. He may expect staff attitudes and behavior to be similar to those he experienced in his family, school, and neighborhood. He may view staff as the people who will punish him for imagined or actual sins. Expecting punishment, he may protect himself by attacking first or by withdrawing into isolation. A child who is masochistically inclined may try to evoke punishment to allay guilt feelings. A child may also hesitate to establish close and significant relationships with adults because of the fear that if he loves them or is loyal to them his own parents will resent it, or because of a feeling that he will again be rejected and subjected to another separation. Similar reactions may be experessed in relation to other children in the group.

The older child in placement, especially the adolescent, faces additional difficulties. The general instabilities which pervade adolescence are aggravated by separation. Intensified feelings of ambivalence toward parents may then be nourished by actual or fantasized feelings of parental rejection. The resolution of the dependence–independence conflict becomes more complex and difficult. Negative feelings are more readily displaced or projected. Child care workers are drawn into the vortex of the emotional turmoil that accompanies the strivings for independence. They may become the object of defiance and rebelliousness, rationalized by such expressions as "You can't tell me what to do. You are not my parents!"

Orienting the Newcomer

The impact of separation on the newly admitted child should not be minimized. The outward lack of concern may simply be a defense to control inner anxiety. Child care workers require preparation for the new arrival. The greater their understanding, the better equipped they will be to cope constructively with the child's feelings about leaving his home, friends, and neighborhood. Upon admission, the child finds himself to be a stranger in the group. The other children should have been prepared for his arrival. With the best of preparation, however, it is not certain how they will react to him. Some may view him as an intruding sibling, others may exploit him, some may tolerate him, and some may accept him. The child care worker helps him become acquainted with all the children, and specifically with those children who will be ready to befriend him and help him adapt to the climate and to the expectations of the peer group. The worker also orients him to routines, rules, and expectations of the center and introduces him to the various programs. The child should be assured of the worker's availability whenever he needs it.

The child has to be helped to develop a sense of security and belonging. This may be facilitated by encouraging him to participate in the group's activities. If he tends to be socially insecure or inhibited, he should not be pressured. He will need time to become comfortable with the other children. If he has special skills or talents, he should be encouraged to express them in the group's activities. This may enhance his acceptance by the other children.

A child's behavior following admission may not reflect his true feelings about placement. One child may cover up his anxiety about separating from his family by a false enthusiasm for peers and staff; another may hide his insecurity by a facade of bravado. One should be wary about such behavior. It dissipates quickly. It is then replaced by the real feelings that emerge after the honeymoon period. The following case is an example.

Billy, aged twelve, was admitted through family court because of chronic truancy and uncontrollable behavior at home. During the court hearing, he verbally welcomed the recommendation that he be placed in a residential treatment center. During the first week following his admission, he seemed content, expressing enthusiasm about the cottage and school. His workers were pleased. However, John, the senior worker in the cottage, felt that "it's too good to be true."

Within ten days, a marked change occurred. Billy began to complain about everything and pleaded to be permitted to go home. "After all," he argued, "I asked to be sent here. Now I think I've learned my lesson and I want to go home." He threatened that he would act so "bad" that he would be "kicked out." Billy's worker listened patiently, sympathizing with his feelings but did not support his plea for discharge. John, senior worker, told him he understood he was anxious about separating from his family and worried that the bigger kids might hurt him. He assured him that everyone feels anxious at first and that if he gives himself the chance, things will work out to his benefit. Billy was not comforted and ran away that night. When his parents brought him back, he participated in a meeting with staff and his parents. The parents reassured him of their affection, talked about the separation anxiety they experienced, but were firm about Billy's need for residential treatment. He cried and protested but finally agreed to "give it a try." He did so successfully.

Anxiety may also be experienced by children at discharge from care. The prospect of leaving friends and facing an uncertain future reactivates separation anxieties and may precipitate acting out. For example:

Jim, aged seventeen, surprised peers and staff by violating a fundamental rule of the school following the graduation ceremonies. He had been awarded one of the highest honors as "the boy who had made the greatest improvement" during his residence at the treatment center and was to be discharged the following week. During the night following the graduation ceremonies, he sneaked into one of the girls' cottages. When he was apprehended hours later by night staff, he made no excuses for his action. The following day, he was seen by the clinical director, Dr. K., who recommended deferment of his departure. In a subsequent discussion with Mr. Jones, his child care worker, the latter wondered why Jim had fouled up his discharge.

"It was stupid of me and I still do not understand it fully," Jim replied. "Dr. K. had asked whether I felt comfortable about going home. I told him that I had been somewhat anxious about it, especially since I find that I still have difficulty in getting along with my mother. She still nags and wants me to do everything she demands. In addition, the prospect of going to the public high school worried me. I'm sorry I caused all this trouble because I've been treated very well here. I think I can use the summer months to work on this matter. I don't know what got into me Sunday night. Don't worry about me. I think I can make it with some extra help."

Staff changes reactivate children's separation traumas. When a worker departs from his job, the children in his group experience to varying degrees the loss of a significant person. The worker feels a reciprocal loss. Staff changes are inevitable because the rate of turn-over among child care workers is high. Since such separations cannot be avoided, they should and can be made less painful. For example: Staff at the Ohalla Center for Children and Families at Tolego, Oregon, have evolved a helpful procedure (Miller 1979). The departing worker informs the children two weeks in advance of the departure date and talks about it throughout the remaining period of time. Other child care workers help the children plan a going-away party. Staff is encouraged to talk in front of the children about their feelings regarding the pending departure. Children are reassured that the other workers are staying on and suitable replacement will be assured to compensate for the loss of the departing person. The children's families are also informed. On the final day, staff and children participate in an exercise to share their feelings.

Similarly, peer discharges are an everpresent phenomenon. During a child's residence, he may witness departures of many peers within his group, some of whom may have become friends. He may sense their anxiety of separating from staff and peers. This not only reactivates previous separation traumas but also raises anxieties about his own departure. There is, therefore, a need to neutralize the pending separation trauma for the child who leaves and for those who remain. A good-bye party similar to the one for departing staff can be helpful. Planning of a party provides a period of involvement of staff and children in the separation process, so they can become accustomed to the physical event of departure. The party itself, with its sharing of refreshments, receipt of gifts, and farewell sentiments expressed by the child who leaves—as well as by staff and the other children—provides a framework of rituals that binds or neutralizes anxiety. Because it is experienced collectively, this process, can be very supportive to all concerned.

Parental Feelings

Feelings about separation permeate all families and affect all family members (Adler 1970). Fathers and mothers, siblings and relatives may be shaken by the fragmentation of family cohesiveness as a result of having one or more children placed. Feelings of guilt and anger generated by inner conflicts are intensified by outside pressures. Prevalent community attitudes are generally unsympathetic to parents who place their children. Such persons are viewed as inadequate, not "good" parents. Consequently, the parents' own guilt feelings and sense of failure become intensified. This state of mind may be further reinforced by staff who convey to the children by implication, or directly by word or deed, that they are "rescuing" or "protecting" them from their "irresponsible" parents (Mandelbaum 1962). Such an attitude is not justified; it is unfair and counterproductive. We should be sensitive to parental feelings about separation and supportive of their sense of loss.

Observations

Following admission and subsequently as appropriate, the worker should report to members of the interdisciplinary team his observation of a child's reaction to separation. For instance:

1. Does he seem to be homesick (cries easily when family is mentioned, when he receives mail or a telephone call from home)?
2. Does he say he prefers being here to being at home?
3. Does he engage worker in frequent talks about his home and family members?
4. Does he seem not to accept placement, refusing to cooperate with institutional requirements?
5. Has he made an adjustment to group living, his peers, and workers, but sporadically expresses a desire to be at home, indicating ambivalence about placement?

STRUCTURE

The child who comes into group care has generally experienced failure in many aspects of his life. He needs to establish order in his disorganized mode of living. To achieve harmony from disorder, he must first experience ordered and planned living. "Structure" represents a fundamental therapeutic component of group care, providing a life rhythm of routines and expectations. Conflict thus tends to diminish because there are fewer individual choices about routines of daily living. Concreteness is represented rather than vagueness, certainty rather than confusion, and simplification instead of complexity.

Another aspect of structure is protection against destructive impulse expression. Just as society prescribes rules of conduct and laws for the protection of all, so does the group program provide its children with external controls against impulses which may be inadequately controlled from within. Acts against oneself, against others, and against property are dealt with quickly and effectively. If this is not done, adult inaction may be interpreted as indirect approval of destructive behavior. This may convey adult weakness and indecision to children who require adult firmness and strength.

Because structure is imposed and restrictive, it tends to evoke anxieties and frustration. It should therefore be clearly interpreted and consistently administered. Children who have conflict about it should have an opportunity to discuss it. Adolescents, in particular, are more apt to accept it and conform to its requirements when they are convinced that rules are not arbitrarily set by each individual adult but are responsibly planned. (Mayer 1972). When structure is equivalent to controls, without considering therapeutic needs of children, when it has no flexibility to adapt to an individual's developing capacity for greater responsibility, it becomes rigid, stultifying, and loses its therapeutic value. When overemphasis on controls is motivated by the need of an institution's staff to maintain order and to avoid trouble, it may not be constructive as a method of rehabilitation. An inflexible program dominated by rigid rules and sanctions may suffice for containment purposes. It may achieve superficial conformity and adaptation to the institution's standards because of fear of adult retaliation, but it will not generally promote inner change. The street-wise youngster may pay lip service to the adult-dominated social structure. He is capable of manipulating adults for his benefit. Although his adjustment may seem impressive, it is superficial. He adapts but he does not change. If he has leadership capabilities, he may in fact rule his group in accordance with an accustomed delinquent code and hinder others from benefitting from a rehabilitation program (Polsky 1962). Structure should not be fixed or rigid. It should have a built-in flexibility for the youngster who has demonstrated a capacity for greater responsibility and independence.

It is not sufficient for staff to be familiar with the structure of the program and to carry out its requirements with efficiency. Acceptance and understanding of its therapeutic purposes is essential. The adults must have the capacity to convey these feelings to the children with conviction and firmness but without hostility or defensiveness. If a worker is dissatisfied with a prescribed rule or routine and therefore finds it difficult to enforce, he should discuss it with his supervisor. Changes or deviations from established practice cannot be left to the discretion of an individual. It requires prior discussion among staff and, wherever feasible, with the children as well.

AUTHORITY

Every individual relates to authority figures. Parental authority as well as parental affection are essential aspects of parenthood and parental guidance. Children's ambivalence about adult authority is an age-old phenomenon. Recent years have witnessed increasing parental ambivalence about exercising authority. Mayer (1972: 484) states:

> What has made the handling of adolescents complicated in our time is not that today's adolescents are so much more opposed than in the past to the use of authority (Socrates complained about the unruliness and rebelliousness of the young), but rather that adults have become so much more uncertain and guilt-stricken about using authority.

To be constructive, the adult acting in an authority role cannot be authoritarian, meaning despotic, rigid, unsympathetic, or cruel. If he is, he will be feared but not respected. Neither can he be corruptible or subject to manipulation. If he is, he may be subject to seduction by the shrewd, exploited by the strong, considered hypocritical by all, and respected by no one.

The child care worker by his very role and function represents authority. He can expect to evoke ambivalent feelings among all of the children and overt resistance by some. This is particularly pertinent in relation to the delinquent-oriented adolescent who views adults, with the exception of his delinquent associates, as tyrannical authority figures. He tends to express his hostility by defiance and destructive acts. In group care, such a youngster may be helped to modify his distorted attitudes by making available to him benign, firm, and uncorruptible adults with whom he may establish a significant relationship. There must also exist an atmosphere of respect for authority. If a child care worker conveys to children the impression that he is conflicted about authority or feels guilty about expressing it, he cannot be effective. He may, in fact, fortify conflicting feelings toward authority.

Group care is reality-oriented, emphasizing corrective socialization for children who are either unable to cope with reality or who attempt to avoid its demands and restrictions upon their pleasure-seeking urges. Goals of group care include provision of "care, guidance, restraint and protection of such quality that infantile omnipotent strivings are frustrated, dependent object-love relationships with staff are established and tension releasing activities are guided into socially approved ego-building forms of expression" (Simon 1956). Child care workers play a crucial role in realizing these goals. To be effective agents in this endeavor, they need to feel comfortable about upholding established structure, setting limits, and exercising restraint on children's impulsive behavior. If a worker is fearful that the exercise of his authority will antagonize the children and harm his relationships with them, he will most likely be insecure about using it. Authority can be abused and misused. Appropriate use of authority serves to strengthen relationships with children and "can contribute to the achievement of several worthy goals: to provide order and security, to reflect the larger social order in which the clients will eventually live, or to aid in the development of inner controls" (Watkins 1979: 213).

As a group leader, the child care worker represents authority within his group. His personality and nature of involvement with the children as a group will affect the quality of group life, its sense of cohesiveness, social responsibility, and security. In research studies on leadership, three types have been identified (White and Lippitt 1953):

1. **Authoritarian** leadership characterized by arbitrariness and control. This type of leader is dictatorial. He dominates, is strongly directive, gives orders, does not explain plans or task he imposes on individuals and the group. He rewards conformity and discourages initiative. He is aloof from involvement with individual children but may designate "assistants" who enforce his orders. Whether children submit or rebel, the consequences are destructive to individual, groups and group socialization.

2. **Laissez-faire** leadership implies lack of adult direction, friendliness but not closeness, and overall passivity. The adult exercises minimal control.

3. **Democratic** leadership encourages the participation of the children in planning and decision-making through group discussion. There is open and free communication with adult availability to all the children. Individuality is respected and initiative encouraged. Cooperation rather than competitiveness is stressed. The group atmosphere is one of friendship and pride in the group and the physical setting. Democratic leadership requires (a great deal of) effort and investment on the leader's part. In the long run, it contributes to healthier child development. This does not mean that the child care worker cannot or should not act with authority. This degree will vary with the nature of the group. Some children need more direction and outer controls than others.

As an authority figure, the worker needs the support and backing of the "structure" of the group care program. The routines, rules, and regulations specify standards of expectations and set limits on acting-out behavior. Since it is "nonpersonal" in character, it provides the worker with "legitimate power" in his limit-setting role (Jacobs and Schweitzer 1979). This status should be made clear to a child upon admission, so that from the beginning he is aware that the "control" component is set by the program and is not the consequence of the worker's subjective whim or "hangups." Some children may forget this clarification because of their need to project blame on their child care workers and perceive them in negative terms as authoritarian and depriving adults. This can be counteracted by reminding a child of the true source and purpose of the limit-setting mechanism-structure. ("These are the requirements and expectations in this place . . . I did not make these rules.") How these controls are interpreted and enforced will depend on the worker's understanding and acceptance of structured living for the children, on his skill and personality. This is analogous to the parental role in child-rearing and is consistent with the principle that healthy growth requires development of inner controls. When a parent provides the necessary guidance "in a consistent loving manner," he provides the outer, age-appropriate measures of controls his child requires for healthy development. "This serves as a model for the child's developing an inner control system, reinforces the degree of self-control he has achieved, and provides external controls where inner ones are not as yet developed" (Jacobs and Schweitzer 1979: 249). Children in group care who have not experienced this type of relationship in their own families require it. To be effective as a modeling agent, a good working relationship between worker and child is essential. The harmonious interactions of structure, authority, and relationship is the essence of effective group care.

There is also the question of free choice. Certain tasks in group life are mandatory. Group discussion on whether essential tasks should be done or established routines followed is not advisable. It is valid, however, to involve the group in determining how best to do them and to evaluate performance. A worker must also act quickly and decisively in crisis situations and emergencies. This justifies authoritative intervention. A laissez-faire approach may also be valid at certain times—when, for example, there is no programmed activity or during free playtime—to enable a child to make independent decisions or to find his own way as long as it is not damaging to others or to himself. This implies "planned passivity" rather than disinterest or lack of involvement as is the characteristic of laissez-faire leadership.

EMPHASIS ON HEALTH

No matter how disturbed a child may be, he has vestiges of health within him which have to be identified and nurtured. Children's recuperative powers are strong. When transferred from pathogenic environmental conditions, they have a chance to develop their healthy potential. The assessment of a child's strengths is most important. It complements diagnostic understanding of his disturbance or handicap by identifying potential sources of health. This is useful in planning a program of activities for him which will match assigned tasks with his capabilities. It will enhance the likelihood of success in developing physical, intellectual, and social skills. Mastery opportunities built into the residential program include learning and work responsibilities in the cottage, at school, and in leisure-time activities. Geared to flexible standards of expectations, they help increase a sense of adequacy and self-confidence. Adults convey to the children the feeling that they believe in their capacities and potentials. To do so involves an understanding of a child's strengths, a readiness to help him with problems of mastery, and a flexible increasing scale of tasks and expectations.

INDIVIDUALIZATION AND GROUP LIVING

Individualization is of prime importance in group care. It is based on the individual characteristics of each child and the assessment of his maturational level. A six-month old infant expresses his need for food, drink, or a sense of discomfort differently than the three-year-old who has verbal skills; the three-year-old, differently than the ten-year-old or the adolescent. The developmental level of children in group care is not necessarily represented by their chronological age. In fact, the term "he is old enough to know better" or "he doesn't act his age" is generally not applicable to these children. Most, if not all, have experienced a lag in their emotional and social development. This may be due to the fact that few, if any, have had their basic physical and emotional needs (for acceptance, belonging, affection, control, and so on) met adequately. Because they have not had a satisfactory nurturing relationship during infancy, they are unable to express their needs, desires, and feelings openly and directly. Not having experienced a sense of basic trust during their early years, they tend to be distrustful and wary about getting involved. Not having been cared for adequately, they may feel that they must not be worth caring for. Such children have developed defensive mechanisms which influence their attitudes and pattern their behavior, often making them easily frustrated and tending to avoid learning.

Through observation and information about a child's history, the worker is cued in regarding his level of developmental functioning and begins to understand his unique way of expressing inner needs. The overt behavior which is generally defensive may mask the underlying feelings of insecurity and anxiety. As the worker learns to read the meaning behind the behavior or the nonverbal messages representing feelings, he will be in a position to set goals in accordance with the child's capabilities. With reference to group life, the workers will have to establish and maintain an environment of security, trust, acceptance, care, and support so that the children can freely express their needs, work through their developmental lags, and achieve a higher level of maturation.

The child care worker has to be sensitive to the struggle the child is going through while learning and mastering tasks. For example, a child might become antagonistic toward his devoted worker and say or do things which might hurt the latter's sensibilities. It may represent a transference reaction or a projection. It may be a manifestation of the surfacing of a deep sense of hurt. The child expresses this hurt by projecting his feelings onto the worker. Therefore, the worker cannot always interpret negative behavior toward him literally. In his efforts to help the child in his growth, he must also guard against overprotection or hasty alleviation of frustration. In helping him master physical, intellectual, and social skills, the worker "stands by," giving support, encourages effort, and helps directly as needed rather than by doing things for the child. All of this represents individualization.

Often child care workers are troubled by what seems to them to be clinician's pressures for "individualizing" without due regard for the realities of managing a group of troubled and troublesome children. It is not uncommon to hear a worker say, "I understand that (Johnny) requires more of my attention but to give it, I have to neglect someone else . . ." or "If I give Mary this additional privilege, the other girls will accuse me of favoring her and of not liking them."

This is an understandable dilemma. However, there need not be a dichotomy between individual needs and the group. The uniqueness of the individual must not be neglected for the benefit of group control. Although group living should be designed to provide optimum growth possibilities for each child, one cannot expect child care workers (or teachers) to disregard group needs to meet an individual child's excessive needs for physical care or special treatment. When such a child is brought into a group, he will require special attention. It is essential that additional staff be available to assure adequate coverage so that the regular staff will not be overburdened nor the other children neglected.

It is important for staff as well as children to accept the principle that individualization is a prime focus of group care. The group, as a dynamic balance of interacting individuals, serves as a medium which enhances individual development. This implies educating everyone, especially the children, to understand the concept of individuality—that each one is cherished as unique, and as much as it is possible, every child's needs will be respected. If a child needs something "extra" or some special attention, it does not mean that it is given at the expense of the others, that the motive is to be unfair, discriminating, or "undemocratic." When a child accepts this interpretation and can act upon it, he has matured from self-interest to respecting others' needs, from distrust to trustfulness, and demonstrates a readiness and capacity to share a significant adult with another child without feeling rejected.

There are innumerable examples in group care to illustrate individualization. One deals quite differently with two children who may commit the same type of offense against established rules. For example, when a psychotic child is "out of place" from his school program, one takes into consideration that he is a disoriented child who frequently forgets where he is and what he is supposed to be doing. Such a child is helped to get back to his class. When a sociopathic-type youngster tries to manipulate himself out of the classroom situation in order to do as he pleases, he is treated with firmness and may be punished if the offense is repeated. One individualizes in many other respects—the number of times a child is seen in individual therapy, the type of school program to which he is assigned, his cottage group placement, his recreation group assignments, and so on.

However, overall group structure sets the outer boundaries beyond which individualization is not possible. If these limits are over-extended, the total program might be threatened by disorganization. For example, delinquent acting-out cannot be condoned. Consistent and uniform attitudes must be conveyed against runaways, against destruction of property, and against physical assault. Neither should the structure of daily routines, such as getting up on time, cleanliness of the cottage, mealtimes, bedtime, and so on, be discarded because of individualization.

IDENTIFICATION

Identification plays a major role in human development. Unlike imitation, it operates unconsciously. The individual strives to pattern himself after a person or persons significant in his life by incorporating that person's attributes, beliefs, and values. Many of the children in group settings have not experienced wholesome relationships with adults within their own families. Consequently, their identifications may be confused, diffused, or faulty through association with asocial or antisocial models. In group care, efforts are made to help them overcome their reservations and resistances so they can form significant relationships with adults. This may pave the way toward positive identifications. Esthetic and ethical values are important in achieving constructive and mature identifications.

Esthetics pertain to a sense of the beautiful. A person's physical environment affects his state of wellbeing. It also is a determinant in the development of his creative potential. It is the agency's responsibility to make available to children a living situation and activities that evoke and encourage creative expression. This may be done by making the children's physical surroundings attractive, and by actively sensitizing staff and children to esthetic values in relation to cleanliness, appearance, and tidiness in cottage, group home, and classroom. The key factor seems to be the attitudes of the adults around them. If they set sound standards and are actively involved in attaining and maintaining them, they will convey to the children that they care for them and that they, the children, are worth caring for. On the other hand, the children tend to respond with apathy or even destructiveness to drab and shabby physical surroundings. Maintenance of standards may have to be an ongoing struggle for many workers because of children's inability or unwillingness to comply, but standards should not be compromised.

Ethics may be viewed as the quality that integrates human beings into a society. Ethical values are a gauge of a civilization's spiritual and social achievement as well as man's counterforce against the pressures of destructive inner impulses. Laws representing established ethical and moral values have been in existence throughout man's recorded history. Children are taught to respect them. They inevitably become aware of the existence of a gap between the ethical values they are taught and expected to follow and their violations by adults in daily life transactions. When this occurs, they may begin to view adult teachings with skepticism. It is unlikely they will incorporate adult values unless they are convinced that the adults themselves adhere to them.

Cultural, ethnic, and religious factors are important aspects of a person's sense of identity. The group, consisting of children representing a diversity of cultural, ethnic, and religious backgrounds, can serve and enhance such identifications and correct prejudices. An essential requirement for its realization is staff attitudes and values. If a child care worker has confused identifications and manifests prejudicial attitudes, he will convey this to the children. This may result not only in confusion on the children's part, but at its worst, an enhancement of prejudice. Awareness of one's own attitudes and values is helpful. A genuine expression of tolerance and respect for differences by the adults will be felt by the children. In time the exposure may help them modify their own prejudicial attitudes and behavior toward others who are different.

VALUES

According to Kohlberg (1975), "moral," ethical, or value development parallels maturational growth. He formulates three progressive levels of moral awareness:

1. **Preconventional level**—An individual is oriented toward obeying rules and avoiding punishment, a state determined by parental guidance to conform to their value orientation. Parents reward behavior that they approve, and they disapprove, verbally or through punishment, behavior contrary to their values. As a consequence, young children learn to judge behavior that is rewarded as "good" and behavior that is punished as "bad." Satisfying one's needs is also an important determinant of what is the right action. Thus, control of conduct is *external.*

2. **Conventional level**—The orientation is initially to conform to family and then to peer-group standards. During adolescence, when the wish for peer-group acceptance may outweigh the need for family approval, there may be a conflict between family (and the societal values they represent) and peer-group values. Another aspect or stage in this level is orientation to values of the existing social order. At this level, control of conduct is still external since the individual still adheres to standards of others; however, the motivation to comply with these expectations is *internal.*

3. **Postconventional level**—Control of conduct is internally determined. Decision to act is based on examination of issues, and includes careful thought and judgment concerning ethical matters. The capacity for self-evaluation and self-criticism is more developed; the rights of others and the validity of mutual agreements are respected. Flexibility and adaptability to changing values have also been assimilated.

In group care, workers are involved with children whose value orientation is either in Level I or Level II. Intervention techniques in reorientation toward Level III, which is an ultimate goal in child-rearing and rehabilitation, must take into consideration the level of a child's value orientation. Behavior modification seems to be more appropriate to children and adolescents in Level I. Positive as well as negative reinforcement techniques are used to redirect these children from socially undesirable behavior and attitudes to more adaptive levels of functioning. Group discussion and other educational methods would seem more appropriate for adolescents who function on Level II.

It is important to differentiate between genuine or "true" values and professed values, particularly because children in group care are quick to assess whether a worker practices the values he attempts to convey. It may be helpful to workers to be familiar with more objective criteria for evaluating a true value. The following are suggested by Group Child Care Consultant Services (1978: 53–56).

1. The value must be freely chosen from among a number of alternatives.
2. The consequences of the alternatives (on other people) must be considered.
3. The person must be ready and willing to act on the value repeatedly. This action demonstrates a commitment to it.
4. When the value is affirmed through action, it tends to help the person achieve his potential and indicates that it has become integrated into the person's total value orientation.

These criteria reflect Level III of Kohlberg's classification. Most children in group care have not achieved it. They act in accordance with their accustomed values. Once a child's value orientation is established, the worker is in a position to formulate ways to help him strengthen constructive values and to modify destructive ones which he may have brought with him or learned since his arrival. There should be statement of values upheld by the program which become expectations for staff as well as the children.

A value system should have a degree of flexibility. Changing conditions may require modification. A periodic review by administration of established values supplemented by staff discussion regarding recommended changes should initiate the review process. A representative staff committee from the various disciplines would then meet to draw up a consensual statement of basic values which would be presented to the children's groups. The children should not be asked whether or not these values are acceptable because they will need time to think about them and evaluate them with their child care workers. Children should discuss how they, along with staff, can implement the values in group living—that is, what specific steps should be taken, whether they should be enforced, and how?

In formulating value expectations, the following may be considered:

1. *Physical security*—Everyone needs the assurance of protection from physical abuse. Fighting, attacking, hurting among the children, assault on the staff, and corporal punishment of children by staff is not acceptable and will not be tolerated.

2. *Emotional security*—An atmosphere of acceptance, respect, and caring for all is desirable. Emotional abuse of children as well as staff will not be tolerated.

3. *Self-reliance*—Responsibility for oneself (taking care of personal appearance and hygiene, clothing, etc.) on the basis of one's capability and potential is an expectation.

4. *Social responsibility*—A responsible attitude toward others and the program is a goal to be worked for.

5. *Communal work*—The scope of work responsibilities varies with age level.

6. *Learning*—Education and learning is encouraged. Expectations are in accordance with ability to learn.

7. *Ethics and esthetics*—Development of a cooperative spirit and of esthetic sensibilities should be valued goals.

Value differences are inevitable in group living. The child care worker, like a parent in his family or teacher in the classroom, is faced with conflicting values, especially with adolescents. Differences will surface regarding dress, attitudes about education and work, peer relationship, goals, and so on.

The child care worker not only has his own value system to which he is committed but also the group values he is expected to uphold. When a child's behavior is contrary to the standards or rules of the group care program, his child care worker is obligated to deal with it. The process may be helpful to the child and to the relationship between worker and child. The following approach has been found to be sound.

First it is essential to determine whether the child is familiar with established standards and expectations. If he is not, he should be informed and told that he is expected to conform. There are occasions when a child will request that an exception be made in his case. The worker has to assess whether this is a justified request or a manipulation. If it is the former, he may wish to take the matter up with his supervisor or administrator; if it is the latter, he should point it out. In either case, the worker makes it clear that he does not have the authority to make an exception to an established rule which everyone is expected to follow. In the case of a first offense, the worker may decide to defer disciplinary action and inform the child accordingly, indicating that if he does it again, he will have to enforce the rule and discipline him for violating it. The worker may use the occasion to explore why the child is unable or unwilling to conform to expectations and, in the process, offer to help him work out his differences with established values. Hopefully, the offer will be accepted. If it is, the worker can proceed to present his point of view or the rationale for established values. It is essential that it be presented clearly and concisely without lecturing or moralizing, which tends to antagonize.

The burden for change is left with the youngster. The worker has offered a different outlook and suggested alternative ways of thinking and behaving. One can only hope that the impact will shake the child's commitment to questionable values and generate a receptivity for change. Of course, the most effective way of modifying values is to model the desired behavior—practicing rather than professing values. The children are alert judges of adult behavior and quickly spot a "phony." The best way to get children to adopt one's values is through maintaining a caring, trusting relationship.

INTEGRATION

In group care, no one can be fully effective working in isolation. Positive results can be achieved only through collective effort and cooperation. Such integration goes beyond sharing of information among the various disciplines. It involves joint planning and evaluation of a child's treatment plan, a capacity to work together, respect for contributions made by each member of the residential team, a common conception of the work, and an understanding of the complementarity of each other's roles and tasks. The clinical and environmental programs must function as a unified therapeutic effort through participation of all the disciplines in planning for each child, implementing individual and group treatment goals, and evaluating the overall program of the institution.

Disunity and role confusion among staff is not helpful to children, especially to those who have witnessed parental disharmony. One area of confusion in relation to role may arise when there is no common base of reference about basic terminology. For example, the term "treatment" in designating the institution as a treatment center may mean different things to teachers, social workers, child care workers, or psychiatrists. If it is viewed in its specific circumscribed meaning, connoting individual psychotherapy rather than the broad growth-inducing and rehabilitation services the institution makes available for the children, the essence of residential treatment is distorted. Treatment signifies the total encompassing atmosphere and practice and includes all of the aspects of the therapeutic milieu and clinical services. All personnel in group care working with children should function "therapeutically." This means that each one addresses himself to the individual needs of the child within the context of his area of responsibility, with awareness that he is part of a collective treatment effort. The child care worker's contribution encompasses his varied tasks related to group living. The teacher contributes by conveying knowledge of subject matter, developing the child's mastery and skills in educational areas, and providing additional opportunities for positive identification. The caseworker or therapist helps the child achieve greater self-understanding.

This description of allocating specialized functions to different disciplines sounds like parcelling out parts of a child among a number of specialists. Such an impression is not intended; it would be unrealistic and incorrect. Everyone involved in a continuous relationship with a child must not lose sight of the *wholeness* of the individual. While exercising his particular role, the child care worker, caseworker, teacher, and recreation worker must do so in the context of the child's total personality and his interrelated needs. This is stressed in staff training, supervision, and integration conferences. It requires continuous communication among the members of the residential treatment team. Because many people are involved in a child's residential life, integration is not easily achieved. This is especially true in large residential settings where the ratio of staff per child is low, where relationships between the disciplines are not close, and where scheduling is not flexible. Small residential treatment centers, generously staffed, are more likely to achieve a higher degree of integration.

There are group programs that reduce integration problems to a minimum. For example, the psychoeducateur model developed in Montreal (Guindon 1973) integrates a number of functions in one professional. He encompasses four disciplines—child care, counseling, education, recreation—as well as coordination of any other services that may be required. This calls for a highly competent, dedicated, educated, and experienced professional. Training of the psychoeducateur, which includes field work as well as academic subjects, takes three to four years in the School of Psychoeducation in the University of Montreal (Guindon 1973).

CONFIDENTIALITY

There are two aspects of confidentiality. The first has to do with information that identifies children. This information should not be divulged to others in conversation, table talk, or gossip because it violates a fundamental right of every child to be protected from the dissemination of personal information about him. Neither should staff discuss children in their presence unless the children are included as participants in the conversation.

The second aspect relates to confidences conveyed by children. If dealt with constructively, they can be helpful to children as well as staff. The following case situations illustrate:

"I am worried about Mary, Miss Adams," said Mrs. Jones, Mary's housemother. "She's moody, avoids me, keeps to herself most of the time, and gives the impression that something is bothering her."

"I've noted a change in her as well during our last two interviews, but I haven't been successful in getting Mary to talk about it," replied Miss Adams, Mary's social worker. "She denies anything is wrong, and whatever she does discuss is of little significance. Why don't you talk with her? She thinks highly of you and trusts you," Miss Adams urged.

"All right, I didn't want to take the initiative with her before I consulted you. I know something is not right with Mary," Mrs. Jones replied.

The next day Mrs. Jones asked Mary to accompany her to the housekeeper for some supplies. On the way she remarked, "Mary, you seem to be troubled about something. Is there anything wrong? It might help to talk about it." Mary began to cry, "Yes, there is. But I cannot tell you unless you promise not to tell anyone."

"You know I can't give you an unconditional promise, Mary," said Mrs. Jones. "But what's the big secret that you don't want me to share with anyone?"

"I feel I have to talk to someone and I trust you. But I'm afraid it will get me into trouble with administration if it becomes known. It may also get someone else in trouble," Mary said.

"So it's that serious," exclaimed Mrs. Jones. "Is the other person your boyfriend David?"

"Yes," admitted Mary. "I don't think we are doing anything wrong, but it is against the rules."

"You know, Mary, I can't withhold information from administration if it's harmful to children or the institution," said Mrs. Jones.

"Well," Mary said. "I can't go on without feeling very guilty and anxious. I'm afraid we'll get caught one day."

"Caught doing what?" questioned Mrs. Jones. Because Mary hesitated, she indicated to her that it might make her feel better if she talked about it. She could not promise that she would keep this confidential but she hopefully could be of help.

"O.K.," said Mary. "I've been sneaking out of the cottage after lights out to meet David. We've done nothing more serious than kissing and some petting. But I'm not sure if it continues it won't go further. Then I'm worried and scared that we might be expelled or returned to court if we are caught. I'd like to put a stop to this, but I don't know how to handle it with David."

Mrs. Jones advised that Mary should put a stop to this activity and talk to David about her misgivings. They had better consider the consequences of these clandestine meetings and the effect it may have on their future. She further suggested it might be good for her and David to talk to their social workers. As for David's reaction, Mrs. Jones felt that if David really cared for her, he would understand. And if he didn't, maybe she would have to reconsider whether she wanted to be involved with him. In any event, she would be glad to talk to Mary about it.

She concluded by saying, "You know that it's wrong to violate this rule. There's good reason for having it." As for the disciplinary consequences, the fact that she had talked about it at this time was in her favor.

"All right, Mrs. Jones," Mary said. "I'll talk to David today and Miss Adams tomorrow. But won't you please hold off about this information until then? I'd like to have the chance to handle it myself."

"All right," said Mrs. Jones. "I'll do that."

"And I promise to do my part," said Mary, quite relieved.

Children's confidences should be respected unless they involve risks to life and safety or destruction of property. If a child informs a worker that he has something to tell him but will not do so unless it is kept confidential, then the latter must explain that he cannot keep certain things confidential. He can assure the child that he will help him think the problem through and also help him decide whether to convey it personally to his caseworker or to administrative persons who must be informed about it. He may offer to do so himself, with or without the child present. To do otherwise and keep the secret may represent to the child approval of destructive behavior. For example:

> During his Monday morning therapy session, Ben was restless and unusually anxious. He said that he had to tell Mr. S. something very important but could not do so unless he was assured it would be kept confidential. Mr. S. promised and Ben revealed that the previous day he had broken into the school canteen and stolen a large sum of money. The discussion then focused on an examination of the dynamics of the act and what motivated Ben to steal and did not deal with realistic issues such as return of the money and the unreality of keeping this act a secret. When the theft was discovered during the afternoon, the whole institution was shocked because of the nature of the offense and the scope of the loss. Ben's therapist had kept his promise not to divulge the secret, but Ben subsequently told several of the boys in his cottage. This led to his exposure.

The fact that a child has a need to confide a planned or actual wrongdoing indicates that he may not only want to share it with someone because it troubles him but also implies that he wants to be prevented from doing something he knows is harmful. This might include running away, suicidal attempts, assaultive acts, setting fires, stealing, or destroying property. It is logical to assume that a child would not reveal a secret for which he may be punished unless he is masochistically inclined. Revealing it even with the proviso that it be kept confidential implies that the hidden motive is not to conceal the act but to seek intervention.

REFERENCES

Adler J. 1970. "Separation—A Crucial Issue in Foster Care." *Journal of Jewish Communal Service* 46, no. 4: 305–313.

Group Child Care Consultant Services. 1977. *The Basic Training Course for Residential Child Care Workers*, Student Manual "Discipline." Chapel Hill: University of North Carolina Social Work.

Guindon, J. 1973. "The Psychoeducator Training Program." *International Journal of Mental Health* 2, no. 1: 27–32.

Jacobs, B.J., and R. Schweitzer. 1979. "Conceptualizing Structure in a Day Treatment Program for Delinquent Adolescents." *American Journal of Orthopsychiatry* 49, no. 2 (April): 246–251.

Kohlberg, L. 1975. "The Cognitive Developmental Approach to Moral Education." *Phi Delta Kappan* 61: 670–77.

Littner, N. 1956. *Traumatic Effects of Separation and Placement.* New York: Child Welfare League of America.

Mahler, M.S., and K. La Perriere. 1965. "Mother–Child Interaction During Separation–Individuation." *Psychoanalytic Quarterly* 34: 483–497.

Mandelbaum, A. 1962, "Parent–Child Separation: Its Significance to Parents." *Social Work* 7, no. 4: 27–34.

Mayer, M.F. 1972. "The Group in Residential Treatment of Adolescents." *Child Welfare* 51, no. 8: 482–493.

Miller, J. 1978. "How Do You Say Good-bye?" In *Focus* 2, no. 4.

Perlman, H. 1979. *Relationship: The Heart of Helping People.* Chicago: University of Chicago Press.

Polsky, H. 1962. *Cottage Six: The Social System of Delinquent Boys in Residential Treatment.* New York: Russell Sage Foundation.

Simon, A.J. 1956. "Residential Treatment of Children: Unanswered Questions." *Social Service Review* 30 (September): 260–267.

Watkins, T. 1979. "Staff Conflicts Over Use of Authority in Residential Settings." *Child Welfare* 58, no. 3 (March): 205–215.

White, R., and R. Lippitt. 1953. "Leader Behavior and Member Reaction in Three Social Climates." In *Group Dynamics—Research and Theory*, edited by D. Cartwright and A. Zander, pp. 585–611. Evanston, Ill.: Row Peterson.

Whittaker, J.K. 1979. *Caring for Troubled Children.* San Francisco: Jossey-Bass.

7 DISCIPLINE

Discipline and punishment are interrelated but not synonymous. Discipline may be broadly defined as the degree of established order to facilitate group living. Punishment is "a planful attempt by adults to influence either the behavior or the long range development of a child, or a group of children, for its own benefit, by exposing it to an unpleasant experience" (Redl 1966: 363). "Punishment emphasizes penalty. . . . discipline, on the other hand, emphasizes the educative value of the disciplinary measure to the wrongdoer" (Gardner 1973: 163).

Punishment is an imposed action; discipline, a learning process whose aim is achievement of self-control. A person may be considered disciplined when his actions and behavior are self-regulated. Discipline cannot be imposed; it develops over a period of time through relationship with others, and involves incorporation of a value system. Thus, a child in group care may learn to become disciplined through his relationship with his child care worker(s). He becomes receptive to the worker's teaching, responsive to his guidance, amenable to his value orientation and conduct which he may begin to model. Teaching discipline requires patience, effort, and concern (for the child) and integrity on the part of the worker. For the child it involves a slow process of trial and error, a developing sense of trust in the worker, and motivation for change. Working through this process enables the child to strengthen control over inner impulses and gain a capacity to adapt to the demands of outer reality.

Discipline in group care may be defined as the "educational process of establishing and teaching an orderly way of life which will maintain and protect the integrity of the individual and the group" (Group Child Care Consultant Services 1977: 23). The "structure" of the group care milieu provides the framework for education in orderly living—namely, a planned stable life rhythm throughout the day, designated limits, and stated expectations. To help children adapt to its requirements and to profit from its therapeutic objectives, the group setting relies on the development of significant relationships among children and staff.

Education in orderly living for most of the children in group care implies a process of "unlearning" established patterns of maladaptive behavior and replacing them with more socially constructive behavior—for many, often a painful process filled with resistance to the new ways. But through individual and group discussion they should be enlightened about the need for structure, the rationale for limits it imposes, the necessity to comply with established rules and regulations: in other words, why control of undesirable behavior is essential. Offenders should be forewarned about consequences of repeated violations. Reward for acceptable behavior should be emphasized. Actual punishment or deprivation of privileges should be the final step or action taken in the process of teaching discipline.

According to Ginott, most discipline problems consist of "angry feelings and angry acts." Each has to be dealt with differently. "Feelings have to be identified and expressed; acts may have to be limited and redirected" (Ginott 1965: 94). Handling the feelings by acknowledging them and then talking about them may diffuse the anger and prevent the undesirable behavior reaction. For example:

When Dean (age twelve) was observed by his child care worker, Mrs. Bates, to be roaming around the cottage living room looking tense and angry, she asked him to come into the staff office. He impatiently cried, "Leave me alone," but when she persisted, he followed her.

"You look angry," said Mrs. Bates.

"So what!" Dean challenged.

"You seem very upset," Mrs. Bates added.

"I feel mad!" said Dean.

"At whom? Did anyone do something to make you angry?" Mrs. Bates asked.

"You did," replied Dean with tears in his eyes. "You are letting Jimmy go on his home visit a day earlier than me. It's not fair."

"So you believe I favor him more than you?" she asked.

"Yes," said Dean, beginning to cry. "I've been better than he, but you like him more."

Mrs. Bates put her arm around Dean and said, "You have been good; and I do not play favorites. Why did you not talk to me about this before? Whenever you feel I've been unfair to you, you should talk to me about it. It helps to talk about feelings that make one feel bad inside. Now, let me explain about Jimmy's home visit. . . ."

She then told him about the special circumstances in Jimmy's family that required him to go home earlier. Dean accepted them. He said that Mrs. Bates was right. If he had asked about the visit before getting so angry it would have been better.

By helping Dean talk about his frustration, a blow-up was avoided. Had she arrived on the scene later, just as Dean was about to assault Jimmy or another child who was the target of his anger, she would have intervened physically by firmly demanding, "Stop it, Dean!" and removing him to the office where in time she would have gotten Dean involved in a similar dialogue. But in this type of situation the behavior had to be dealt with first, followed by diffusion of Dean's anger through discussion.

Child care workers also have to deal with their own angry feelings. It is inevitable that a child care worker will get angry with children. The often intense emotional pressures in dealing with disturbed children are pervasive. A worker is subject to a bombardment of displaced and projected feelings, expressed in varied forms of provocation ranging from denigrating and insulting epithets, hostile attitudes, and aggressive acts. Frequently a worker faces such provocations in the presence of other children and feels "put on the spot" by such challenges. At times his anger may be aroused by planned or spontaneous disruption by a group of children. Even the most experienced workers may "lose their cool" and react angrily. It is unrealistic for a worker to expect of himself total and unconditional control of his emotions, especially anger toward the children. It is neither a sign of meanness or weakness to do so. In fact, an expression of anger can be constructive and helpful to children who may not be sensitive to the hurtful feelings their actions may evoke or provoke.

In her study of "Constructive and Destructive Anger in Child Care Workers," Helmer (1978: 310–312) describes a sequence in experiencing and expressing anger: A worker subjected to continued provocations by a child begins to *accumulate* increasing frustration which is finally triggered into an angry outburst against the child by some hostile comment or aggressive act. The worker loses control and reacts with behavior ranging from verbal to physical abuse toward the child, such as screaming, shaking, or hitting. He might even turn his anger against himself, punching the wall, thus injuring his hand. This is classified as destructive use of anger. Although it may stop a child's provocation or destructive act momentarily, it damages relationships, generates guilt feelings on the worker's part, or intensifies a feeling of helplessness or inadequacy.

Constructive use of anger involves understanding of the child who provokes it and a readiness to express feelings. The worker who experiences anger at a youngster's provocation avoids becoming the target of displaced emotions, avoids counter-transference reactions, or avoids falling into the trap set for him. Instead of "blowing his top," he might say to the child, "It seems that you are trying to get me angry. Well, you're succeeding! I'd rather talk about what's bugging you than fight. Maybe I can help. Let's talk about it." The worker educates the child about feelings, suggests a constructive way to deal with them, conveys understanding, and demonstrates self-control and a caring attitude. The child might then be helped to express his feelings and deal with frustrations which have been problematic to him and to others. Problems can then be defined and the process of resolving them begun through examination and resolution rather than explosion and exploitation of others. Using this approach, a worker may serve as a model for handling feelings of anger constructively.

DEALING WITH DISRUPTIVE BEHAVIOR

Child care workers are confronted with a diversity of disruptive behavior, ranging from minor violations of established routines to physical assault, abusive behavior, suicidal attempts, vandalism, and fire-setting. In a recent nationwide study of group child care programs, "Coping with Disruptive Behavior," Russo and Shyne (1980) researched the scope and methods of control of such behavior. They classified them into sixteen categories, including verbal and physical abuse, self-destructive behavior, loss of impulse control, drug and alcohol abuse, hyperactivity, stealing, running away, refusal to attend school, destruction of property, inappropriate sexual activity, and fire-setting. Findings included the following:

1. Aggressive, assaultive behavior and use of drugs were considered by staff as the most troublesome. Verbal abuse and loss of impulse control were rated highest in occurrence.

2. There has been an increase in all categories of disruptive behavior during the past five years, possibly reflecting the escalating numbers of older and more disturbed children entering the group care system. The highest increase was in use of drugs (53 percent), physical abuse of others (45 percent), verbal abuse (43 percent), stealing (28 percent), and fire-setting (20 percent).

3. A wide range of methods to control disruptive behavior are used. The most frequent is talk—discussion with individual children as well as groups. Others include withholding of privileges, separation from the group, payment for damages, medication, physical restraint, secure confinement, and discharge.

4. Excessive talk, staff's reactions of anger, and physical restraint were deemed least successful in controlling disruptive behavior; restriction of privileges, a consistent relationship with children, counseling, and separation from the group were rated as the most successful methods.

5. The primary determinants of successful management of difficult behavior seemed to be the combination of type of method used and the attitudes and skill of the adults implementing them.

Punishment

There is a parallel between punishment and frustration. Frustration is a universal human experience and, in tolerable doses, essential for health and mature development. Disciplinary measures, not unlike frustration, can be constructive if they are consistently imposed, if they do not exceed the frustration tolerance of a child, are not arbitrarily imposed at the whim or impulse of the adult, and are not accompanied by hostility or motivated by a sense of revenge.

In group living situations, punishment is generally instituted following repeated breaches of established rules. It is essential that the rules be clearly stated so that both children and adults understand them. To avoid confusion among the children and conflict among the staff, rules must be consistently enforced by all the workers involved with a particular group of children. Reminding a child about violations of expectations is generally advisable and should precede punishment. The actual mode of punishment may involve suspension of privileges, extra work assignments, restriction to the cottage or to one's room, and other types of deprivation.

Avoiding Power Struggles

Power struggles may result in an impasse and consequent misuse of punishment. With seriously disturbed children a power struggle may lead to such a rigidity of reaction on the part of the child that irrationality will replace any reasoning capacity the child may have when not under severe stress. It may even lead to uncontrollable temper tantrums. In such situations, the child care worker who becomes involved in an irrational confrontation risks being the loser. The loss involves important consequences to his relationship with the child and his status in the group. The other children may lose respect for the worker's authority. Some of them may become anxious because the sense of security that adult authority provides has been shaken by their perception of the worker's loss of control. Diamond (1973) offers the following suggestions:

1. Don't become involved in any confrontation unless you are sure you can win.
2. Don't make threats you will not follow through.
3. Don't make threats you cannot follow through.

Preventive Intervention

Actual punishment may at times be avoided by preventive intervention. A child care worker may interfere in a volatile argument between children before it reaches explosiveness or physical assault. He may initiate group discussion about irritating situations which contribute to group acting-out in destructive ways.

Redirecting a child's or a group's attention and energies from potential explosiveness to constructive, anxiety-diffusing activities can avoid crises. The following examples by an experienced child care worker (Dryer 1978) illustrate the effectiveness of this method:

1. On different occasions, situations would flare up on the floor that needed my immediate attention. My approach was to remain calm and try to understand what precipitated the behavior. When a child is very angry with either peers or child care workers, it becomes difficult for him to express himself without getting hostile, defiant, and very frustrated. Reprimanding a child at that precise time doesn't always solve the problem. Redirecting a child, when she or he is in a crisis has worked for me tremendously. For instance, Patricia was a very disturbed and depressed child; she constantly would be irritable with peers and child care workers. Pat couldn't tolerate any changes in her daily routines or structure. If so, she would become destructive and abusive and go into a raging temper tantrum. I was able, most of the time, to cope with pat's behavior and motivate her interest by redirecting her. Giving Pat a particular project to do and compliment her on it was an excellent way to deal with her. Pat did splendid work with her hands, such as needlepoint and sewing. When calm, she was able to communicate and verbalize her feelings about how she had played a part in provoking and manipulating the incident at hand. Patricia had many good qualities that I admired about her. I nicknamed her "Busy Bee," because of her many talents. It's essential to try and establish a relationship with each child. In that way, the individual child would respond in a more positive manner to you.

2. Being involved in group activities can play an important part in a child's behavior. But regardless of what you do at times, the girls can still become emotionally upset "at the drop of a hat." One afternoon, I had a cooking activity going on with a group of girls; we were baking cookies. In the midst of preparing the ingredients, a fight started with two girls. In trying to separate the girls, the whole floor became chaotic. I had to focus my thoughts on how to regain control without adding "more fuel to the fire." After separating the girls, I tried to explain to them that fighting only created more anger, and talking about the problem was the best way to solve it. I decided to discontinue the cooking lessons because the children needed a more active, stimulating activity. I decided to organize a disco show; the girls enjoyed dancing, and once again, I was able to maintain order.

If a worker becomes aware of a potential delinquent act by an individual or group, he should intervene by bringing the issue into open discussion. He should be willing and ready to state categorically to a potential runaway: "I am not going to let you do it. I will not stand by and let you hurt yourself" or "I am not going to let you hurt him" or "I am not going to let you destroy that."

If a child seems to be working himself into an uncontrollable temper outburst which might result in injury to himself or to others, he may have to be isolated from the group for a brief period to give him time to calm down. He should be returned to the group when the worker feels he has regained control and when the child feels he can rejoin the activities without further disruption. When this "take-over time" method is not effective and the child continues to behave in a seriously disturbed and unstable manner, recommendations should be made to the supervisor or administrator on duty to transfer the child out of the group to an "isolation" room in the infirmary, if one is available, or to a similar facility where he would be under adult supervision and observation. He should be given the opportunity to talk to his child care worker, caseworker, or psychiatrist, as needed.

This often helps a child over a serious emotional crisis, and it avoids the need to transfer him temporarily to a psychiatric hospital.

PUNISHMENT CRITERIA

Before deciding on a specific punishment, the worker should consider whether it will help the child to learn not to repeat the offense. If it will not be effective, then it is improper. If a particular punishment is destructive to the relationship between the child and the worker, an alternative should be chosen. Other considerations include:

1. Punishment should be administered as soon as possible after the offensive behavior has been exhibited. Delay may cause the child to forget what he did to deserve it. He will not connect his responsibility to the consequences and will project blame on the worker, considering him unfair.

2. Excessive punishment is unfair as well as abusive. The child will focus on the unfairness of the adult, rather than on his own responsibility.

3. The disciplinary act should not be motivated by vengefulness or hostility. If it is, the child senses the hostility and views the punishment as vengeance rather than justice.

Schaefer (1976) offers these additional guidelines to assist child care workers "in thinking about and evaluating their effectiveness in punishing children":

1. A generally supportive relationship between worker and child will enable a child to meet the worker's expectations regarding appropriate behavior or conformity to rules and values.

2. Before blaming or imposing punishment, encourage the child to evaluate his behavior and its consequences to himself and others.

3. Before deciding on a child's culpability and punishment, one should have all the facts about the offense.

4. Threats should be avoided.

5. We should expect some expression of rebellion against adult authority or nonconformity to rules. It is part of growing up and independence. One should not overact and take it as a personal affront.

6. The worker should follow through on his warning. "Mean what you say."

7. Child should not be punished by two or more different people for the same offense.

8. Reprimands should not be administered in public.

9. At times a child should be given the option to decide his own punishment.

10. Preventive action can be taken if one can identify situational patterns which contribute to breakdown of discipline.

11. The action should be geared to ensure effectiveness.

12. The worker should be explicit about the punishment to avoid misunderstanding or distortion by the child as to why he is being punished. The misbehavior, the rule or principle that is violated, and the punishment to be received by the child should be clearly identified.

13. When meting out punishment, state what alternative would have been appropriate and acceptable in that situation.

14. Positive reinforcement is preferable to negative action. Punishment should be instituted only as a last resort.

15. It is important to observe a child's reaction to a punishment.

16. Inconsistencies in applying punishment should be avoided. This applies to the individual worker as well as to the team staff.

Some offenses may be neurotically motivated. For example, stealing or lying may be an expression of neurotic conflict or need. It is unlikely that punishment will help to stop this behavior. In such cases, the worker should involve the child's therapist or caseworker to deal with this symptomatic behavior. In contrast, there are children who lie and steal because they do not consider it wrong. This may be a consequence of identification with established values in their families or neighborhoods. Because these children view punishment for such offenses as unjust, punishment itself will not suffice. A more appropriate approach is to focus on reeducation from delinquent to ethically and morally acceptable values. This takes time and will be accomplished only when these children form identifications with significant adults who represent socially acceptable values.

The nature of the child's personality, his cultural background, and the degree of his pathology need to be considered. The caseworker or therapist can help the child care worker to differentiate between the significance of disciplinary action to, for example, a sociopathic youngster who strives to avoid it, a neurotic child who wants to be punished to have his guilt alleviated, and a masochistic individual who views punishment as pleasure.

GROUP PUNISHMENT

As a rule, group punishment should be avoided. Redl (1966: 359) states: "An intervention technique . . . should at least be 'harmless' in terms of its effects on the group, or at worst, it should not produce more negative group effects than we can handle." Group punishment is especially inappropriate as a means of forcing a group of children to expose an unknown culprit. The concept is contrary to the adolescent group code and is perceived as blackmail to force them to turn against a peer.

The following situation is an example:

When Barney came upstairs Monday morning to wake the boys, he was struck by a lingering odor which puzzled him. He said nothing until his partner Jack arrived.

"Do you smell anything?" he asked.

"Sure, I bet it's marijuana," Jack exclaimed.

"Who could have brought it in and who could have organized a pot party last night? We better take some action before it gets known on campus," said Barney.

"You know that no one will tell us if we ask the kids," said Jack. "We have to get to the bottom of this quickly. Administration's going to be furious when they find out, so we better call a cottage meeting before the boys go off to school today."

After the boys returned from breakfast, Barney called for order and told the boys about the suspected pot smoking. "You know the rules," he said. "You know who distributed the pot. So let's have it. We'll have to inform administration. Maybe if you tell us, we'll be able to get a break for the guy who did it."

The response was complete silence. Then Jimmie asked, "How do you know it was pot?" Tim added laughingly, "Why not! Most people smoke pot. Why do they make such a fuss if kids do it? It's a double standard. They can do it; we should not!"

"Shut up! This is serious. You know the rules. Besides, pot is not good for you. A guy will start with pot and then end up as a junkie," Jack said in a serious tone.

"Tough luck," someone smirked in the background.

"Now let's be serious," said Barney. "You guys know the truth. We want to know who is responsible. It will protect you from consequences." When there was no response, Barney said, "O.K., everyone is restricted to the cottage except for meals, until you guys come to your senses."

"But that's group punishment," cried Billy. "It's unfair."

"It's blackmail!" others exclaimed.

"What one of you guys did was also unfair. So don't tell us what is right or wrong. It's up to you to come across with the truth. The meeting is over, and now get ready to go to school, but remember when we get back by lunchtime, I will expect to be told the truth," Jack concluded.

After they left the boys at the school building, Barney said, "I don't think we'll get the truth. I will be surprised if anyone confesses."

Barney's prediction was correct. There was no confession and no resolution. The group's recreational activities, including TV-viewing, was restricted for several days. The boys were surly and angry at their workers. One wonders what might have happened if, instead of an ultimatum and threats, the workers had convened the meeting, expressed their concern about pot smoking and violating the institution's rule about bringing in drugs, and then encouraged discussion of the issues involved. Disciplinary action could still be meted out through administrative intervention. However, the channel of communication between workers and the group would not have been blocked and the issue of drug abuse would have been expressed openly. It is even possible that eventually the wrongdoer might have revealed his identity.

Even if the use of "strong-arm methods" or threats of group punishment are successful, the price the worker pays in loss of respect, resentment, and hostile feelings more than counteracts the gains or adult "victory." Even if there had been a confession, there was no assurance that it actually confirmed the culprit. In a delinquent group an innocent youngster, generally the group's scapegoat, may be forced to confess to an act he did not perform to protect someone in a favored or power-status position. Workers who know their groups are not easily fooled by such subterfuge and thus can avoid punishing the innocent.

The peer group should not be utilized as judge and jury of an individual offender. Disturbed and delinquent children do not make objective juries nor benevolent judges. They can act as cruel executioners. Consequently, trial by peer courts should be outlawed rather than encouraged. Such kangaroo courts do not represent democratic processes, nor are they a constructive aspect of student government in institutions for disturbed, delinquent children.

PHYSICAL PUNISHMENT

Physical punishment as a method of control or as a means of asserting adult authority is inhumane and for the most part does not work. According to Karl Menninger, "The sock-it-to-'em theory (punishment to deter crime) of controlling frustration and anger and greed is futile and self-defeating. It isn't just unfair or unjust. It is ineffective" (Menninger 1968: 1). At best it may temporarily suppress an undesirable behavior or displace it. Children view physical punishment as personal attacks. For the emotionally disturbed child, it seems to be an inappropriate reinforcer of learning because it feeds his distrust of adults, hindering the development of positive relationships.

The provocations constantly faced by child care workers cannot be minimized. When a worker reacts physically to extreme provocation it is understandable because everyone's threshold of tolerance can be breached. Children should be made aware of this. But as a prevalent technique of intervention, corporal punishment is neither educational nor therapeutic, and, in fact, is prohibited by law in children's institutions in most states. In the event that a staff member is provoked to react physically, he is required to write a detailed statement regarding the incident.

Agency policy regarding discipline should clearly define what staff cannot do to a child and should suggest alternatives. It must also be firm about what children cannot do to the staff. Child care workers feel strongly about this. It is not uncommon to hear a child care worker ask, "What am I supposed to do when I'm threatened? How should I react when I'm physically attacked? How should I stop a big bully who is beating on a younger, weaker child?" Such questions must be taken seriously by supervisors and administrators, and guidelines provided for realistic and effective action. Not unlike other adults in the general population, there are child care workers who continue to believe in the platitude, "Spare the rod, spoil the child." However, most child care workers are not in favor of corporal punishment as a method of control. Nevertheless, it is not unusual to hear workers who deal with severely disturbed, impulse-ridden children and violence-prone youth express the wish that they had the option to react physically against extreme defiance and provocation. They complain that many of these children take advantage of existing policies against corporal punishment, knowing that they cannot be handled roughly. King (1976: 48) states, "The flaunting of rights is the single most provocative weapon that these kids use, particularly when it's coupled with an expression of guilt-lessness, of open contempt for the very considerations they are being offered."

In seminar sessions conducted by the author, this concern was frequently expressed. A number of very pertinent questions were raised. "Is it not better to hit a kid who drives you to desperation by his defiance, threats, negativism, or abuse of other children than to hate and reject him?" "How are these youths, who won't listen to us, to learn right from wrong?" "If talking and teaching by example does not convince a boy (or girl) that his (or her) destructive behavior is not good for him (or her), what can we do?" Several workers with decades of service in child care talked with fondness about visits from their former charges who reminded them of long-forgotten incidents of painful confrontations which they still considered had been most helpful to them. One man had told his cottage mother, "I never forgot the beating you gave me—it hurt but I knew you did it because you cared. It helped to 'straighten' me out."

The common threat weaving through all of these reminiscences was a genuine adult concern and caring for the children they had hit. This, rather than the physical act of punishment, could have been the significant factor that registered and turned out to be beneficial for the young man quoted above. It was obvious that none of these workers had enjoyed hitting children; all had felt badly afterwards; no one was sure physical punishment would have worked equally as well for other children in their care.

A discussion followed of the danger inherent in allowing individual discretion regarding use of corporal punishment. Some expressed concern that it might be abused. Some workers might punish cruelly, to "get back" at kids who were disliked; for others, it might serve as an easy way to achieve conformity and stability in a cottage group. It might be "nice" for staff but harmful to children. In view of these reservations, many of these workers expressed themselves in favor of retaining the prohibition against corporal punishment.

There must be a firm agency policy regarding physical assault on staff by children. Such a policy should specify the scope of physical restraint that is permissible, should clarify questions related to staff defense against assault, and should provide training opportunities for staff to enable them to cope constructively with physically threatening situations—especially in settings serving the violent-prone adolescent, the severely disturbed emotionally, and mentally retarded patients.

Educational and training aids are available to deal with critical violent situations. Among them are two recent 16 mm. films and manuals available for rental at a modest fee from Motorola Teleprograms, Inc., 4825 N. Scott Street, Suite 23, Schiller Park, Illinois 60176. The first, "One Step Ahead," explores various types of emotional crisis situations confronting mental health workers, including physical assault situations. Specific instruction is given on to handle trauma and physical pain. The second film addresses itself to "Classroom Crisis Control" which instructs teachers how to respond to the acting-out or potentially violent student, verbally and physically. Although these films are not specifically related to children in group care, much of their content is applicable to crisis control in group care, and should be helpful to child care workers in dealing humanely and therapeutically with crises of physical violence.

The broader issue of physical contact with children is a troubling one to workers. Frequently, physically (in contrast to verbally) oriented children seek out physical contact with their workers for "fun" reasons. This "horsing around" can get out of hand, especially when the child is emotionally disturbed and has poor impulse control. Losing control because of overstimulation, he may strike out and hurt the worker or may accuse the worker of hurting him. Some children may seek closeness for sexual reasons. In both cases a worker should be aware of the child, the motives, as well as potential consequences of becoming involved in the physical contact of "play," and know how far to go and when to stop such activity. In contrast, there are children who are fearful of human contact, and their need for physical distance should be respected until they show evidence of reaching out. Finally, there are youngsters who do not respond readily to a worker's verbal requests or admonitions because in their past experience they only knew physical reprimand if they did not conform. They have feared or respected the adult who was stronger and more forceful physically. Workers may feel that they can't achieve results with such children through verbal discussion and that grabbing such a youngster, squeezing him forcefully, or shaking him seems more effective. The most important issue here is by whom, how, and under what circumstances this should be done. It may not be traumatic or hurtful to the child if this physical communication is conveyed firmly and without hostility. Neither should it be done excessively. A child is more likely to judge the adult far favorably for his actions if they are motivated by caring rather than "hating," by firmness and strength rather than defensiveness.

THE VIOLENT-PRONE YOUTH

The child care worker's dilemma regarding management of the violence-prone youth without resorting to counterviolence may be controlled by agency policy prohibiting physical punishment. However, the worker's conflicting feelings may persist. King suggests "the necessity for constant team cooperation, review, supervision, and direction towards the objective of bringing into disciplined play the understanding of feelings in the work with these youths" (1976: 51). He urges training in the recognition of sensitivity to the causes that generate these feelings. In a confrontation with a defiant, aggressive youth, the worker must be ready to tell him how he feels about provocation. If counterviolent feelings are evoked, they should be expressed but assurance given that they will not be enacted. Thus, "You are getting me very angry but I'm not going to hit you. It is better to talk things out. How about it?" The violence-prone youth expects counterviolence from others. He has to be convinced that those who care for him can control him without resorting to violence. He has to be helped to substitute thought for impulsive action. In this way, "these youths can begin to learn to cope with the frightening violence that controls their lives by surviving new experiences in a different way, and by incorporation of the new way into their styles of life" (King 1975: 143).

Nadler's (unpublished) suggestions (paraphrased here) may be helpful in dealing with children who become violent.

1. *Don't panic*: It is important for the worker to realize that the child who is (or is about to become) violent is probably upset. The pent-up feelings of frustration or the accumulated anxiety becomes intolerable and must be drained off. They find it easier to have an external object—staff and peers—against whom to react rather than to tolerate the unpleasant feelings. Consequently, "Do your best to minimize yourself as a target."

2. Whenever possible, *isolate the child.* By removing him from an audience whose presence may stimulate violent actions, some of the motivation may be reduced. This is particularly applicable in cases of a defiant youngster who wants to impress peers with his bravado. It may enable the youngster to back down in private.

3. *Try not to escalate the violence.* If at all possible respond to the violent acting-out with firmness rather than counteraggressive behavior. This includes threats, getting too close, insulting or demeaning comments, pushing, or hitting. Violence can also be escalated by confrontation that cannot be followed through, anxiety reactions that imply fear or weakness, and threats that cannot be carried out.

4. Emulate a degree of *confidence* that conveys to the child, through verbal and nonverbal expression, that the worker is serious about not tolerating the violent behavior. The child may not hear what is said, but he may get the message from the way it is conveyed—a firm, clear, "cool" delivery. It may be helpful to state that he will not be touched or hurt if he stays where he is, that he will be respected if he deescalates the violence, and that one is ready to talk over with him how to resolve the problem(s) that upset him. Some children's attention may be distracted or diverted from continuing violence by asking them to describe how they feel or suggest that they think about the consequences of their action.

5. The worker should be ready with *alternatives*—to call for reinforcements when he feels he can't handle it alone. He may have to request that an isolation facility or sedating medication to be prepared. If physical restraint is necessary, one should have sufficient force available to achieve it quickly and with minimal hurt. Here skills and techniques in dealing with physical assaultiveness can be very helpful. For example, it is best to seize the violent youngster and hold him from behind with arms pinned against his back. While holding him, address him quietly and firmly, assuring him you are not trying to hurt him, that you want him to quiet down so you can let him go.

ALTERNATE APPROACHES

Children who are highly impulsive, who have difficulties in communicating verbally, who do not think clearly because of organic deficits, psychosis, or mental retardation, cannot assume responsibility for self-discipline. They require a high degree of structure, adult direction, and supervision, and behavior management techniques. These approaches have also been found helpful in controlling impulsive, delinquent-oriented youth who initially require a tight structure before they are able and ready to assume greater responsibility for self-discipline.

These children tend to react to disciplinary action with confusion, lack of connection between their offensive behavior and consequent restriction, or anger against the worker who imposes it. This may initiate a cycle of escalating provocation and punishments which is harmful to all—child, staff, and peer group. Behavior modification, utilizing positive reinforcement techniques, sets up a process through which children may learn that their behavior is the determinant of reward or punishment rather than an arbitrary punitive system or the personal feelings or prejudices of their workers. Rewards ranging from praise, tokens (which can be exchanged for candy, beverages, and other items), money, or extra privileges are given when the child or youth conforms to expected behavior. Ignoring the maladaptive or disruptive behavior while rewarding the expected behavior may also help to extinguish it in favor of rewarded behavior. Hopefully, these techniques are temporary. Otherwise, there is the danger that the child will behave as expected only because of the reward. Behavior management should not be an end in itself, but rather a means to help a child to learn self-discipline on the basis of learning to make choices between destructive and adaptive behavior.

Another technique in teaching discipline involves *contracts.* Thus, a child care worker may contract with a child regarding certain expectations. They negotiate a mutually acceptable agreement designating each party's responsibilities. For example:

Jane, a finicky eater, loves desserts. She refuses to eat vegetables. When one of her workers threatened to stop her desserts unless she ate vegetables, she refused to eat altogether. A contract technique was recommended, and one of the workers discussed it with Jane, who agreed to it. Both formulated the terms which were written down and signed by the worker and Jane. It stated that during the subsequent two weeks Jane would commit herself to eat vegetables. She would be rewarded with an extra dessert whenever she ate the vegetables served at mealtime. Desserts would be curtailed if she did not. Jane made an effort, and with encouraging praise from the workers and a number of her peers she managed to comply with the contract. She was proud when she received the contract with "Satisfactorily completed" written across it by the worker. Subsequently, she was able to eat all of her meals including vegetables without the incentive of extra desserts. Through this method the worker had helped Jane to become involved in a self-help process, to make a decision to oversome a handicap, to test her capacity to achieve it and experience success.

ROLE OF ADMINISTRATIVE STAFF
IN DISCIPLINE

Supervisors and administrators are not significantly involved in the daily life of the children and, therefore, are at a greater social distance from them than their child care workers, teachers, and social workers. Administrators are, however, important as symbols of authority to children. They play a role in establishing and maintaining the structure of the residential program and delegate to others enforcement of its requirements. Rarely are they involved as disciplinarians. Some situations, however, may require direct intervention by higher administrative authority, especially in crisis situations which have an impact on the institution as a whole. Direct involvement by the chief administrator with a child or group of children is advisable in cases of individual or group vandalism, car theft, burglary, or assault within or outside the boundaries of the institution. This serves a number of constructive purposes: It conveys to the offender(s) the concern of the highest level of authority for them as individuals, as well as for all the children and staff of the institution; it reaffirms staff responsibility to uphold standards for the safety and protection of persons or property; and it symbolizes the help the institution is ready to extend to children in order to help them curb destructive behavior. This "talking to" needs to be supplemented with opportunities for "talking with" in order to involve children and staff in coping with crises. Discussions with children and staff may stimulate rethinking of important issues related to communal living. The interactional processes which this stimulates may contribute to a greater sense of cohesiveness, and social responsibility.

Examples of crisis situations, not uncommon in residential settings, are offered for purposes of illustration:

1. A group of adolescent boys leave their cottage late at night and burglarize a staff apartment.

2. Youngsters from the institution get into difficulties in the neighboring community by stealing a car, burglarizing a store, or fighting with neighborhood children.

3. A group of girls runs away from the institution.

4. Children returning from home visits bring in dangerous drugs for use and for distribution to other children.

5. A recently admitted boy is severely beaten by his cottage peers during initiation rites.

6. A secret kangaroo court in a cottage metes out severe physical punishment to a child.

All of the examples involve a group of children whose behavior is harmful to themselves and to others; all are destructive acts, violating institutional regulations and structure and acceptable social values; all require staff intervention. The traditional way of coping with such behavior is generally limited to disciplinary action against the offenders. This may be temporarily effective in deterring repetition of the offensive behavior. Its efficacy in effecting lasting modification of destructive attitudes and behavior is questionable.

If the goals of residential treatment are rehabilitation and (re)education in the service of mature personality development, punitive measures which at best maintain surface control over disturbed children do not suffice. Structure and behavioral standards are essential in residential treatment, and disciplinary consequences for violations of institutional requirement are in order. Other methods of education in values, however, are necessary supplements to disciplinary action. Residential treatment has the advantage of group living and the group processes available for therapeutic purposes. Children and staff, including the offenders, can be involved in organizing discussion groups to examine pertinent issues. The whole institution, mobilized for free interchange of ideas, may become a symbol of common oncern and mutual aid for constructive change.

Appropriate matters for group discussions in the crisis situations just mentioned might be:

Example 1, breaking into a staff apartment, represents a threat to a basic human right—a sense of personal security. Group discussion would provide an opportunity to examine: causes of such behavior; its impact on children and staff; its threat to the essential atmosphere of security; the rationale for structure to curb destructive, impulsive behavior; and the need for everyone to have a sense of social responsibility and mutual aid.

Example 2 provides an opportunity to acquaint the children with the relationship of the institution to the neighboring community, the importance of maintaining a good-neighbor policy with the people who live around them, and the consequences of destructive acts which elicit community hostility against the institution. The group could also formulate ways in which children could demonstrate to the community their regret about the harm done and plan activities for making restitution for the damage.

Discussion related to Example 3 might deal with the harmful consequence of running away. This would include exposure to danger, exploitation by those who might "pick up" a girl on the road, clarification of the meaning of running away as "acting out rather than talking out" frustration, and the fact that running away disrupts the continuity of treatment.

Example 4 provides an opportunity to discuss the dangers of drug use and traffic, perhaps leading to the development of a drug education program.

Examples 5 and 6 involve the elemental issue of safety and freedom from physical attack, the minimum a residential setting must guarantee to each child and member of its staff. Adult surveillance and punishment for violation of this principle are not in themselves effective deterrents to the expression of the sadism and group aggression which these examples illustrate. Both the attack on the child during initiation rites and the kangaroo court were rationalized by the children who participated in them as being socially accepted practices imitating the initiation rites practices in college fraternities and social clubs. Such rationalization does not justify the cruelty of the action, which must prohibited formally by administration. To prevent such occurrences from going underground, however, group discussion should be initiated to help the children understand the destructive consequences to all who are involved, including judge and executioner (Adler 1971).

REFERENCES

Adler J. 1971. "Interpersonal Relationships In Residential Treatment Centers for Disturbed Children" *Child Welfare* 50, no. 4: 208–217.

Diamond, A. 1973. *Child Care Orientation Manual.* Unpublished booklet, Pleasantville Cottage School of Jewish Child Care Association, New York.

Dryer, M. 1978. Statement by Senior Child Care Counselor, Childville of Jewish Child Care Association, New York.

Gardner, R.A. 1973. *Understanding Children.* New York: Jason Aronson.

Ginott, H.G. 1965. *Between Parent and Child.* New York: Macmillan & Co.

Group Child Care Consultant Services. 1977. *The Basic Training Course for Residential Child Care Workers*, Student Manual "Discipline." Chapel Hill: University of North Carolina Social Work.

Helmer, J. 1978. "Constructive and Destructive Anger in Child Care Work: An Exploratory Study and a Conceptual Schema." *Child Care Quarterly* 7, no. 4 (Winter): 310–312.

King, C.H. 1976. "Countertransference and Counter–Experience in the Treatment of Violence-Prone Youth." *American Journal of Orthopsychology* 46, no. 1 (January): 43–61.

_____. 1975. "The Ego and the Integration of Violence in Homocidal Youth." *American Journal of Orthopsychology* 45, no. 1 (January): 134–145.

Menninger, K. 1968. *New York Times*, October 30 : 1.

Nadler, R.P. 1978. "Suggested Response of Staff to Violence." Edenwald Center, New York. Mimeo.

Redl, F. 1966. *When We Deal with Children.* New York: Free School Press.

Russo, E.M., and A.V. Shyne. 1980. *Coping with Disruptive Behavior in Group Care.* New York: Child Welfare League of America.

Schaefer, C.E. 1976. "Some Guidelines on the Effective Use of Punishment." *Child Care Quarterly* 4, no. 4 (Winter): 307–313.

8 TASKS OF THE CHILD CARE WORKER

"Life with children" encompasses the child care worker's tasks: Therapeutic care is his function; rearing children is his preoccupation. He is not a parent but exercises parental functions; he is not a teacher but educates; he may not be a recreation worker but he plays with children and organizes leisure-time activities; he is not a housekeeper but has responsibility for orderly functioning of the children's living environment. In all of his taks, the child care worker has opportunities to contribute to healthy development of children. These tasks include the following:

1. He participates in daily living routines. Throughout the day, from waking to bedtime, the child care worker guides the children in establishing and maintaining health promoting and socially desirable habits regarding personal hygiene, grooming, mealtime behavior, leisure-time activities, and interaction with peers and adults.

2. He supports the maintenance of standards regarding adequate diet, clothing, leisure-time activities, and pleasant, attractive, and comfortable living conditions.

3. He provides a sense of security and safety for each child in group living by assuring protection from being hurt physically or abused emotionally.

97

4. He is concerned about children's health needs. Under medical or nursing supervision, he may care for a child who is indisposed, or he may give first aid and dispense medication.

5. He encourages and as necessary assists children in their formal education by consulting with teachers, helping with homework, and conveying a positive attitude toward learning.

6. Through participation in maintaining physically attractive and clean housing conditions, he helps children develop constructive attitudes toward work as well as pride in their living environment.

7. He is involved in planning with the children the organization of leisure-time activities. He encourages participation in group games and development of game skills.

8. Through objective observation, sensitivity, and a readiness to meet children's emotional needs, he conveys a sense of empathy and encourages a trusting relationship between children and himself.

9. He interprets to children the institution's policies and requirements.

10. He consults, shares information, and participates with members of other disciplines in planning and evaluation conferences on the children in his group (Beker 1970: 3–4).

Within this broad framework of tasks, the worker has innumerable opportunities to motivate children to learn through encouragement, support, praise, and rewards; to teach skills directly by demonstration, participation, and modeling behavior; and to help those who have difficulty in relating to others because of asocial and/or antisocial patterns of interacting, by discouraging such inappropriate behavior and substitution of socially appropriate behavior.

The child care worker represents authority as well as reality for the children who find it difficult to cope with demands of daily living, have problems in relating to others, and controlling inner impulses which strive for immediate gratification. The day's routines may become an arena of conflict if children and workers are in antagonistic roles.

Throughout the day, the child care worker is expected to cope with children's behavior with understanding and firmness, with appropriate responses related to a particular child's personality and treatment objectives. Each interaction between a worker and a child may have immediate therapeutic significance and long-term implications. To live with a group of disturbed children and to cope with the turbulence of their emotions and their resistances—while at the same time meeting the demands of a structured milieu, administrative expectations, and set schedules—is not easy. It requires firmness and patience, organizational skills, competence, confidence, and a capacity to "give" to children without any assurance of reciprocity or appreciative responses.

Since many of the children find it difficult to reciprocate love, care, and concern, it is not unusual to hear a child care worker express disappointment that his interest and devotion is not appreciated by a child. This is not a question of appreciation but a manifestation of the child's disturbance. Such a child may not have experienced the human nurture which promotes trust in others. He may fear human closeness and avoid attachments because he anticipates rejection. His particular behavior may be a defense against closeness with another person. No matter how pathetic, detached, resistive, or hostile a child may appear, he may want to be loved and protected by adults. His resistance and fears may be ultimately overcome by patience and understanding. However, the process of achieving trust may be lengthy and difficult with many children and never realized with some. Mere sympathy for these children does not suffice. Sensitivity based on genuine feelings and caring is required. Emotionally disturbed children with their supersensitivity are masters at spotting devious motivations of adults. If interest in them is not genuine, they will become aware of it very quickly. The child care worker must be concerned for the whole child and not simply a segment of him which may be to his liking.

A degree of self-awareness in this respect can be productive. It is a most valuable asset for a child care worker to be able to see himself objectively, to be aware of his feelings and of the responses that the children's behavior evoke in him, and to be capable of perceiving objectively how the children view him. This is especially important because, as a closely significant person in the children's lives, the worker may become a target of ambivalent feelings and misplaced emotions. Ambivalence refers to the coexistence of opposite or antithetical emotions, attitudes, or wishes toward the same person or situation. Generally, only one aspect of the feelings is conscious or partly conscious, the other remaining unconscious: For example, love and hate toward the same person or situation (American Psychiatric Association 1964: 11).

The child care worker not only represents a giving person but, like a parent, is also a controlling adult. He demands conformity to the rules and regulations which comprise the structure of the residence. In exercising parental functions, he may stimulate transference behavior (Adler 1973). Transference is defined as the "unconscious transfer to others of feelings and attitudes which were originally associated with important figures (parents, siblings) in one's early life" (American Psychiatric Association 1964: 76). When a person's behavior toward another indicates that he is not viewing the other as he actually is, and his behavior is inappropriate to what the situation realistically calls for, he may be considered acting in transference terms. He sees the other person through a screen of past images, and that his attitudes and behavior toward him are being displaced or transferred from a past significant relationship unto the current one. A child care worker's familiarity with a particular child's tendencies to repeat earlier patterns of relationships in his interactions with adults as well as peers may help the worker understand when the child's behavior toward himself represents transference manifestations.

One way of avoiding or minimizing transference behavior in a confrontation with a child is to stick closely to the issue at hand, that is, the situation that evoked the child's reaction. Focus on the reality of the situation may direct the child's attention from drifting into past patterns of transference reactions which inappropriately fuse present perception with past experience.

It is risky to interpret evidence of transference behavior directly. A dramatic example occurred in an activity group when the clinically oriented female leader reacted to a youngster's seductive behavior toward her by connecting it with his supposed incestuous feelings toward his mother. The boy's immediate reaction was a leap to the nearest open window. The leader's quick response in seizing hold of his body which was halfway out of the (second-story) window saved him from serious injury.

The sense of frustration and resentment experienced from being a persistent object of a child's irrational behavior can be great. Angry or even hostile counterreaction is understandable even though its consequences for the child and the child–worker relationship may be harmful. If the child care worker's reaction to the child is subjective or impulsive, it may be considered inappropriate and may also represent countertransference behavior.

Wolstein has referred to transference and countertransference as "bipolar or reciprocal phenomena" (Wolstein 1954: 196). In psychoanalysis, countertransference refers to anxiety aroused in the analyst by his patient. It may involve both positive and negative feelings, irrational dislike or overidentification, linking the patient to some significant person in the analyst's life. If such reactions can occur in trained and "analyzed" professionals such as psychoanalysts, they can be expected to happen in relationships between a child care worker and a child. In intensive, emotion-laden situations, a child's behavior may evoke reactions tinged by either positive or negative transference. The worker's highly subjective response, triggered by a child's behavior, may represent a link to his own past.

This aspect of the child care worker's interaction with the children cannot be avoided, but it can be minimized. The greater the awareness of his own reactions to children's transference behavior, the less likely he will be to respond in countertransference terms.

The following situation is illustrative of some of the above concepts, including transference–countertransference reactions and self-awareness:

During a supervisory conference, Miss Davis expressed concern about her difficulties with Cynthia. They do not get along because Cynthia is provocative, controlling, and argumentative. She is a bright, attractive, 17-year-old, who has some likeable traits which are obscured by her obnoxiousness toward Miss Davis. Her co-worker Mrs. Ames seems to feel differently about Cynthia, and the two of them get along.

"During the half year I have worked in the group residence, I have been able to establish a good relationship with all of the girls except with Cynthia," said Miss Davis. "Sometimes she gets me so angry that I have to exercise extreme self-control not to strike out at her. At times I am so upset that I walk into the office, close the door, and cry. Why is it that she upsets me so!"

"Have you thought about the possible reasons?" asked Mr. Barnes, supervisor.

"Yes," replied Miss Davis. "Mostly it's the way she acts toward me. But there is also something else. I sometimes think that my reaction to her is exaggerated. She always reminds me of a high school friend who gave me a hard time during my teens. She used to belittle me, flaunt her superiority, and she always argued. But she was one of the popular girls in our class, and since I had few friends, I was at times grateful she wanted to be friends with me. So I put up with her obnoxiousness. The similarity between her and Cynthia is striking. So is my reaction to both of them."

"I happen to be familiar with Cynthia's background," said Mr. Barnes. "It's interesting to note that her mother had similar complaints about her. There was chronic conflict between them which, in addition to other problems with peers and at school, resulted in Cynthia's placement."

"Are you implying that both of us are reacting to each other in very personal terms?" asked Miss Davis.

"It may well be that Cynthia is displacing her feelings toward her mother onto staff and thus replicating her earlier reaction patterns. What may aggravate the situation in your case is that Cynthia reactivates in you the frustrating experiences of your relationship with your high school friend," replied Mr. Barnes.

"Why had I not thought of this before?" asked Miss Davis. "It's a plausible explanation. Maybe it's because I repressed the painful experiences of the past. My reaction to Cynthia activated the memory. I only felt the associated anxiety but did not perceive the source and the connection with Cynthia."

"It's good that you see it now. Perhaps it will help you with Cynthia. If you have not talked with Cynthia's therapist about your relationship conflicts, you should, because Cynthia also needs help in clarifying her transference behavior," suggested Mr. Barnes.

"I will do so," said Miss Davis. "But I think I can be of help as well, now that you've helped me see my reactions. I may have greater control over my responses to Cynthia, and this in itself could be the basis of building a better relationship.

Children's judgments of adults can be highly perceptive. Adult failings cannot be concealed from them. When they feel free to express their observations, they are generally objective. This was dramatically illustrated in a group therapy session of a cottage group of adolescent boys who behaved disruptively and with hostility to a child care worker. The following notes, taken by one of the group leaders, summarizes the children's reactions:

> Listed below are some of the criticisms which the group articulated in relation to the cottage father of the couple who were their child care workers.
>
> One was his impulsivity, in that he was quick to lose his temper when frustrated by the group. He often made threats which he did not even intend to carry out and which were not qualitatively or quantitatively appropriate to the incidents which evoked them. They were critical of his lack of consistency, so that the boys were unable to anticipate in any given situation whether his behavior would be similar to what it was in a similar situation previously, or be entirely different. They complained bitterly that this inconsistency paralleled the inconsistencies which they had experienced from their own parents at home.

They viewed the cottage father as weak, having no "backbone," and this reflected upon his adequacy as an adult after whom they were expected to pattern their own responses. He did not give of himself generously. When he "gave," whether in terms of material giving, recognition, etc., there was always an underlying desire on his part to exact some kind of price from the boys to whom he did the giving. He wanted gratefulness from them or exchange of favors, etc. This signified to them that his giving was calculated and therefore not real. Another objection was that they expected an adult to be understanding of their pathology and idiosyncracies, and he was not. This was interpreted by them to represent a genuine lack of understanding in a person working with disturbed kids. Finally, they felt that he played favorites, and also that he was rigid and vindictive; rigid in the sense that they had the feeling that the rules were more important than the children for whom the rules were intended, and vindictive because he felt obliged to retaliate whenever anything was done which reflected upon his power or prestige. They were able to split him off from the established structure of the school. He was capricious in making his own rules relating to conduct in the cottage, despite the fact that he referred to the administration demands upon him as a means of bolstering what authority he had.

The boys correctly assessed their worker's insecurities about exercising authority and resented his attitudes, which seemed to be defensive. Lemay (1974: 7–8) suggests a number of basic attitude requirements for child care workers serving those whose adaptation to reality is precarious:

1. Acceptance and respect for each child as he is without value judgments.
2. Attitude of self-awareness.
3. Attitude of involvement. The worker accepts the reality of living and working with disturbed children without losing his objectivity and orientation to reality.
4. Attitude of evaluation. Through objective observation of daily behavior, the worker becomes aware how a child perceives and deals with reality situations. Through the worker's relationship with the child, he is helped to replace maladaptive functioning with behavior appropriate to reality.
5. Striving for continuity in the relationship with a child during his placement. This involves long-term commitment and regularity of presence.
6. Attitude of genuineness. This emphasizes the fundamental role in a relationship where both transference and countertransference elements have to be recognized and then utilized where possible.
7. Individualization. The disturbed child must not be viewed as a category or stereotype of maladjustment. Each child is a unique personality who has to be understood in terms of total life experience, the mechanisms of

his behavior, and his defenses against meaningful relationships with others.

The child care worker needs to be aware of his strengths as well as limitations. The former will give him a sense of confidence and competence in carrying out his tasks. Awareness of limitations will help him avoid difficulties inherent in working with emotionally disturbed children—countertransference and defensive reactions.

To be an effective worker, then, implies an attitude of *commitment* to children and to one's work. In committing oneself, there is a giving of oneself to something or someone other, not to the exclusion of oneself or through denial, but rather out of the affirmation of oneself (Setleis 1975). The rewards are inner—growth and personal satisfaction—and outer—service to others. Both of these, psychological and social, are interrelated.

The above requirements demand a great deal of a child care worker. Some may even consider them unrealistic or indicative of ivory-tower idealism and therefore unattainable. They are meant to be goals to work toward rather than rigid standards of expectation for all. When viewed as conceptual guidelines, they are useful objectives and as important in the education of child care workers as the specifics of daily child care management. The stark realities of the child care worker's job are not minimized by conceptual frameworks nor by professional goals. We are well aware that the strains of living with disturbed children can at times be overwhelming to the most experienced of workers. The children's impulsivity, self-centeredness, manipulativeness, and provocations can frustrate the most patient of temperaments and evoke anger from the most tolerant. The process of achieving a high degree of effectiveness involves accumulative knowledge, development of skills, and self-awareness. Learning opportunities have to be made available in an atmosphere of support. Mistakes which are inevitable need to be tolerated. Individual supervisory conferences, peer-group discussions, and seminars should encourage frankness in expressing feelings and opinions. It is particularly important for a worker to feel secure enough in his relationships with his supervisor and co-workers to express himself freely. Unless he is ready to describe conflict situations that arise during the course of his daily activities frankly, his supervisor cannot help him learn these experiences.

Understanding and acceptance of the child as an individual have been emphasized, and should not be interpreted as *unconditional* acceptance of children's behavior, including actions which are harmful to themselves and to others. The principles of understanding and acceptance should have a degree of linkage to the principles of growth and development. Regardless of theoretical orientation and treatment methodology, the group care program in its entirety is committed to the active encouragement of adaptive (positive) behavior and discouragement of destructive, maladaptive behavior. An incentive system—whether material or relationship-based, or a combination of both—is essential.

Throughout the broad range of his responsibilities and child-worker interactions, the child care worker is constantly involved in teaching–learning relationships, in utilizing incentive (including restrictive) techniques in encouraging and modeling behavior, expectations, and values. These techniques will be discussed in greater detail in the ensuing sections.

A TYPICAL DAY

The child care worker's tasks involve the children's waking hours, as exemplified by the following example of a schedule in a residential center:

Weekdays

7:30 – 8:25 a.m.	Wake up, wash, and dress, make beds, do room chores such as dusting and sweeping, bring laundry downstairs.
8:25 – 9:00 a.m.	Breakfast
9:00 – 11:55 a.m.	Morning school session
11:55 – 12:00 noon	Wash up for lunch
12:00 noon – 1:00 p.m.	Lunch
1:00 – 3:00 p.m.	Afternoon school session
3:00 p.m.	Afternoon snack
3:15 – 4:45 p.m.	Leisure-time activities in cottage or recreation program.
4:45 – 5:00 p.m.	Wash up for supper
5:00 – 5:40 p.m.	Supper
6:00 – 7:00 p.m.	Study period

7:00—8:30 p.m.	Leisure-time activities such as arts and crafts, scouts, folk dancing, free play, sports activities in gymnasium, etc.,
8:30—9:30 p.m.	followed by evening snacks.
9:30—10:00 p.m.	Bedtime (past 10:00 on discretionary basis when there is no school the next day).

Weekends

8:00 a.m.	Wake up and do house chores.
9:00 a.m.	Breakfast
10:00—4:00 p.m.	Trip program to points of interest. Off-ground activities for older children scheduled.
12:00 noon	Lunch
5:00—6:00 p.m.	Supper
6:00—8:30 p.m.	Some activities scheduled (with resident staff).
8:30—10:00 p.m.	Snack, showers, bedtime—same as weekends.

Each phase of the structured day from wake-up to bedtime is designed to provide a life rhythm of routines and expectations which represent concreteness and order for children who have experienced insecurity, neglect, and disorganization in family and community living. Each phase represents a therapeutic framework, providing the worker with opportunities to help children mature emotionally and socially.

As previously indicated, many children entering group care are not prepared to cope with the routines and (even minimal) expectations. Through observation of children's initial reactions (supplemented by historical information provided by a caseworker) the child care workers need to assess children's capabilities to meet basic demands related to the various phases of daily living. The next step is to formulate intervention techniques to help the children overcome deficits and to develop effective and socially desirable coping skills. These involve workers and children in close and significant interactions which hopefully will serve to strengthen growth-inducing relationships.

DAY'S BEGINNING

Waking from a night's sleep may present difficulties for children in group care. Unlike the child who wakes up in his own home with a sense of family security around him, the child in placement awakens to the realization of family separation. To be awakened from the comfort of sleep and forgetfulness to the reality demands of the day evokes anxiety. The diversity of waking patterns which confronts the child care worker each morning expresses this anxiety. Some children may respond quickly to his call for rising, others lag behind, and some cannot manage without help the process of washing and dressing. Many children tend to wake up troubled. Some are so anxious about the day's expectations that they seem disoriented in terms of time and place. Sometimes a child, upon awakening, explores parts of his body as if to check whether he is "all there"; some may still be under the influence of frightening dreams; others may be resentful of being awakened and may react hostilely.

Waking

Waking the children requires sensitivity, tolerance, patience, and firmness.

One might begin the process in an encouraging manner, rousing each one individually, calling out his name or touching him lightly. Children who do not arise quickly may have to be reminded several times. If this is not effective, one can call attention to the institution's rules regarding morning routines. This approach tends to shift the child's view of the worker as a disturber of his peace to one who reminds him of the requirements that are expected from everyone. It is most important that the worker not compromise established routines. He should persist with firmness, but without anger or hostile actions such as turning over a child's bed or spraying him with water — unwholesome punitive methods which have occasionally been used by workers.

The following illustrates the dilemma experienced by a child care worker during wake-up time and a youngster's feelings about being awakened.

During a conference with his supervisor, Mr. Sayre, Frank talked about his frustration during morning hours in the cottage.

"It's so difficult to get the boys up and ready for breakfast and school," he said. "After all, they are older boys! Even the toughest among them act like babies. They roll up in their blankets, snarl at me when I try to wake them, do not want to be disturbed, and act as if they dreaded to get ready for the day's activities. Then they are so slow in washing, dressing, and doing their morning chores!"

"That's not unusual with teenagers in general and our type of boys in particular," said Mr. Sayre. "But are they all this way?"

"Luckily, no," replied Frank. "The worst offender seems to be Tom. He's the biggest boy in the group and the self-appointed natural group leader. He used to be a big shot in a delinquent gang before he came here. Generally, when I come into his room, I find him curled up in his blanket in a fetal position. When I try to wake him, he growls at me, pulls the blanket over his head, and turns to the wall. With persistence I manage to get him up, but it takes time. And sometimes I get very annoyed because there is so much to do during these hours. At times I'm tempted to turn his bed over."

"Would this do any good?" asked Mr. Sayre.

"I don't think so," said Frank. "It certainly is risky with a big boy like Tom. Anyway I don't approve of such methods. But what do you advise me to do?"

Mr. Sayre agreed that a boy like Tom seemed like a walking contradiction. He appeared strong and adequate, and therefore we expected a great deal from him. But this may represent a tough exterior. His waking behavior indicates that he has a fragile inner self. Tom was a neglected, deprived, disadvantaged child, and these experiences must have left an impact on his personality. So he may have built up some strong defenses against inner insecurity and a sense of helplessness. During waking-up time hours these defenses do not function fully, and this may explain the other side of Tom which is not evident during his waking hours.

"By the way," said Mr. Sayre, "Does Tom still have nightmares?"

"No. They ceased about six months ago," replied Frank.

Mr. Sayre then suggested that Frank talk with Tom about his waking behavior. He cautioned there might be a problem because it is a touchy issue with Tom, and consequently Frank would have to find an opportune moment. "Maybe you could start with the description of his waking behavior and then you might ask him for a suggestion about the appropriate way of waking him," advised Mr. Sayre.

"Supposing Tom tells me not to wake him at all but leave it up to him?" asked Frank.

"Tom knows the rules and the morning schedule. There cannot be a compromise about this matter. He has to get up on time. What we're talking about is the process. If we can get him involved in the procedure, it might be helpful. It may serve to convince him that you care enough to ask his advice and that you want to be helpful," concluded Mr. Sayre.

"O.K. It's worth a try," said Frank.

That evening, after snacks, Tom was in the kitchen helping Frank clean up. As they were working together, Frank remarked about the difficult time Tom seemed to have getting up in the morning. He added, "I know this is a subject you might not wish to talk about. But you know I have to get you up on time. I've been wondering if you could suggest a better way?" remarked Frank.

During Frank's statement Tom seemed tense, but he listened and said nothing.

"You know I'd like to help," said Frank.

Tom replied, "O.K. I'll think about it and let you know. But I want to make one thing clear. Your partner Jim is getting on my nerves about this. He has tried some rough stuff that I don't like, such as lifting up my bed, shaking me roughly, and at time screaming at me to get up. That's not the right way. He even threatened to throw me out of bed next time. Well, he better not or he'll be sorry," threatened Tom. "Would you tell him that?"

"All right" agreed Frank. "But I'd like to postpone my talk with Jim until you give me your answer and suggestion."

"O.K.," said Tom. "I'll tell you tomorrow, but tell that S.O.B. to lay off," Tom said angrily.

Every child care worker is faced with difficult problems during waking hours. Time pressures, multiple demands by children, and the many tasks entailed in getting children ready for breakfast and school can be overwhelming as well as exhausting. It may be frustrating to awaken a young child who resists getting out of bed but not potentially dangerous as the above case illustrates. The workers seem to have erred in judging Tom's capacity and motivation (during early morning hours) in accordance with his chronological age, tough exterior and leadership qualities. Not understanding the other aspect of his personality, namely his insecurity and sense of helplessness, which during waking hours he managed to conceal effectively, their approach was both ineffective and harmful to their relationship with him. Frank's subsequent sensitivity in discussing the matter with Tom evoked a positive response. The message he conveyed through him to his fellow child care worker Jim should not be viewed as an empty threat. There are numerous examples of uncontrolled explosive attacks against child care workers who used physical force to awaken adolescents like Tom.

Sensitivity to the individual child's make-up and needs as well as self-awareness of one's own reactions to frustration can serve to simplify and enhance the process of waking up emotionally disturbed children.

There are situations where children say they cannot get up because they feel ill. If a child complains about not feeling well, he may actually be ill, or he may be manifesting anxiety about going to school that day. A child care worker who knows the children well usually knows who is telling the truth and who is feigning it. Until this knowledge is certain, arrangements should be made for every child who complains about illness to see a nurse. Persistent manifestations of anxiety should be reported to a child's caseworker. Discussion should be held with the manipulative child.

Washing and Dressing

Once all the children are awake, the worker faces problems related to washing and dressing. It is not valid to assume that a child who is slow in these activities is purposely stalling. Some children, while dressing, may slip into day-dreaming fantasies. They seem literally suspended in time between such relatively simple acts as putting on one shoe after the other. They need help to speed up the dressing process. The worker may, for example, list the pleasant activities which the child can expect that day. A "counting" game (Whittaker 1969: 124) may be suggested with the worker counting to see how many seconds it takes the child to put on his socks and shoes. On subsequent mornings, he will be encouraged to reduce the time interval. Praise may be offered or a token reward given as positive reinforcement. Some children may actually need a worker's help in getting dressed. This may be a hardship at a time when the worker is responsible for getting the whole group ready for breakfast. However, teaching a young child to master these skills is very important.

Some children, following awakening, may get involved in masturbatory activity. This should be handled simply by telling the child to "get dressed." If this behavior persists, a plan of action should be developed jointly with the child's caseworker.

Good grooming habits should be encouraged. The well-groomed worker who also demonstrates to the children his own interest in washing, brushing his teeth, combing his hair, and caring for his clothing, teaches by example. The value is then demonstrated rather than professed.

The child who learns self-care habits has the satisfaction of seeing immediate results. When he looks in the mirror, he sees the fruits of his effort. When he is subsequently praised by teachers, child care workers, or caseworkers for being neat and attractive, it reinforces a sense of self-esteem. Achieving success in this personal area may contribute to a sense of security so that he is more inclined to attempt other types of learning. Grooming materials for all children should be readily available and special grooming aids for those who require them. For multihandicapped children or for seriously disturbed children who require individualized help to master basic skills like brushing teeth properly, washing, or combing hair, special incentives might be offered during the course of a grooming program. A complete boxed grooming kit may be the prize for successful completion of the course, with individual items given during the process of mastering each step of the program.

Pre-breakfast Activity

Getting children ready for breakfast can be a trying task. The following is illustrative of a morning scene in a group of very disturbed ten-to-twelve-year-old boys:

When I arrived at 7 a.m., apparently there had been a lot of activity before the official wake-up time. Jimmy, a disorganized but usually not a provocative child, was giving the night counselor a very difficult time, being verbally and almost physically abusive. Everyone was standing around watching, too frightened to do anything. Jimmy, who needs a sense of firm limits set for him and doesn't allow himself to get out of control too often, has the potential to be very destructive. I knew it was important to disengage and redirect him from an involvement with the night counselor. While scanning the other children for any signs of inappropriate behavior, I removed him to his room, taking care not to incite him further. Since talking would calm him down, I attempted to find out what was going on. After several minutes, there was a noticeable decrease in his anger. While trying also to sense the mood of the other children, I was able to influence Jimmy to start his morning routine, which was to take a shower since he usually wet the bed. This further served to calm him and was a signal to the rest of the group that everything was okay now. I then established the morning routine of washing up, getting dressed, and cleaning rooms. The better-functioning boys, like David and Sam, were able to get organized much quicker than some of the others, needing only a show of appreciation and slight direction on my part. Jose likes to be noticed and so needed constant approval and encouragement in getting him into his morning chores. Bill, his roommate, probably least disturbed by the incident, was methodically plodding about his room thankful that no one was bothering him. I encouraged him to keep working with the knowledge that he can be extremely slow in the morning.

Paul and Ben are probably the most fragile boys in the group and, therefore, more easily thrown into disorganization and confusion by any changes from a normal situation. Ben can react to the slightest difference in his perception of something and thus become extremely frustrated, overwhelmed, and provocative. On this particular morning, Ben, one of the boys originally involved in the sneaking from room to room, was relieved that the episode was over and that he could prove himself by getting his room cleaned properly. I pretended not to be aware of him working and so was surprised and happy when he proudly showed me the finished product. Paul, on the other hand, will not recover so quickly. He needed constant encouragement and nurturing in attempting to get himself organized. He was unable to be left alone being continually distracted by anything, so that I had to "spoon feed" him in order to keep his mind on what he was supposed to be doing. Most of the time, Paul is the last one to finish the morning routine and needs an approach in which he feels loved and protected. That day was no exception. After his shower, Jimmy apologized to the night counselor for his outburst. I was satisfied. —

William Kearns, Child Care Counselor, Childville

Since children dress at different rates, some will be ready before others. If there are chores, such as making beds or sweeping, this becomes the focus of the worker's attention. Play activities or T.V.-watching before breakfast may become an issue, especially for those children who have completed their chores and have waiting time before breakfast. T.V.-viewing can become a problem because children may become too involved in a particular program. This can best be handled by telling the children in advance that it is time to get ready for breakfast. Quiet games should be encouraged. "Horsing around," disruptive behavior, and obvious delaying tactics should not be tolerated. The worker must make it clear that this behavior is not acceptable because it delays the group.

Going off to the dining hall (if breakfast is served centrally) and later to school may involve a struggle about appropriate dress. It is the worker's responsibility to make sure that every child is dressed in accordance with weather conditions. Wearing boots or rubbers in rain and snow is frequently resisted but is necessary if the children are to remain well.

Greater understanding of individual children, the group as a whole, and of the child care worker's own reactions can be developed through the following observations:

Questions About the Individual Child

1. Does he awake easily, or is it difficult to rouse him?
2. Is he overly slow—seemingly "half-awake" or day-dreaming?
   a. Does he seem anxious after arising?
   b. Does he seem disoriented regarding time?
   c. Does he examine parts of his body?
3. Does he get through with bathroom duties quickly?
4. Are there problems about washing or grooming?
5. Does he complain he "can't find" items of clothing?
6. Does he dress quickly or require only an occasional reminder?
7. Does he seem to stall to create delay for others and/or a power struggle with worker?
8. Is he slow because he is compulsive or perfectionistic about dressing?
9. Does he appropriately ask for help when it is needed?
10. Docs he refuse help when it is offered?
11. What does he do after dressing while awaiting the call for breakfast? What is his general mood—quiet, jovial, disruptive, cranky, angry?

Self-awareness Questions

1. What is your own mood this morning?
   a. Watchful, pleasant, encouraging, eager to help the children, thus facilitating their own efforts to get ready for the day's activities?
   b. Troubled, moody, angry, impatient with difficult children?
2. Do you react inappropriately to a child's irrational behavior toward you, or do you understand that you may be the object of displaced emotions?
3. Are things well organized to help the children (clothes laid out, bathroom facilities checked and in order, activities planned for those who get ready quickly)?

4. Is continuity assured, that is, have you information from others about the children and their behavior? Is your pattern of routines the same as your co-workers, assuring consistency of approach?

MEALTIME

Emotional Connotation of Food

Food has emotional as well as nutritional significance. *How* one is fed may be more important than *what* one is fed. The feelings accompanying a mother's offering of food to her child evoke complementary reactions resulting in emotional associations with feeding. These may range from feelings of being loved to rejection, pleasure to frustration, tenderness to anger. Withholding of food may be viewed by the child as withholding of love and care. Mealtime experienced in a positive family milieu becomes associated with a sense of family togetherness, sharing of food, conversation, and satisfying social interaction. Negatively experienced, it is associated with frustration, loneliness, rivalry, conflict, and unpleasantness. Thus, anxieties and conflicts experienced by children during meals may give rise to a spectrum of ambivalent feelings toward food as well as toward parent figures.

For many children in residence, mealtime in their homes had been a frustrating experience. They may, therefore, have developed food fads, poor eating habits, and other anxieties associated with eating. They tend to perpetuate accustomed mealtime behavior and to transfer negative attitudes felt toward a feeding person, generally from their mothers to child care workers. A child may dawdle, gorge, or eat with his fingers, eliciting anger from peers and adults; another may complain without justification about the quality or quantity of food; still another may refuse to eat certain foods or not eat enough. The emotionally deprived child may overeat; the economically disadvantaged child may hoard food. Both deprived children will need reassurance that there is enough for everyone and that seconds are available. Limits have to be set for the child who throws food around or grabs the first portion to be served; the child who is unskilled in the use of utensils will have to be taught.

Routines and Expectations

Institutional routines tend to compensate for a child's immaturities. The very fact that meals are scheduled is an aid in preparing children for this event. Children learn that they have to be ready to postpone other activities. They cannot blame the worker's willfulness for interrupting what they are doing. It is advisable to remind children to get ready five or ten minutes in advance. They need a period of preparation to make a transition from one set of activities to another. Hyperactive children may have to be reminded still earlier so that they can calm down.

Mealtime is an important social event. The physical surroundings should be attractive and comfortable. Disorder conveys to children a lack of caring and disrespect for them, and they will react accordingly. A mess breeds messiness; a depressing atmosphere contributes to restlessness, evokes anxiety, and can lead to acting-out behavior.

Seating arrangements are important and should be designated by staff. The location of the worker may have to be flexible. He might sit between two children who easily provoke each other, next to a child who generally initiates conflict situations, or adjacent to one who has difficulty in managing utensils or who is fearful of eating certain foods or of aggression by peers. Thus, the worker may serve in many roles—as buffer, guide, teacher, or protector.

Children should be aware of expectations regarding behavior at table. Every child is expected to eat with the group. Shouting, fighting, and throwing of food are not allowed. Children cannot leave the table without the worker's permission. Table manners should be stressed since they convey respect for others. Some children are unaware of this and require guidance.

Food should be well prepared and be served promptly, quickly, and attractively. How it is served and by whom is generally determined by the degree of the children's maturity. Children may pass it or the worker may serve.

Mealtimes can be used to encourage children to assume responsibility. They should learn to pass the food appropriately and take turns in clearing the table. It is important to prevent disturbances before they start, because once they begin, they affect the whole group. If things get out of hand, it may be advisable to remove the child who is responsible.

Children should neither be deprived of food as punishment nor be forced to eat. Each child has his own capacity, and the worker should be able to individualize the children in this respect. A child who has food fads may take some time to get over his anxiety about a phobic food and may need the help of his caseworker to accomplish it. However, the worker must also be aware of manipulation at meal times. For example, some children may refuse to eat vegetables or the main course in order to fill up with extra desserts. This should not be permitted.

Plans for the day's leisure-time activities may be discussed during mealtime. Story-telling or word games with younger children can minimize restlessness while waiting for food.

The folllowing are suggested guidelines for observation during mealtime:

The Group

1. Do seating arrangement cause problems? Should anyone be moved to another table?
2. Which of the children needs assistance with eating, use of utensils, table manners?
3. What is the general mood of the children—friendly, quiet, tense, noisy?
4. What is the atmosphere today? Has something affected the behavior of the children in general? Of any child in particular?
5. What complaints are there about food? Its preparation? Quality? Quantity?
6. Is it possible to talk with the children about problems occurring at mealtimes and to involve them in resolving them? If not, what and who are the obstacles?

The Individual Child

1. Note individual patterns of behavior during mealtime. Does he eat calmly and quietly? Is he cooperative or does he attempt to provoke you or other children? Does he snatch food? Take too much food? Eat very little? Eat very slowly? Gorge himself? Steal food? Throw food? Use fingers instead of utensils?

2. What are his favorite foods? Does he have food fads? What food does he refuse to eat? If pressured to eat it, how does he react— become agitated? Cry? Use abusive language? Have a temper tantrum?
3. Is he sociable at the table?
4. Is he fearful?
5. Is he cooperative?
6. What is his mood—content, jovial, depressed, etc.?
7. Does he converse with other children? With the worker?
8. Does he try to monopolize the worker's attention?
9. Is he provocative toward the worker? Does he interfere when others try to talk with the worker or with peers?
10. Does he start fights?

Self-Awareness Questions

1. Does your own mood affect the group atmosphere? Positively or negatively?
2. Are you impatient with the children? If so, why?
3. Do you like to eat with the children?
4. Do you find mealtime aggravating or pleasant?
5. When the food is not to your liking, do you express your dissatisfaction in the children's presence? If you have done so, what has been their reaction?
6. How do you feel toward a child who disrupts mealtimes?
7. What methods do you use to control misbehavior at mealtime? Are they effective?
8. Are you comfortable conducting a group discussion about disruptive mealtime behavior?

EDUCATION

The child care worker, not unlike a parent, is closely involved in children's education. He sends a child off to school and greets him when he returns; he helps with homework; through contact with teachers and caseworkers, he learns about the educational achievements or the handicaps of the children in his group.

Learning Difficulties

Many of the children may have problems at school. Learning difficulties arise for a number of reasons:

1. Education emphasizes *reality*. The child whose reality testing is impaired will find adaptation to classroom requirements difficult. Anxiety in its varied forms, evoked by reality demands, will interfere with learning.

2. Education involves *relationships*. One learns most easily through loving and trusted adults. Consequently, the child who has not experienced love and trust has an impaired capacity to relate to others.

3. *Poor impulse control*, a characteristic of many disturbed children, deflects attention from concentration.

4. A child may be handicapped by a *learning disorder* associated with impairment of the central nervous system as a result of brain injury sustained at birth or through infection, accident, biochemical irregularity, mental deficiency, genetic causes. Or he may have a *learning disability* not associated with mental deficiency.

5. Some children may have had a poor educational experience. If they have failed, they bring with them a poor sense of adequacy, a lack of self-confidence, and negative attitudes toward teachers. They may resist education because of fear of exposing their inadequacies.

6. Family and cultural attitudes may also account for lack of educational motivation.

Under optimal conditions, residential schooling occurs within an educational system which is integrated with the clinical as well as the environmental aspects of the total residential program. Such a school makes demands on children in accordance with their capabilities which are identified early in the child's residency. If a child is educationally retarded, acceptance of his level of competency is conveyed to him, and efforts are made to help him overcome deficiencies. Teachers help him compete against himself instead of others. They assist him in developing skills, beginning with his level of competency and working toward achievement of his potential. Teachers may also be helpful when they can convey to the child their understanding of the difficulties which have hindered his learning (Adler 1963: 219-220).

This type of educational program is generally not available for children in community-based group care settings. Unless there are *special education* facilities within the community school, with small class capacity, flexible programming, and teachers trained to work with handicapped children, many of the children will be at a great disadvantage. Other educational resources would have to be made available such as specialized private schools or educational programs associated with day treatment centers. Such resources are not plentiful and are expensive.

The Child Care Worker's Role

Children in general and especially disturbed children cannot be expected to have mature attitudes about the value of education. The children need to feel that the adults around them value learning and take an active interest in their education. Small and Clarke (1979) view the child care worker as a "facilitator" for the school and as the coordinator between school and group care programs for the following reasons: The child care worker is closest to the reality of every-day life, observing children's reactions to learning and school demands, learning styles, strengths, deficits, and motivation. As a highly significant person in the child's life, he may be the most effective person to deal with difficulties related to school and may be a prime motivator for learning. He is also in a position to facilitate education by creating a favorable climate for learning. He may provide reading material (newspaper, books, magazines), structure study hours, encourage viewing of educational T.V. features, and aid children with verbal communication skills.

Depending on the relationship he has with a child, the child care worker may be able to counteract insecurities as well as negative attitudes toward learning through his expressed interest in the child's education and class functioning, the positive values of education he represents, the understanding he conveys, and the actual help he offers. A child may exert greater effort if the worker shows interest. As he incorporates the worker's values, he may gradually evolve a sense of confidence in himself and begin to view education as an asset instead of as an imposition.

The following illustrates child care workers' active intervention to further a boy's education:

"I wish you would speak to Albert about his school work," said Mrs. Lewis to her husband Tom. "I talked to his teachers today. They were discouraged because Albert fights their attempts to teach him. He is defensive and then becomes hostile when demands are made. They feel he has the brains, but not the will."

"He never does homework," said Tom. "I've asked him about it, and he said he hasn't any. But I don't believe him. I wonder why he is so against learning?"

"Well," said Mrs. Lewis, "Albert's social worker believes that he is afraid. He is so far behind that he thinks it's hopeless, then rationalizes that it's not important. Maybe he is afraid to expose his ignorance; maybe he's ashamed to try. I have a feeling he'd like to be educated, but his whole upbringing and lifestyle has been anti-intellectual. But he's fourteen years old! He should be educated while he is here. Maybe we can help. He respects you, Tom; so won't you talk with him about the importance of learning?"

"Oh, I'll try," said Tom skeptically, "But I have to be careful to get him in the right mood."

The following night, Albert asked if he could look at Mr. Lewis's sports magazine. "Sure, come into our living room," invited Mr. Lewis. While Albert was looking at the pictures, Tom began talking about one of Albert's favorite football players. Albert was very interested and asked questions. "Wouldn't it be nice if you could read about it yourself?" said Tom.

"I can read," snapped Albert defensively.

"Don't get annoyed," said Tom. "You know what I mean. Mrs. Lewis talked with your teachers yesterday. They seem concerned that you don't try enough. They think that you could learn to read fluently in a short time. We think so, too. Why don't you take advantage of the opportunities offered you?"

"I don't care. I'm not interested. When I get out of here, I can work," Albert said with feeling.

"You certainly will be able to do that," responded Tom. "But your choices will be limited. You could do better for yourself if you could get over your hang-ups about school work."

"I didn't learn much in that lousy school in Harlem and now it's too late," Albert replied.

"It's not too late for you," said Tom. "To be behind in reading and math is nothing to be ashamed of. You can try to make up for lost time. You think the other kids will laugh at you if you do homework?" asked Tom.

"No one is going to laugh at me. They better not," threatened Tom.

"I know you can take care of yourself," said Tom. "The other kids might even follow your example, if they see you do schoolwork. Mrs. Lewis and I would be proud of you."

Just then, Mrs. Lewis returned from the kitchen, and Albert rose to go. He stopped at the door and said, "I know you mean well. Thanks. I got something to think about."

Disruptive classroom behavior becomes a concern of child care workers as well as teachers. When it comes to the attention of the worker, he should discuss it with the child. Expressed concern, support of classroom expectations, and disapproval of destructive behavior is in order and can be helpful. However, the worker should not be expected to become a disciplinarian for school-related misdeeds nor should he be the executioner for school-prescribed punishment. These domains remain the responsibility of teachers and the school administration.

The Mentally Retarded Child

The child with intellectual handicaps poses special considerations for the child care worker. Because the mentally retarded child has not experienced a sense of basic trust in his relationship with others, he is distrustful. Because failure rather than mastery has been the fruit of his efforts, he is insecure and fearful of learning. He has strong defenses against exposing himself in learning situations.

The worker trying to help such a child faces difficulties and discouragement. A great deal of patience will be necessary as well as persistence in pursuing the educational process in which he engages with the child. The child may test the worker's patience to the utmost before understanding that the former's effort is an expression of a genuine desire to help him learn. Acceptance of him as a whole person, including his handicaps, conveys a positive attitude that he is indeed capable and worthy. This may help him develop confidence to master the tasks in which the worker is involved as helper and teacher. Success here could inevitably help in other areas of learning. If successful, the child care worker could become an important reinforcer of learning within the total education of the child.

The quality that enables the worker to feel what the child must be experiencing is helpful. Indeed, the more he knows of each child in terms of his cognitive shortcomings, the more capable he will be of putting himself in the child's place, empathizing with him for the embarrassment and shame that he surely feels for his inability to follow instructions. Empathy for the child means an understanding of what it is to be like him. Conveying this understanding can help build rapport, the essential ingredient of a relationship through which the child may be motivated to learn (Adler and Finkel 1976).

Observations About the Child

1. Does he seem to like school? Is he indifferent to it? Does he dislike it?
2. Is it difficult to get him to go to school? For example, does he complain about not feeling well, does he forget his books, dawdle, and so on?
3. What is his attitude about homework—does it efficiently, compulsively, has to be admired, does it sloppily, refuses to do it?
4. Does he ask for help with schoolwork? Does he refuse help when offered? Will he accept help but not ask for it?
5. Does he read books or newspapers? Is his reading limited to comic books? Or does he not read at all?
6. Does he have a special educational or vocational interest or goal?
7. Does he speak favorably of his teachers? Does he like anyone in particular? Dislike them all?
8. Is he concerned about his school performance? Anxious about grades? About taking examinations?

Religious Education

The extent of religious education and religious services in a given setting is determined by the philosophy of the institution which in turn may be influenced by legal requirements, sectarian affiliation, or board and administrative conviction. The predominant attitude that religious education is necessary for the spiritual development of children and that religious training is regarded as a parental responsibility extends to group care.

Child care workers exert a direct as well as an indirect influence in relation to religious training. They generally accompany children to services, are involved in decorating the cottages for holidays, and participate in religious celebrations. Indirectly, a child care worker may have an even greater impact on children's attitudes because children learn more by example than from instruction. The worker who identifies with the religious philosophy and practices of an institution may, by his very presence and actions, encourage children to do the same. In a nonsectarian institution, a worker should not only be familiar with the concepts and practices of the different religions represented by the children in his group but he must also convey a sense of tolerance for all religions. By doing so, he demonstrates respect for all of the children, regardless of their cultural, ethnic, or religious background. He also contributes to the modification of existing prejudices and to the acceptance of differences. The sense of tolerance conveyed helps create an atmosphere of cultural, religious, and ethnic pluralism which is the heritage of a democracy.

WORK

Group living provides opportunities for the learning of skills, self-care, and social responsibility. Success at work tasks in the cottage may give a child confidence in his ability to contribute to group living, to develop manual and social skills, and to maintain a sense of pride in his surroundings.

Unless children are very young, they should be expected to do personal chores such as making their beds and keeping their rooms orderly and clean. They should also share responsibility for maintaining cleanliness and order in common rooms such as kitchens, bathrooms, porches, living and dining areas, as well as in the immediate grounds. These tasks convey a sense of obligation and contribution to their "home," which in a family represents the collective responsibility of parents and children. Unless child care workers convey a sense of dedication to maintaining attractive living space, the children cannot be expected to approach their tasks enthusiastically. Whenever possible, children should participate in planning work assignments, and evaluation of the group's success in carrying out its responsibilities for maintenance should take place at the weekly meeting. Workers should be available to help those who require assistance during cleanups and should offer objective criticism, including approval, for jobs well done.

Children may be constructively involved in beautifying their surroundings Enthusiasm can be evoked for decorating bedrooms, common rooms and grounds when staff and children plan and work together. Adult guidance and supervision is essential because children in residence may be unrealistic in their initial conception of a project — of the work involved and the materials they request.

For example, boys in one adolescent cottage decided to paint their rooms. No one told them there were unacceptable colors. Several of the boys wanted to paint their rooms in "way-out" colors such as deep red or dark brown, and were angry when their choice was disapproved. One night a boy defiantly painted his ceiling and walls a deep brown. Similarly, a girl who was deeply depressed following her father's death and had suicidal thoughts, painted her room and her bed black. Symbolically, she had converted her room into a tomb. In both cases, pathogenic factors rather than esthetic consideration determined the selection of colors. Depressing surroundings were not good for these children, and the rooms had to be repainted.

If a project is not geared to the children's capacities and available resources, their initial enthusiasm may wane quickly. In addition to guidance in planning, they will need support, help, and supervision in completing the project.

The value of work and respect for it can be conveyed to children if adults demonstrate concretely through actual participation. A worker who asks children to do work which he himself does not do is disrespecting the concept of the positive value of work. Indirectly, he conveys the attitude that work is something to be avoided or to be imposed on others. A child care worker who rationalizes his demands on children to clean their rooms or do assigned house chores on the basis that this is required by administration conveys a negative attitude about work as an essential part in group living and influences children to view work as an imposed burden. The worker who demands order and cleanliness in children's rooms while his own is messy is neither respected nor readily obeyed.

Workers' Observations on the Group

1. Are the children involved in planning for household tasks, rotation schedules, and distribution of work assignments? Or is this achieved by posting designated assignments without involving the children?
2. Are the children involved in evaluating their performances in household tasks through weekly cottage group meetings?
3. Do the children care about the appearance of their rooms or common living areas?
4. Are they cooperative in carrying out such tasks?

5. What are the disruptive elements that prevent a sense of group cohesiveness around the physical appearance of the cottage?
6. Are there any particular children whom you resent because of their negative attitude toward work?

Workers' Observations on the Individual Child

1. Does he enjoy doing the work assigned? Does he carry it out responsibly?
2. Does he passively accept a work assignment without motivation to carry it out?
3. Does he resist doing assigned chores?
4. While working, does he easily get discouraged, frustrated, or angry?
5. Does he seek help from the child care worker?
6. Does he learn a task easily?
7. Does he ask for approval?
8. Does he rationalize mistakes?
9. Does he blame others for his failings?

Self-Awareness Questions for the Worker

1. Do you believe in the value of the work you ask the children to perform?
2. Do you feel that too much work is expected of the children? Too little?
3. Do you like working with them, or do you limit your role to supervising and checking whether the work is done?
4. Do you convey respect for the value of work orderliness and cleanliness through action rather than words?
5. Do you prefer assigning chores and work projects to involving the children in discussion about planning, execution, and evaluation of achievement?

CLOTHING AND GROOMING

Clothing has social and emotional connotations in addition to its practical functions of protecting the body. The former takes on greater significance as the child gets older. Clothing that is drab, worn out, shabby, and dirty does not necessarily represent economic poverty. To a child, it may signify lack of concern and care on the part of adults, and it contributes to a sense of feeling inadequate, worthless, and rejected.

Children in residence reflect prevailing peer attitudes regarding clothing and this may become an arena of conflict between children and child care workers. Even young children want to be dressed in the current style, a need which becomes even more important among pre-adolescents and young teenagers. Nuances of individuality seem to become more important in later adolescence. Child care workers have to be sensitive to children's attitudes and preferences regarding style of dress. They should not condone extreme fads in clothing which are socially unacceptable, contrary to the rules established by the institution, or which involve excessive costs. Child care workers can help in the selection of appropriate clothing and in its maintenance. Children usually need to be reminded to lay out clothes before bedtime so that they will be easily available the next morning. They need to be taught proper attitudes and skills to keep clothes clean; they should be directed to wear appropriate protection against rain and snow; and they should have their clothing checked for repair and replacement. The child care worker frequently accompanies children on shopping trips and helps them select the best available quality items at the most economical prices. Relationships with children can be enhanced by the interest expressed in their appearance.

The following excerpt from an institution's policy on clothing illustrates the significance of the child care worker's role:

> The manner in which clothing is provided has implications far beyond that of merely keeping the children adequately clothed. For example, the concern we have in seeing our children adequately clothed, the pains we take in developing in our children a feeling of pride and dignity in their appearance is the real substance which makes for relationship between a child care worker and child. Too, there is real educational value in helping our children shop for clothing, realize what clothing costs, and appreciate the responsibilities of taking care of their belongings. . . . From the day of admission on, the child care worker will have the major responsibility for the child's clothing, its upkeep, repair and replacement in accordance with the demands of the basic wardrobe. . . .

> All items of clothing belonging to a child are clearly marked with the child's name. This has value for recovering clothing items which may be mis-

placed or get mixed among another child's clothing. It also has value in giving the child a feeling of individual possession and can foster a sense of responsibility on the child with respect to his clothing. From time to time, it becomes necessary to check through the children's clothing for marking, since with wear and cleaning, the names can rub out, and of course, all new items of clothing should be marked immediately. . . .

When a replacement is necessary, the child care worker may arrange a shopping trip. The purpose of shopping trips with the children is to give them experience in using stores, making selections of merchandise and to gain some appreciation of the cost of clothing. The child care worker is responsible that the clothing purchased be in good taste, appropriate to the particular child, and of good fit. Therefore, a shopping group should be small enough to be easily manageable so that the child care worker is able to give the necessary time and attention to each child.

Factors not directly related to clothing such as child's feeling of deprivation, neglect, difference from others need to be considered in planning purchases, but they have to be related to the reality of the institution's clothing policy. . . .

Child care workers should train children to meet their responsibilities for taking care of their clothing. This should include washing, mending, ironing and using the washing machines. . . . This training is of real educational value in helping our children maintain self-respect and developing a sense of pride and dignity in their daily appearance. Certainly, all of them, if they are to live in the community, will have to be able to do such things in order to maintain themselves properly.

About one week before the date of discharge of a child, the child care worker will go over the child's complete wardrobe with the child present and participating. The child care worker will especially check to see that all clothing presented by the child is in fact hers and not another child's. The child should leave with sufficient clothing. If necessary, additional purchases should be made (Edenwald School 1973).

Like clothing, personal hygiene and grooming represent a person's self-image. Children need adult guidance to develop and maintain good standards of caring for their bodies. Younger children may need direction and help in developing skills and establishing habits of cleanliness and grooming, such as washing, bathing, brushing teeth, care of hair and nails. The child care worker provides reminders for those children who need them constantly, supports others in their efforts to establish good grooming habits, and expresses approval for those who demonstrate satisfactory performance.

SPENDING MONEY

Child care workers have the responsibility for budgeting children's spending money. The amounts may be small, but the burdens and emotional strains are great. Money, like food, has symbolic connotations, generates strong emotions, and creates tensions in cottage living just as it does in families.

All children receive spending money. Older children who depend wholly on the relatively modest monthly allowance given by an institution may find it insufficient. Some who spend it before the end of the month complain, resent those who have money, and frequently ask their child care workers for advances on next month's allowance or on fantasized sums which they say come from home. Denial is difficult, and not infrequently child care workers subsidize children from their own earnings because they cannot bear to see a child without a longed-for candy bar or ice cream, or doing without extras on a cottage trip, while others have more than enough. The following case example illustrates such a dilemma:

After the children went to bed, Bill and Tom talked about their trip to the zoo.

"This was a good day," Tom said. "The kids were well behaved and they all seemed to have a good time."

"Yes. They really enjoyed the animals, especially the elephants," said Bill. "Did you see how thrilled little David was when the bull elephant waved his trunk at him through the iron fence? He fed him peanuts. I'm so glad I gave him extra twenty-five cents to buy the peanuts."

"What do you mean, you gave him money," asked Tom? "Didn't we give the kids fifty cents each for refreshments? Did you forget that cottage staff is not supposed to give their own money to children?"

"True," replied Bill. "Something happened to make me change my mind about this. You know that David comes from a poor, disadvantaged family. Unlike some of the other boys, he gets no spending money from his family. I saw David spend twenty-five cents on a package of food to feed monkeys. He had only twenty-five cents for a coke to eat with his lunch. So I knew that he had spent his money we gave him. He was the only child who had given up part of his refreshment money to feed the animals. After lunch, when we got to the elephant enclosure, David seemed enthralled by the big animals. He looked so longingly at Danny who had bought a big bag of peanuts with which he was feeding the elephants. Danny refused to give some to David. So I gave him twenty-five cents. You should have seen his face and his delight as he fed the elephant.

By the way, we ought to talk to Danny about concealing money which he should have turned over to us for his cottage account. . . . I guess the contrast between David's poverty and Danny's affluence was too much for me, so I broke the rules."

"O.K.," said Bill, "I can understand that. But despite the sentimentality of the situation, you were taking a risk. Suppose another kid saw you give David extra money, and asked for the same, what would you have done? You can't go around subsidizing the kids," he exclaimed.

"That would depend on the particular situation," answered Tom.

"But you face the possibility that you'll be accused of being partial and playing favorites toward David and those kids you give money to," said Bill.

"That's true. But then I would have to explain the reasons to the children. Anyway, we face problems about spending money. The agency really doesn't give the kids enough pocket money per month. The consequence is a class system. The poor kids suffer compared to the kids who get supplemental spending money from their parents," Bill said.

"The kids have to get used to the fact that there is no economic equality, and you have to get used to the fact that that's life. Maybe the agency should give more money, but they can't. So you can't take it upon yourself to right the wrongs of society," said Tom.

"I know," replied Bill, "but in this case, I just couldn't resist the look of longing on David's face."

Child care workers have tried to cope with such situations by interesting the children in establishing a common cottage fund derived from the sale of cottage-produced crafts or from other money-raising efforts. In some institutions where a child cannot keep more than a token amount, violations have been dealt with by confiscating the excess for inclusion in common funds. Problems are created when, during visits, parents give spending money to children rather than to the child care workers, when they send it in letters, or give it to children during home visits. Such situations with the parents must be handled expeditiously by caseworkers or by the child care workers during visiting time. Clarification and explanation of the rationale for the regulations suffices for most, but not for all. Those who feel antagonistic to the institution or excessively guilty for placing a child may as compensation continue to give money surreptitiously in excess of suggested amounts. Other parents cannot cope with their children's pressure or manipulations and give in to their demands for money.

Children may use their money to compensate for insecurities. They may purchase luxury items which they flaunt before the others, buy excessive amounts of sweets, or "buy" friendships. They may tempt others to steal their money and then complain about the theft.

In a group where there is a wide range in spending money among the children, it is possible but not always convincing to try to convey the reality of economics to "have-nots." The child from an impoverished slum family may be able to understand intellectually that some children have more to spend because their parents are able to provide it, but few can accept it. They feel that they are treated unfairly; some view it as rejection by their parents; all resent the inequity between their poverty and their more affluent peers. Child care workers cannot do much about this except to appeal to administration for higher amounts of spending money and to try innovative methods to enrich the common funds.

When money is stolen or used for destructive purposes such as financing runaways, or purchasing alcohol or drugs, disciplinary problems arise which have to be dealt with appropriately. Caseworkers and administrative persons have to be involved. The acts as well as the consequences create strains and instabilities in group living. Action against the offenders is necessary. Meetings to discuss issues which interfere with harmonious group life are advisable.

CHILDREN'S MAIL

Mail from home or from friends is important. It symbolizes continued interest on the part of family and peers, and a sense of caring by others. Mail should be distributed to the children as soon as it is received. Usually, child care workers pick up the mail after the children go off to school and distribute it when they meet again. In general, mail is not and should not be opened and read before delivery to the child. There may be exceptions. For example, if child care workers or caseworkers observe a markedly disturbed reaction by a child after receipt of a letter, the matter should be discussed with the child. If there is conviction that mail from certain sources is damaging to him, a clinical and administrative decision can be made to open his mail before delivery. Evidence that unauthorized money is being sent in letters should be discussed with the child as well as the parents. If it continues, then letters may be opened to confiscate the money.

Children should not be forced to write letters home. When parents express anxiety about lack of mail, the matter should be discussed with the child. At the recommendation of a caseworker, a child care worker may ask a child whether he has written home, but at no time should he pressure him to do so. It may be advisable to designate a time during the week for letter-writing. This schedule may serve to remind children who are careless about correspondence to communicate with their families.

PLAY AND RECREATION

Play, individually or in groups, organized or unplanned, is a universal phenomenon in human life. For children, it provides outlets for physical energy, emotional expression, and fantasy. It provides opportunities for education, skills, incorporation of values, and socialization.

Disturbed Children's Use of Play

Disturbed children, whether they are withdrawn or hyperactive, anxious or apathetic, may not feel the exuberance, joy, and fun generally experienced by children during play. The withdrawn child may find greater security in individualized play which seems to provide a refuge from group living requirements. The hyperactive child, motivated by anxiety to dominate or win, deprives himself of experiencing a sense of pleasure and relaxation. For the aggressive child, play may serve as an outlet for hostile feelings.

Since disturbed children generally do not know how to plan or utilize free time constructively, adult planning and involvement in their play and recreation is essential. In one sense, play can be viewed as authorized regression to more immature behavior. It provides a stage upon which children are permitted to enact impulses which are otherwise unacceptable. Verbalizations and actions which cannot be permitted in everyday living are acceptable when expressed in play. For children whose personality is restrictive or immature, it is important to make available certain periods in which they can relax their controls in play situations. Planned recreation provides an opportunity in which a child can relax, can reorganize his ego strengths, and then return to the more serious business of the day's activities.

A recreational program should provide different types of activities or forms of play adapted to meet the therapeutic needs of different kinds of children. For example, a hostile, aggressive child in a group game such as baseball or basketball will tend to make it an intense rivalry situation. Because of group disapproval or other sanctions employed against any of his efforts to disrupt the game, he will begin to see the usefulness of rules and required behavior in group play. This provides education in cooperative activity. A youngster who is inhibited can be helped to use play to drain off a great deal of repressed hostility which may immobilize him. Participation in group games regulated to his capacity may gradually help him express suppressed aggressive impulses in constructive ways and at the same time serve as socializing experiences.

The child care worker involved in play with children, whether it is in group activities or in the formal recreation program, has opportunities to teach skills, game rules, sportsmanship and, through active participation, to strengthen his relationship with children. His observations have significance for diagnostic evaluation and treatment planning, and his views should be shared with his co-workers during appropriate conferences.

Whereas most younger children can be interested in organized recreational activities available in the institution or in off-ground trips, sporting, cultural, or entertainment events, many adolescents will resist becoming involved, preferring to be left alone to do as they wish. This laissez-faire attitude generally ends up in television-viewing, hanging-around, often listlessly, and frequent complaints of being bored because there is "nothing to do." It is not surprising that child care workers get discouraged by lack of responsiveness to their efforts to interest the residents in recreational activities, or at times angry as a result of hours wasted in isolation or in unjustified griping.

This negativism, lethargy, and apathy may be manifestations of the youngsters' emotional difficulties rather than being attempts to frustrate their workers. To counteract this behavior, discussion is suggested, individually and in groups, about the reasons for it. Forced participation is generally ineffective and counterproductive. Encouragement of planned activities may counteract the anxiety and lethargy present in many adolescents. This constructive alternative is within the scope and responsibility of the therapeutic milieu.

Leisure-time Activities

Even in large institutions, where recreation is centralized through a recreation department and takes place outside of the cottage living situation, there are free hours within the cottage which can be used constructively and enjoyably in activities programmed by child care workers. A supply of material and skill training is a prerequisite and must be provided by the institution. The worker's interest and investment in planning and participation with the children is crucial. According to Whittaker (1969: 103–112), the worker's enthusiasm and enjoyment in a creative activity, game, or sport "provides a model for the children of how a person relates to an activity." Before deciding on a particular activity, a number of variables should be considered, including skill competency of staff, availability of the necessary materials and tools, sufficiency of staff coverage, the children's interest and motivation, and the particular mood of the group. The nature and timing of the event is also important. Thus, physically active and stimulating games should be avoided prior to bedtime; quiet games, group singing, or story-telling for younger children are preferable. A diversity of activities, including imaginative innovations of the rules of established games, may stimulate children's interest and enthusiasm. Flexibility in switching from one activity to another is advisable if the one that had been planned does not seem to evoke a positive response from the children.

A comprehensive activity program contributes to individual and group development. It includes arts and crafts, group games and sports, creative work projects, dramatics and music, nature walks, and camping.

Arts and crafts offer a diversity of interesting and meaningful opportunities for developing skills in working with materials, creating outlets for excess energy, and deriving satisfaction from completing a creative task. Abundance of materials is essential, though they need not be expensive. Newsprint, scrap materials such as cloth remnants, plastic, and wood can be used imaginatively in such activities. Drawing, painting, and clay modeling are particularly appropriate for individual children who are reluctant or not quite ready for sports or group games. They provide constructuve outlets for frustration, draining off tension and anxiety. Some children may be fearful about using certain materials or tools and will require guidance, skill training, and encouragement. Others, who get discouraged easily, lose interest, and want to terminate a project which they started, will require adult support to continue working. The child who is restless and impatient should be started off with a simple type of activity which he can complete rather quickly and which does not require too much concentration. Success in the simpler tasks may give this child a degree of confidence to try more complex activities.

Games and sports promote social interaction, an experience in cooperation, an education in following the rules of the games, and an outlet for physical energy. Some groups may need more supervision and structure than others. Emphasis on enjoyment rather than on competitiveness, playing the game rather than winning, should be encouraged.

Musical activities, ranging from listening to records together to group singing, musical games, and rhythm bands, also provide group participation and enjoyment. Puppetry and dramatic performances require more preparation and are excellent outlets for individual talent, for teamwork, and satisfaction for both performers and spectators.

There are activities which can be planned for leisure hours which not only provide recreation but also contribute constructive work projects within the children's living space. These would include decorating individual rooms, common rooms, the outside of the cottage, including gardening or construction of game or play areas. Such activities offer extensive opportunities for joint planning between children and staff, skill development, cooperative work, esthetic development, and a sense of achievement in beautifying one's surroundings.

Finally, there are outdoor activities like walks, hikes, and camping which expand children's perceptions about nature. Special consideration must be given to children's fears and anxieties evoked by overnight camping. Sufficient staff must be available for coverage in emergencies.

The camping trip, the dramatic performance, the joint cottage project, all culminate in enjoyment for the children. The process of planning and carrying out these activities contributes to socialization and individual growth. For example, in one residential setting, a cottage of young children and their child care workers have had a tradition of planning a two-week camping trip during the summer. They work all year on projects to finance it. They have made arts and crafts objects for a cottage fair, and had lunches and parties which earned them money to buy camping equipment and supplies. Parents have also become involved, and the institution has matched the children's earnings. It has been an exciting, constructive experience for all, especially the children who felt that their effort and labor made the summer camping trip possible.

Fundamental to leisure-time activity planning is assessment of individual and group needs. This is particularly pertinent with younger children, the emotionally disturbed, and developmentally handicapped. They are not well served by mass recreation programs geared to normal children. Many of these children are poorly coordinated and lack basic skills. They are also poorly motivated and they are afraid to try because of failures experienced earlier. The child who cannot run well, hit, catch or throw a ball has experienced ridicule from peers and adults. He not only needs encouragement but individual instruction to acquire basic skills. They can be helped through a program of simple exercises and fun games to enhance coordination and develop mastery of fundamental skills. Workers may wish to use Blake and Volb (1964) or Flugelman (1976) as source books where the suggested games prepare children for team sports.

The following Leisure-time Activity Profile suggests an outline for a leisure-time activity assessment. Since child care workers are closely involved with the children's activities, it is suggested that they complete the profile for children in their group. The child care workers' observations and participation with children in leisure-time activities will contribute significantly to planning and implementation of a child's needs. The profile should be available at the time of the initial planning conference where goals and strategies for implementing them would be formulated. These would be evaluated, extended, or modified in accordance with a child's needs during subsequent inter-disciplinary evaluation conferences.

Leisure-time Activity Profile

Name of Child:_____

Age:_____

Group Care Unit:_____

I. *PROFILE* (To be completed by child care staff by time of initial evaluation conference)

   1. *Activities and Interests* (check all those that he/she participates)

Outdoor sports	____	Music	____
Gym activities	____	Socials	____
Art	____	T.V.	____
Crafts	____	Other: (specify actual or expressed interest)
Hobbies	____	_____
Quiet games	____	_____

2. *Strengths* (check those applicable)

Well coordinated _____
Good playing skills _____
Positive attitude toward activities _____
Positive attitude toward staff in activities _____
Positive attitude toward peers in group activities _____
Good leadership qualities _____
Other: (Specify) _____

3. *Coordination Problems* (check appropriate item)

None _____
In running _____
In jumping _____
In hand dexterity _____
In finger dexterity _____
In catching ball _____
In throwing ball _____
In batting ball _____

4. *Motivation to learn skills* (checkone)

Eager to learn _____
Gets anxious about it _____
Is not cooperative _____
Refuses instruction _____

5. *Attitude toward leisure-time activities* (check one)

Positive _____
Fearful _____
Hostile _____
Indifferent _____

6. *Degree of Participation in Group Activities* (check those applicable)

Initiates peer group activities _____
Participates actively _____
Needs encouragement to join group activity _____
Refuses to participate _____

7. *Behavior in Group Activities* (check one or more)

Is always involved in it _____
Seems to enjoy himself/herself _____
Is cooperative _____
Is highly competitive _____
Gets frustrated easily _____

Is mostly quiet and passive _____
Is angry most of the time _____
Gets into fights _____
Is disruptive _____
Seems anxious most of the time _____

8. *Leadership Qualities* (check one)

Is leader, using his role constructively _____
Is leader, using his role destructively _____
Is a follower _____
Is an isolate _____

9. *Acceptance by Peers in Activities* (check one)

Is liked _____
Is tolerated but not liked _____
Is disliked _____
Refuse to play with him _____

10. *Attitude Toward Staff* (check one)

Seeks out staff _____
Avoids contact with staff _____
Rejects staff attention _____
Is indifferent to staff _____

II. *GOALS* (formulated at initial conference and evaluated periodically)
Determined at scheduled interdisciplinary case conference.
List them in terms of priority:

1. _____

2. _____

3. _____

III. *MEANS and STRATEGIES* to achieve above goals and designation of person(s) who is most suited to work with child to achieve goals.

1. _____

2. _____

3. _____

_____

_____

Television

Television-viewing is an important leisure-time activity in our society for children as well as adults. Unfortunately, it can be misused. It becomes an obstacle to relationships when it is used as a substitute for personal interaction. When children are indiscriminately exposed to inappropriate, frightening programs and films of violence, T.V. is harmful.

Its use in residential living to fill empty leisure hours is evidently poor planning of cottage activities. A television set kept running throughout the day and evening, serving as a shelter for children who cluster around it for hours on end, is an example of adult thoughtlessness. Unplanned and unstructured television-viewing can be destructive because children will frequently select programs that stir up anxiety. Younger children, exposed to horror films—especially before bedtime—may have difficulty falling asleep and may have frightening dreams or nightmares. The same films may serve to reinforce aggressive tendencies in older children.

Children who are highly suggestible, have poor impulse control, and poor reality judgment, may reenact destructive scenes viewed on television. For example, this occurred in a girls' cottage. The girls had asked the child care workers for permission to view the film "Born Innocent" which portrayed some gruesome scenes, insensitive staff attitudes, and a rioting group of girls in a girls' institution. The following night, two of the girls organized a reenactment of the riot scene and influenced most of the other girls to join them. Though some of the girls had questions about it, they followed the delinquent leaders' requests because they were afraid of retaliation. During the disturbance, they messed up the cottage but did not physically hurt the child care workers. Intervention by administrative staff stopped the rioting and reestablished controls. The girls spent hours cleaning up the mess, and the leaders were disciplined. During subsequent discussion with staff as well as the girls, it became clear that it was an error to let the girls view this film.

Staff control of television-viewing is important because it minimizes the risks enumerated above and because it ensures appropriate use of a potentially educational and therapeutic instrument. Through familiarity with television programming, a child care worker can plan constructive use of television viewing. The weekly T.V. guide should enable a worker to determine which programs are appropriate for his group and which ones should be avoided. Children can be involved in selecting programs from those deemed acceptable by the cottage staff. If a child or a group desire to see programs of sadism and violence, the request should not be granted. However, reasons for the refusal should be stated clearly. Sometimes a confrontation can be avoided with a touch of humor or exemplified by the following incident:

Throughout the day, a number of boys were talking about a movie "Devil's Force" which was scheduled to begin at 9 p.m. that night on Channel 4. Arnold and Lou, the child care counselors, felt that this gory, violence-ridden, frightening movie was not a suitable program prior to bedtime. They so informed the boys, offering substitute programs. At 9 p.m., one of the boys switched to Channel 4. When Arnold firmly insisted that the movie was not appropriate, that it would be frightening to some of the boys, that there was no point seeing it for half an hour anyway, several of the boys disagreed and argued for seeing it. However, Arnold turned the channel.

The atmosphere became tense. One boy argued that the 9 p.m. hour was "O.K. because it is considered family (viewing) time and if this is all right in families, why not in the cottage?" Arnold replied, "This may be family time for T.V.-viewing, but it doesn't mean we have to turn family time into "poison-time" by subjecting children to such programs." One of the boys began to laugh because the term "poison-time" struck him as a funny joke. This started others laughing. Another boy then argued, "It's not your T.V., it's ours, so you can't tell us what to watch." Arnold jokingly asked, "You have a receipt to prove it?" This evoked hilarious laughter from the boys. "Did you hear that? He asked him for a receipt!" "Tell us another joke," others said to Arnold. With this, the tension subsided, and jokes were passed around by all. No one watched T.V., and at 9:30 p.m., the boys went to bed quietly.

Staff participation in viewing television with the children can be constructive. It represents participating and sharing time together; it also provides opportunities to talk with the children afterwards about the content of a program. The discussion may be educational in nature or reassuring if some of the scenes were frightening. Even a film like "Born Innocent" which, in the case described above, stimulated destructive acting-out, could have been utilized for constructive purposes if the staff had been ready to talk about the film after it was over. The anxieties and negative feelings that were stimulated could have been exposed; feelings and attitudes about institutional living and what it means to the children in the group might have been expressed; comparisons could then have been made between cottage living in the film and the girls' real cottage.

The child care worker cannot be the guardian of television at all times. Many times he may be the only worker on duty, or he may be busy with a problem situation, or preparing snacks, and so on. At such times, he may have to depend on the television set to occupy the children. There is nothing wrong with this, but the children should be told that they are being left on their own and that the worker expects them to behave. Whenever possible, the worker should make a periodic check to insure that everything is going well.

(For more detailed activity programming by child care workers, the following references are suggested: Chapter 12, "Developmental Programming for the Worker," and its Appendix, pp. 203–257, in Foster et al. 1972; and "Program Activities, Their Selection and Use in a Therapeutic Milieu," pp. 100–119, in Whittaker 1969.)

Observations on the Individual Child

1. Does he prefer individual play or group activities?
2. Is his play reality-oriented or primarily make-believe or fantasy? If predominantly make-believe, does he switch back to reality quickly? Does he do so reluctantly or with difficulty?
3. What kind of group activities does he prefer? Active or passive games? Competitive or noncompetitive activities? Athletic or esthetic, such as dance or music? Does he prefer watching T.V. to playing games?
4. Does he have any special interests or hobbies?
5. Does he have any special skills or talents? Is he eager to learn new skills, or is he fearful or evasive?
6. Is he a leader or a follower in games?
7. Is he well coordinated? Poorly coordinated or clumsy? Inhibited? Spontaneous?
8. Is he destructive with toys or equipment?
9. Does he conform to the rules of a game? Try to dominate a group activity? Cheat or try to, in order to win? Try to avoid getting into group play? Blame others if the team loses?
   Is he aggressive, even hurting playmates? Disruptive in a game?
10. Does he have fun, enjoy himself at play?

11. Is he fearful of getting hurt?
12. Is he reckless, accident-prone?
13. Is he accepted and liked by his playmates?
14. What is his attitude toward recreation staff—friendly, hostile, ambivalent, or indifferent?

Observations on the Group

1. Is it easy or difficult for the group as a whole to get involved in group activities?
2. Are there subgroups (two or three children) who enjoy playing together?
3. Is the group responsive to planned activities?
4. What kind of activities or group games do they prefer?
5. Is it easy or difficult to get them involved in planning group activities?
6. Are they responsive to workers' suggestions?
7. Can they function as a team, a cohesive group?
8. Does the group have a natural leader?
9. Are there isolates who do not get involved in group activities?
10. Is anyone treated as a scapegoat by the others?

The Worker's Self-Evaluation

1. Do you enjoy organizing play activities?
2. Do you feel insecure about organizing group activities?
3. Do you like to play with a child individually, with small groups, or with the total group?

HEALTH CARE

The child care worker plays an important role in protecting children's physical wellbeing. He supervises and guides them in maintaining standards of personal cleanliness and grooming, eating well-balanced meals to assure adequate nutritional needs, getting physical exercise through recreational activities, and wearing clothing appropriate to weather conditions. He has to be alert to signs of illness or side effects of medication, sensitive to children's physical complaints, and ready to act quickly when a child becomes ill suddenly or sustains an injury. The child care worker's contact with agency medical staff is generally limited to the nurse(s), but he may have to contact a doctor in the nurse's absence, or may have to take a child to a hospital emergency room. He is also expected to be familiar with established medical procedure, which he is expected to follow as needed. The following abstract from the medical procedures of a residential treatment center (Childville, 1976) exemplifies such directives:

> Children should be observed for any unusual signs of illness, i.e., colds, cuts, bruises, nosebleeds, swellings, rashes, etc., and brought to the attention of the nurse. Any abnormality is to be referred to the nurse immediately.
>
> Children should be ready for clinics on time and should be appropriately dressed.
>
> All illness or emergencies should be called to the nurse's attention when she is on duty.
>
> In the absence of the nurse or nurse's assistant, Dr. D _____, telephone no. _____, is to be called in all cases of illness. This means if a child has an elevated temperature; if he complains of any aches or pains; if he vomits more than once, has a cough, etc.
>
> If a child sustains injury of any kind, falls, or has pains that might indicate internal injury, has sprain or fracture, contact nurse or doctor. In their absence, take child to _____ Hospital Emergency Clinic.

For minor cuts or scrapes, wash with soap and water, apply a small amount of bacitracin ointment and a bandaid.

For major cuts or lacerations, cover with sterile gauze and take child to hospital emergency room.

For a cold, child should be kept indoors, at rest, and encouraged to drink fluids. Temperature should be checked morning and later afternoon.

For fever (rectal temperatures above 101°), call the answering service to report to the doctor. Should the temperature rise rapidly and cause discomfort, while awaiting the doctor's instructions, give 1 tablet Tylenol every 4 hours as needed. For rectal temperatures between 100° and 101°, the child should be observed unless there is abdominal pain or severe headache, in which case doctor should be called.

For headache, put child to rest in bed and check temperature. If there is fever, follow directions as in item above.

For sore throat, check temperature. Without fever, if associated with cold symptoms, follow procedure as item for a cold.

For abdominal pain that persists, note other symptoms such as vomiting or diarrhea, temperature, and report to doctor.

For nausea or vomiting without abdominal pain, give nothing by mouth for 3 or 4 hours. Child may be allowed to suck on ice or hard candy. When nausea and vomiting stop, give teaspoonful of any of the following clear liquids every 20 minutes: coca cola, ginger ale, fruit juice. As child improves, these fluids may be increased in amount slowly. If nausea and vomiting recur, stop all fluids and repeat as above. If vomiting continues, notify doctor.

For diarrhea, stop all food except the following: rice, skim milk, banana, pot cheese, farmer cheese, skim milk cottage cheese, dry toast, saltine crackers, clear broth, orange juice, Dezerta gelatin.

For nose bleed, keep child in sitting position with head tilted forward over a sink or basin. Pinch nose on the affected side or sides very firmly and continuously for 5 minutes. During this time, child will be breathing through his mouth. Should nose bleed continue or recur, repeat this process. Do not pack nose, do not apply cold compresses.

For burns, immerse part in cold water or apply cold wet compresses. Dry gently and apply Bacitracin ointment and cover with sterile gauze dressing and bandage roll. Tape may be applied on outside of bandage roll. If there is blistering or raw areas of skin, follow same procedure and report to doctor.

For head injuries associated with loss of consciousness or repeated vomiting, take child to emergency room of _____ Hospital.

For injuries to extremities where normal motion is limited or normal weight bearing is not possible, take child to emergency room of _____ Hospital.

For toothache, give Tylenol, apply cold compress externally, and rinse mouth with lukewarm water every half-hour. Check temperature, and if elevated, call doctor.

For eye problems:
   a) All cases of eye injury with pain should be taken to emergency room of _____ Hospital.
   b) For foreign body in eye, take child to emergency room of_____ Hospital.
   c) For eye discharge, compress eye with warm water (use cotton balls).
· *For earache*, check temperature, give Tylenol and call answering service of doctor.

All temperatures should be taken rectally.

If any of the above occur, please indicate this in the log book.

A question may be raised about the desirability of the information described above because it implies that child care workers should be performing nursing functions which are beyond their capacities and therefore risky to children's health. This is not the case. Medical procedures and guidelines for child care workers are essential for the protection of the children in group care. This worker, like a parent, should be acquainted with children's symptoms, information on how to deal with minor ailments and when to act expeditiously when a child is injured or ill.

Medication

Medication is prescribed for the relief of excessive anxiety and control of impulsive behavior. The overanxious child is unable to cope with the requirements of daily living; the impulsive child is constantly in difficulty because, lacking sufficient inner controls, he cannot adapt to the requirements of social living. Both experience inner turmoil and outer frustration because they cannot concentrate on work or learning, and their behavior often results in social rejection.

Prescription of medication is a psychiatric responsibility. The five major categories of medication for children (Nichtern 1973) include the following:

1. **Tranquilizers** such as **Thorazine, Mellaril,** and **Stelazine** are phenothiazines. They sedate, relieve anxiety, and decrease impulsivity. Thorazine and Mellaril are generally prescribed for the agitated child; Stelazine seems more effective with the depressed and withdrawn child. These phenothiazines have been found to be most effective in treating disturbances of childhood and adolescence associated with the schizophrenias.

Librium and **Valium** are considered milder forms of tranquilizers than the phenothiazines. They are useful in reducing tension and anxiety evoked by distressful situations. **Benadryl** seems effective for the young hyperactive and impulsive child.

2. **Stimulants** including amphetamines such as **Benzedrine, Dexedrene,** and **Ritalin,** given in proper doses, have a calming effect on children, whereas they produce stimulating "highs" in adults. The amphetamines make the hyperactive child quieter and more relaxed; they decrease mood swings, improve attention spans and relieve tension. They seem most effective with children who have neurotic problems which are expressed in hyperactive behavior. Ritalin is effective in children diagnosed as having minimal brain dysfunc-

tion or whose behavior is characterized by distractibility, impulsivity, hyperactivity, specific learning disabilities, and perceptual impairment.

3. **Anti-depressants** such as **Elavil** and **Tofranil** are used for relief of symptoms of depression and for depression accompanied by anxiety. This includes restlessness, sleep disturbance, and phobias. Tofranil has also proven to be effective in controlling eneuresis in children.

4. **Sedatives** in the form of barbiturates are not generally prescribed for children because they tend to decrease alertness and loosen controls. However, they are used as behavior-modifying agents for brain-damaged children.

5. **Anti-convulsants** such as Dilantin help control seizure reactions. There may be adverse side effects depending on the type of drug used. Children seem to be less affected than adults. When side effects occur, they can be modified quickly by changing dosage. The child care worker should be aware of these physical manifestations, and when observed, they should be quickly reported to the child's caseworker or the psychiatrist who prescribed the medication.

Some of the major *side effects* of these drugs are:

1. *Thorazine*: Drowsiness, usually mild to moderate, may occur, particularly the first or second week, after which time it generally disappears. Jaundice may appear between the second and fourth week of therapy. It is usually reversible upon withdrawal of the medication. Allergic reactions may occur, especially to sunlight; occasional dry mouth, nasal congestion, constipation, and sore throat are other manifestations.

2. *Mellaril*: Drowsiness tends to subside with continued medication or a reduction in dosage. There may be dryness of mouth, blurred vision, nausea, jaundice, and occasional tremors of limbs.

3. *Tofranil*: Hypertension, tingling of extremities, dry mouth, blurred vision, urinary retention, rash, and nausea may occur.

4. *Stelazine*: Drowsiness, dizziness, skin reaction, rash, dry mouth, insomnia, and fatigue may occur.

5. *Ritalin*: Restlessness and insomnia are the most common adverse reactions initially, but are usually controlled by reducing dosage and omitting the drug in the afternoon or evening.

6. *Valium*: Side effects most commonly reported are drowsiness, fatigue, and sleep disturbance.

7. *Elavil*: Disturbed concentration, hypertension, dry mouth, blurred vision, and skin rash may occur.

BEDTIME

In the same way that waking poses anticipated difficulties for some children, bedtime evokes anxieties because sleep implies uncertainties, helplessness, and loss of control. Some children are fearful of potential nightmares; a few may be afraid that once asleep, they may not awaken the next day; others may perceive sleep as a threat because they will not be in control of what goes on about them while they are asleep.

Fear of falling asleep was dramatically exemplified by ten-year-old Marcia who, after admission to the residential treatment center, would cry and complain she could not fall asleep unless the child care worker on duty was near her bedside. It was not certain at first that this might be related to the fact that Marcia's twin sister (who had been ill with leukemia for a number of years) had died in her sleep. Nightly, the worker reassured Marcia that she would watch over her while she was asleep. Subsequently, Marcia told the worker that she had been afraid to fall asleep because she believed that like her sister, she would die. Reassurance by both child care workers and Marcia's therapist that she was physically well, that no one would hurt her while she was asleep, and that she would awaken each morning, finally dispelled the child's anxiety. She could then fall asleep without the physical presence of an adult guardian whom she trusted.

Anxiety Manifestations

Most young children require adult reassurance that they will be safe when asleep. For some, to be tucked in by their worker conveys that the adult cares and will protect them. A warm "goodnight" is reassuring. A child anxious about going to sleep will generally express it in behavior which conveys stress. He may stall, cry, demand a drink of water, or go to the bathroom frequently. To postpone going to bed, he may insist on watching television, or he may get himself involved in play. Some children may even start fights; others may try to monopolize the worker's attention either by clinging or by provocative behavior; some are afraid of the dark; others will anticipate bad dreams; some will go through a number of compulsive rituals such as excessive washing or arranging items of clothing in a particular way.

Children's Objections

Some young children, especially those who had no regular bedtime hours at home, resist going to bed because they are used to staying up late, playing, or watching television. While this may be understandable, the worker cannot compromise the regular bedtime hours. Actually, the time set for young children's bedtime is not unreasonable, and this fact should be explained to them. Occasionally, exceptions may be made by staff when there are special community events or educational television programs which the workers feel would be of benefit to the children.

There are realistic difficulties with bedtime hours for adolescents, especially in relation to the economics of staff time rather than the children's needs. If child care workers' schedules end at 9:30 p.m. or even 10:00 p.m., complaints by the children that bedtime is too early, especially on weekends, may be valid.

During many years of the author's experience in a residential treatment unit for emotionally disturbed adolescent boys, there were interminable arguments against a 9:30 p.m. bedtime. We could not say, "You are growing, active boys and need more rest." To do so would have been hypocritical. The honest explanation about staff scheduling seemed more acceptable to the boys. This unrealistic bedtime also nourished an underground night life of disruptive behavior. Eventually, bedtime was extended to 10:30 p.m., and later for weekend dances and party activities.

Preparation

Advanced planning is necessary to create a peaceful, calm atmosphere for the group in general. Helping the children prepare for bedtime contributes to reduction of tensions as well as a greater closeness between children and adults. Staff could remind the children in advance to terminate play and television-watching, they could supervise showers and putting out clothes for the following day; they could talk with the children. Tucking in the younger children, reading or telling a bedtime story, offering reassurance that one will see them the following morning, are all helpful. If there is a policy or established routine that after lights are out, there is to be no running, playing radios, or loud conversation, it should be enforced. It is advisable for workers to bed-check.

Adequate night coverage by administrative personnel and infirmary staff, as well as by child care workers, is essential for security and safety. This serves to deter acting-out among older children in the forms of intercottage visits (especially in coed settings), runaways, kangaroo courts, abuse of individual children, and vandalism. Night staff should be especially informed regarding any special difficulty an individual child or group has experienced during the day and any anticipated problems.

Because going to sleep is not easy for children who are emotionally distressed, sending a child early to bed as punishment, is, at best, a questionable procedure. According to Gardner (1973: 185), it is not appropriate to associate sleep with punishment. First, it is ineffective because although one can send a child to bed early, he does not necessarily go to sleep; second, it is destructive because using early-to-bed as a punishment reinforces the notion that there is indeed something bad about getting to sleep. For young children, especially, use of early bedtime as a disciplinary measure is risky, and sleep problems may develop as a consequence.

Observations About the Child

1. Are there any problems about getting him to bed? Does he dawdle, object to getting ready, become disruptive, start arguments, or try to manipulate the worker into letting him stay up?
2. Does he express anxiety about anticipated nightmares, or that he might be hurt while asleep, or that he is fearful that he might not awaken the following morning?
3. Is he enuretic and, if so, does he express anxiety about it?
4. Does he masturbate after going to bed?
5. Once asleep, does he sleep through the night or is there restlessness, talking in his sleep, walking in his sleep, or frequent awakening to go to the bathroom?

RECORDING

The "case record" generally refers to recording by clinical staff—namely, social workers, psychiatrists, and psychologists—and rarely contains recorded material by child care workers. When there are references to a child's behavior in his living group, it is generally second-hand reporting recorded by caseworkers.

Child care recording does have value. Its immediate importance is communication of information about an individual child or the group. Without the written record, workers have to rely on memory which is not fault-proof. Consequently, the course of a child's adaptation to group life and his individual growth may not be traced with accuracy. The written record also provides information for new staff or part-time workers. Finally, records are essential for research purposes, essential for systematizing knowledge in the field of child care, for developing theory, for rationalizing the need to professionalize child care, and for funding group care programs.

The form and content of the child care record depend on established requirements of the group care program, time available, and manpower resources to achieve it. Recording may simply be a daily log with brief entries regarding individual children or group behavior, which may be supplemented by concise or even process recording of crisis situations.

The following are examples of actual log entries:

5/20/79—8 p.m.   Jimmy was in good shape today. He functioned well in school, got along with all the children and staff.

5/22/79—9 a.m.   Fay was upset this morning, was irritable with everyone, refused to eat breakfast or do her chores, and cried before going to school. She would not tell me what was wrong. I accompanied her to school and then told her teacher about it. Her caseworker will see her today.

These are concise examples; some may consider them too brief. Ideally, log notes should not only be descriptive of specific behavior crisis, emergency, and so on, but should also tie in this information with the child's overall functioning in accordance with expectations and treatment planning. Log notes should be written at the end of the working day and should be available to all staff working directly with the children.

Charting

Observations may also be recorded on charts that graph a child's activity in relation to daily activities. Charts may be used solely for staff purposes to track a child's functioning in accordance with treatment planning or they may be shared with children to appraise them of their functioning or to motivate them in their progress in a planned program. Krueger (1978: 67–95) specifies and elaborates upon a number of charting techniques. He cautions staff to be objective about scoring behavior, basing it on realistic expectations, on assessment of a child's capabilities rather than subjective reactions, and generalized standards applicable to all of the children in a group. For example, David and Sam are roommates. David is a slow learner and poorly coordinated. Sam has excellent work skills and is highly proficient in doing assigned chores when he feels like it. He has to be prodded by his worker while David tries very hard to do what is expected. In judging their performance, should not motivation be a weighted factor in awarding points for grooming, room and house chores? If the boys were judged by the final product rather than levels of capability and motivation, Sam would always earn more points than David. The children's workers have agreed to weigh positively David's motivation in awarding points and to weigh negatively Sam's lack of effort. When Sam complained that he deserved a higher point score than David, he was told not to compare himself with David because he is more capable than David and that he would earn higher scores when he performs up to his own ability.

Crises

The recording of crises is important because it provides ongoing follow-up by other disciplines. The following is a concise statement of a critical incident on a weekend:

> On Sunday evening following return from a Thanksgiving visit with her mother, Melissa was restless, annoyed the other children, and was unresponsive to my efforts to control her. When Mrs. M. entered the cottage living room, Melissa assaulted her physically, calling her abusive names. Together, we had to physically restrain her and remove her from the room.

This entry, read by the workers who came on duty the following morning, alerted them to the need to deal with Melissa's disturbance.

Promptly conveyed to the child's caseworker, it helped clarify what had occurred to precipitate the outburst. Melissa had had a highly disappointing visit with her mother who had neglected her in favor of her paramour. Apparently, Melissa was very angry but could not express it while at home. Subsequently, she acted out her frustration, first toward her peers and then in the attack against the child care worker. Her perceptions had become so blurred by the traumatic experiences at home that when Mrs. M. walked into the room, Melissa perceived her to be her mother. The attack was a manifestation by a borderline psychotic child at a time of stress when her perception of reality was blurred. Her anger with her mother was misplaced upon another woman whom she knew and liked but who resembled her mother (in color only). The workers had not known the facts of the home visit but had sensed that the assaultive outburst on Melissa's part was not a personal attack but an irrational outburst by a very disturbed child.

No matter what the form the recording takes, it should be clear and concise. In selective situations requiring process recording, it is important that recording be done daily and that time be made available for it.

REFERENCES

Adler, J. 1973. "The Child Care Counsellor as 'Target of Transferred Behavior.'" *Child Care Quarterly* 2 July, no. 2: 98–106.

Adler, J., ed. 1963. *Hawthorne Cedar Knolls Schools Clinic Manual.* Mimeo.

Adler, J., and W. Finkel. 1976. "Integrating Remedial Methods into Child Care Practice." *Child Care Quarterly* 5, no. 1.

American Psychiatric Association. 1964. *A Psychiatric Glossary.* Washington, D.C.: APA.

Beker, J.; P.M. Gitelson; P. Kaminstein; and L.F. Adler. 1970. *Critical Incidents in Child Care.* New York: Behavioral Publications.

Blake, W.O., and A. Volb. 1964. *Lead Up Games to Team Sports.* Englewood Cliffs, N.J.: Prentice–Hall.

Childville. 1976. *Health Care Policy.* Mimeo.

Edenwald School. 1974. *Manual of Policies and Procedures.* Mimeo.

Flugelman, A., ed. 1976. *The New Games Book.* Garden City: Headlands Press Book.

Foster, G.W.; K.D. Vanderven; E.R. Kroner; N.T. Carbonara; and G.N. Cohen. 1972. *Child Care with Emotionally Disturbed Children.* Pittsburgh: University of Pittsburgh Press.

Gardner, R. A. 1973. *Understanding Children.* New York: Jason Aronson.

Krueger, M. A. 1978. *Intervention Techniques for Child Care Workers.* Milwaukee, Wisc.: Franklin Publishers.

LeMay, M. 1974. *The Functions of the Specialized "Educateur" for Maladjusted Youth*, English translation by Vivian Jarvis, Green Chimneys School, Brewster, N.Y. Mimeo.

Nichtern, S. 1973. "Psychopharmacotherapy for Children." *Pediatric Annals* 2, no. 3: 43–59.

Seitleis, L. 1975. "Commitment." Address at Wurzweiler School of Social Work, New York. October 15, 1975. Unpublished.

Small, R.W., and R.B. Clarke. 1979. "Schools as Partners in Helping." In *Caring for Troubled Children*, edited by J.K. Whittaker, pp. 155–185.

Whittaker, J.K. 1969. "Managing Wake-up Behavior." In *The Other 23 Hours*, edited by A.E. Treischman; J.K. Whittaker; and L.K. Brendtro. Chicago: Aldine.

Wolstein, B. 1954. *Transference.* New York: Grune and Stratton.

9 PROBLEMATIC BEHAVIOR

Life with disturbed children is full of problems. The child care worker is a constant witness to and, not infrequently, the object of children's conflicts which express themselves in troubled and troubling behavior. Problem behavior encompasses a broad spectrum, ranging from withdrawal and passivity to hyperactivity, anger, hostility, and aggression; it weaves through the daily routines and interaction among the children and the adults.

Child care workers also have to cope with more serious problems which are very stressful. These include temper tantrums, bedwetting and soiling, lying, stealing, and running away. Although administrative and clinical personnel become involved in crises related to such behavior, the child care worker may feel very much alone, left to struggle with extremely difficult situations and their consequences on the individual child who expresses it and the group that witnnesses it.

TEMPER TANTRUM

A temper tantrum can be as overwhelming an experience for the adult who is the object of it as it is for the child who acts it out. These tantrums are irrational, tumultuous, and exhausting. The child acts as if he is oblivious to the reality of his surroundings. He may cry, scream, throw things, use abusive language, threaten assault; he may jump up and down, throw himself on the ground, thrash about, kick, pound the floor, bang his head; he may scream invectives, threats, and accusations at the child care worker who is nearby blaming him for the frustrations that triggered the outburst. It is rare that the child attack the adult physically. He is more likely to injure himself.

The temper tantrum is generally preceded by a "rumbling and grumbling phase" (Treischman 1969: 176)—the child seems tense and restless, exhibiting a build-up of anxiety, a deepening sense of discomfort which he tries to alleviate by seeking an issue which will provide the outlet for his accelerating inner tension. The slightest frustration can trigger the outburst. The observant worker, sensing the child's restlessness and irritation, may be able to intervene in time to prevent the temper tantrum. He may, for example, suggest to the child that something seems to be bothering him and that he would like to be helpful. If the child has had previous temper tantrums, the worker might remind him that it would be better to talk about it before the feelings build up to uncontrollable proportions which usher in a very unpleasant situation. If this is not done, or if the worker's efforts are unsuccessful, the temper tantrum will run its course.

One child care worker has described a temper tantrum (Alterman 1973: 3)

> I usually could sense when a temper tantrum is imminent, for Danny was more than usually provocative. When I saw this sort of thing developing, I usually tried, if possible, to defuse it before it started, either by isolating him for a time or reasoning with him. If this failed, however, my first thought was always to get a physical hold on Danny. Sometimes this was necessary for purely protective reasons, for he would many times pick up weapons or throw things with anger; but I did it in any case to provide him with a physical manifestation of the control which we were providing for him. At first, I merely would hold his wrists and let the screaming run its course while attempting to remain relatively passive myself. As time passed, however, I found it more efficacious to pinion him some way and let him know he would be released from the uncomfortable position as soon as he controlled himself. He is always quite provocative and abusive in a tantrum, but I always tried not to lose my temper, although I was not always successful. When the incident was over, he was repentant and quiet, and I usually would punish him in some minor way (such as staying in the cottage for a while), making the distinction to him that he was being isolated, not for being angry, but for handling his anger in a harmful and uncontrolled way.

The child's temper tantrum represents loss of inner controls. Expression of sympathy, involvement in dialogue, or negotiation to influence him to stop his behavior is futile. He does not seem to hear what is said to him. In fact, he may react more negatively and contrary to the suggestions. Threats of punishment of hurting him should also be avoided because the genuine temper tantrum is an involuntary act, the child being unconscious of the inner conflicts that produce it. He must be protected from hurting himself or others, which can be done by holding him tightly and firmly and removing him from the scene if other children are present. This avoids aggravating the intensity of the tantrum and protects the others from witnessing its course. It is not an easy task to hold a wildly thrashing, abusive child. It may evoke anxiety and, not infrequently, anger. There is no harm in conveying to the child that one does not like his behavior and that it is making the worker angry. He should be told that he will not be hurt and that he will be held until he is able to reestablish controls which the worker feels he is capable of. Gradually, the irrational behavior will subside, after which the child will seem exhausted physically. Generally, he wants to be left alone and if he requests it, his wish should be respected. He should be told, however, that the worker will be nearby and will be glad to talk to him.

Some children seem to feel guilty afterwards and even apologize for the trouble they have caused. Some act as if the temper tantrum had never occurred. As soon as the child is sufficiently recovered, it is advisable to talk over wih him the events leading up to the tantrum. He may be asked to try to remember what made him feel so tense and to describe the feelings that preceded the outburst. One could suggest an alternative way to handle his feelings such as talking things over with the worker. He should be encouraged to ask for help in the future before he "blows his top." The event should also be reported to the child's caseworker, and the child should be advised to discuss it in his individual therapy sessions.

In the case of Danny described above, there may have been a connection between the temper tantrums and the boy's relationship with his disturbed, inconsistent, and sexually seductive mother. It may have symbolized the sado-masochistic relationship between the two. Alterman (1973: 6) states:

Danny will have engineered, out of anger, some situation in which he has been frustrated or in which he has provoked someone—an adult or another child—usually into striking him. Apparently, as soon as he is struck (or some other physical contact is made), he begins to scream very loudly in the vilest obscenities possible. I have noticed that these obscenities usually refer to mothers, a fact which undoubtedly has some significance. At this point, a staff member usually has to remove him from the premises physically since he will continue to scream at the cause of his anger and struggle.

I see these explosions as a sort of culmination of most of this child's characteristics. In them, he gains attention, manipulates a reaction, and tests an adult's concern for him. He shows his extreme anger and lack of impulse control and of course he frequently masochisticly provokes others to reject and punish him.

Some temper outbursts resemble but are not actual temper tantrums. For example, when a phobic child is exposed to the object of his fear, whether it be an animal or a frightening situation, he experiences a massive surge of anxiety which breaks down his inner controls. The resulting behavior triggered by panic resembles a temper tantrum. However, as soon as the phobic object is removed or as soon as the child is removed from the fearful anxiety-provoking situation, the disturbed behavior ceases. Psychotherapeutic treatment which gets at the causal conflicts responsible for the phobia may eliminate such anxiety attacks (A. Freud 1965: 111). Behavior modification techniques ("systematic desensitization") may eliminate the symptoms. Staged or feigned temper tantrums also occur, and they should be handled with firmness. A child who has been successful in getting his way through a temper tantrum may learn to use it in a manipulative way to force reluctant adults to give in to his unreasonable demands. Knowing the children, a worker will soon learn if a temper tantrum is genuine or faked. In the latter case, the so-called "rumbling and grumbling" phase is not in evidence. The behavior may be precipitated by an adult's refusal to give in to an unreasonable demand. If the outburst does not stop on request, the child should be isolated. The behavior may continue but if ignored and does not bring the wanted results, it will subside. The child may also be disciplined for such behavior in order to reinforce awareness that it is inappropriate and unacceptable.

What is crucial in both the actual or feigned temper tantrum is for the adult not to get frightened nor show anxiety or irrational anger. The child may have been successful in the past in getting his way primarily because the adults, generally parents, became frightened and gave in to avoid the discomfort of witnessing the tantrum or struggling with the consequences. The child has learned to exploit the adults' fears.

There are also situations where a child has learned to stage a temper tantrum in order to get attention from neglectful or disinterested parents. Apparently, the only way the child can attract their attention is through the shock of a temper tantrum. He may perpetuate this behavior with child care workers until he is convinced that they are not like his parents. His tantrums may then cease because he no longer views the workers in terms of his experiences with his parents. Should the child succeed in evoking behavior on the part of the child care worker similar to that of the parents, the destructive reactions will probably be reinforced.

BEDWETTING AND SOILING

Enuresis, the medical term for bedwetting, is a disorder of the urinary function involving involuntary passage of urine. When it occurs during waking hours, it is "diurnal enuresis" and during sleeping, it is "nocturnal enuresis." Enuresis is defined as "bedwetting or clothes wetting in persons over the age of three who fail to exhibit the reflex to pass urine when the impulse is felt during waking hours and those who do not rouse from sleep of their own accord when the process is occurring during the sleeping state" (Pierce 1967: 1380).

It has been estimated that 88 percent of children have ceased wetting by age four and a half, 93 percent by age seven and a half, and 99 percent by age seventeen. Wetting occurs twice as frequently among boys as it does among girls. In about 10 percent of the known cases, an organic defect may be the principal cause. Consequently, when a child has both diurnal and nocturnal enuresis, a thorough medical examination is in order to rule out organic causes. When organic factors have been eliminated, wetting may be considered as a manifestation of emotional disturbance, developmental immaturity due to faulty or inconsistent habit training, or a combination of both. The enuretic child may use his symptoms to get attention from or express hostility toward a rejecting or neglecting parent or to perpetuate infantile dependency on a mother who may consciously or unconsciously encourage it (English and Pearson 1945: 216–219).

Treatment methods include medication like Tofranil, psychotherapy, habit training suggestions such as limitation of fluids before bedtime or interruption of sleep to go to the bathroom, behavior modification or the use of conditioning devices which awaken the child by a buzzer as soon as a drop of urine contacts a wired pad on which he sleeps.

The enuretic child bears the burden of shame. He is chided or ridiculed for being unable to control a function which consciously, he ought to control; he begins to feel demeaned, helpless, ashamed, or angry at himself or his critics. A child in residential treatment who is enuretic is at a disadvantage because this symptom is not easily concealed in group living. Adult impatience with the management problems and peer ridicule aggravate the child's feelings of insecurity. He may deny the symptom, attempt to avoid its discovery by hiding his wet underwear and linens. Shaming, scolding, or punishment must be avoided. It is not only useless as a measure of control but may actually reinforce the intensity of the condition. The situation should be called to the attention of medical and clinical staff for evaluation and planning of a course of treatment to which the child care worker becomes an important contributor. He may dispense prescribed medication, limit fluid intake before bedtime, or awaken the child during the night. If at all possible, treatment should not be imposed on the child against his will but achieved with his cooperation.

Patience and encouragement on the part of the child care worker is vital. If the child wets the bed during the night, he should be allowed time to shower and to deposit the soiled linen in a special container to be sent to the laundry. If wetting occurs during waking hours, he should be asked to change his underwear. The hope should be expressed that the child will be able to achieve control as soon as possible because of the social difficulties that lack of control creates. Encouragement should be accompanied by an offer to help him in his efforts to overcome the condition. The slightest lessening of the frequency of wetting should be rewarded by praise or any other appropriate rewards.

Soiling (medically known as encopresis), is considered a symptom of emotional disturbance when organic causes have been ruled out by medical examination. The incidence is not uncommon among preschool children following toilet training. "Accidents" may occur during periods of excitement or stress. The older the child, the more serious is the problem and its solution. Soiling may represent a reaction to strict and rigid toilet training, a fear reaction against a punitive parent, defiance or rebellion against rigid parental authority.

Shaming, blaming, or punishment is, again, not helpful and may serve to aggravate the condition and add additional conflictual problems.

Soiling makes group living difficult for the child himself, his peer group, and his child care workers. The child who suffers from encopresis is an unhappy child who has experienced shaming, rejection, and ridicule. He tries to hide the evidence but is unsuccessful because of the smell. He may stuff soiled underwear down the toilet, causing overflows, or he may hide soiled underpants in drawers or secret hiding places. He evokes child and adult impatience and anger and, as a consequence of his condition, may become the group scapegoat.

Once a plan of treatment is formulated, the child should be encouraged to follow it. He is expected to shower after each soiling incident, to go to the toilet more frequently, to change his underwear, to rinse the soiled underwear, and to deposit it in a closed container which is sent to the laundry daily. Patience, acceptance, and encouragement are essential. However, not every adult can cope with this problem. A worker who feels he has reached a limit in his capacity to deal with it should discuss the matter with his supervisor to determine whether anything else could be done to make living more tolerable for himself and the children in the group. In some cases, it may be necessary to transfer the child to another group where there is greater tolerance and ability to deal with this symptom. A transfer should not be considered a serious failing by the worker. The inability to continue to care for a child with serious encopresis must be accepted as an understandable human limitation.

A program of intervention designed for a child who wets or soils should take into consideration the emotional factors associated with the disorder. If it is reactive to separation anxiety or relationship conflicts with a parent(s), staff dealing directly with the child would have to concentrate on maintaining a positive relationship; helping to support and encourage the child, and reduce anxiety-evoking situations that would trigger the onset of the bedwetting or soiling symptoms. As indicated, this task may not be easy for some people, especially a child care worker who finds it difficult to cope with the unpleasantness of the cleaning up or the negative peer reactions associated with severe bedwetting and soiling. However, these children are highly sensitive about their problem, feel defensive, and easily identify people's reactions. If reactions are perceived as negative by the child, he will feel rejected and resentful. A child who has developed secondary satisfaction from the symptom because it was found to be an effective weapon against a rejecting parent, may replicate this pattern in group care. Such parents' punitive reactions reinforced rather than "cured" the symptom. The child may then react similarly to child care workers who are overanxious, become hostile to the child, and convey to him that he is "bad" because he "refuses" to give up the symptom. In such cases, the error is the adult's because the control of the symptoms may not be within the child's *conscious* capability. It may take a long time for the child to gain insight about the source of his wetting or soiling and to understand his reactions toward staff as transference reactions. The expectation is that all staff who are aware of this analysis will make an effort not to be drawn into the child's transference projections. If they were, they would not only be feeding the original source of anxiety but would also be evoking the (unconscious) secondary satisfaction of defeating the adult who is associated with the depriving parental figure.

Consistency in attitude and physical handling is important in dealing with the psychological as well as the mechanical (medication, control of fluids, waking child at night, etc.) intervention techniques. Charting progress can be helpful to staff for assessing effectiveness of the intervention strategies and supportive to the child who is making progress. The child's involvement in planning the program and his active participation in the process as well as in its evaluation is essential.[a]

LYING

Lying, prevalent among children in residential treatment, is a persistent irritant to child care workers because it interferes with orderly group living, contributing instead to confusion and dissension. As a falsification or denial of truth, lying takes on different forms. Anna Freud (1965: 116–117) classifies lying into three categories:

1. *Innocent lying* — This is exemplified by the very young child who may deny or ignore painful impressions, thus protecting himself from anxiety. Since the anxiety-provoking situation or frustration is excluded from consciousness, it cannot hurt him.

a. For a comprehensive review of the literature and therapeutic approach to enuresis and encopresis, see pages 177–217 in Schaeffer and Millman (1978).

2. *Fantasy lying*—When an older child or adult faces excessive frustration, he may cope with the realities which they represent by denial, avoidance or distortion of the truth. This is a regressive form of behavior to avoid intolerable anxiety.

3. *Delinquent lying*—This is resorted to as a defense against a fear of punishment, to gain advantage which a child feels he cannot otherwise achieve or is a wish for aggrandizement.

A child may resort to all of these forms at one time or another. A psychotic or borderline psychotic child may act as if he is lying when actually he is responding on the basis of misperception or misconception of reality. He is not consciously falsifying the truth for personal gain. His response, as well as those of children who indulge in "innocent" or "fantasy" lying, will have to be dealt with differently from the lies of those who consciously distort or deny the truth, either as a defense against insecurity or for purposes of personal advantage.

The basis for delinquent lying may be manifold. Some children simply perpetuate a pattern which they have learned in their own families where not telling the truth was practiced as an established mode of interpersonal interaction. Others, especially those who have grown up in disadvantaged neighborhoods, may perpetuate peer patterns which were practiced in order to protect children from adult authority, to avoid punishment for delinquent activities, or to manipulate others for material advantage. Lying may also represent a defense developed in dealing with rigid parental authority. Thus, a child may lie because he fears severe punishment for the slightest infraction of adult expectations. Lying may also be a manifestation of insecurity in relationships. A child may lie because he believes that he will not be believed when he tells the truth. A feeling of inadequacy may have to be compensated by lying or boasting to boost one's sense of adequacy or to impress others and enhance one's status in the peer group. A child may also cheat in competitive situations or games because he feels he cannot achieve on the basis of his own competency.

Understanding the form in which lying is expressed or the basis for its utilization should facilitate constructive and effective reactions by the child care worker.

The child care worker should convey to the children the expectation of truthfulness. While it may be unrealistic, it is a constructive goal to uphold. By his own actions in support of honesty, a child care worker can serve as a model for the children. The destructive impact of lying should be discussed with the individual child who is involved or the group as a whole. It is not advisable to use group pressure to expose a child who is lying. Not only does this exploit the group as a whole but it shows the children that the child care worker cannot cope with the problem. There should be consequences for delinquent lying, and it is advisable to inform the children that if they tell a lie to cover up a transgression, they may get additional punishment for lying. Consequences should be enforced to emphasize that the child care worker considers both the offense and the lying about it unacceptable. The child who seems to be a chronic liar should be referred for clinical evaluation and psychotherapeutic treatment intervention.

STEALING

Stealing is destructive to group living and creates serious difficulties for the child care worker. A child who steals poses a threat to the other children who cherish the few possessions they have. The worker is the adult they turn to with complaints about loss, demands for restitution, and penalties for the offender. As a guardian of ethical values, the child care worker is concerned about stealing. He may understand the motives of a child's tendency to steal in terms of his personality and emotional difficulties, but cannot rationalize, excuse, tolerate, or disregard theft. The other children view inaction by the child care worker as indirect approval. The understanding is important because it helps to formulate intervention techniques to deal with a child as a whole rather than with his symptomatic behavior.

The very young child who does not as yet understand the concept of property will take his playmate's toys openly or will attempt to take an object which attracts him without inhibitions. This cannot be considered stealing. Through his parents' instruction he will gradually learn that this behavior is not acceptable. Chronologically, a child in care might be expected to have learned respect for the possessions of others or at least to be aware of the moral prohibition against theft. This assumption is not always justified. Children who have been reared in families who either condone or do not disapprove stealing may continue the family pattern; a child who has been a member of a delinquent peer group may continue the delinquent practices in his group; the impulse-ridden child who lacks inner controls will tend to take that which attracts him without inhibition; the child driven by compulsive needs to steal (kleptomania, as an example) will do so despite the knowledge that it is wrong; the psychotic child may take things that do not belong to him because he cannot differentiate between his or other people's possessions; a socioeconomically deprived child who has grown up in poverty may be tempted to take things from others who are more affluent because he does not want to be different from them nor deprive himself of spending money or money which may be required for outings and trips. The emotionally deprived child's stealing may symptomatically represent his search for substitute satisfaction to fill his loveless void.

Children who consciously steal for personal material gain will require re-education in values and disciplinary action to discourage stealing. Positive reinforcement in terms of rewards should be offered when they make an effort to control themselves. The impulse-ridden youngster or psychotic child will require patience as well as growth-inducing nurture to help him establish inner controls and more adequate judgment of reality. The poverty-stricken child should be provided with sufficient material needs so that he does not feel so different from and more deprived than the other children. Finally, the neurotic child will require psychotherapy to resolve the conflicts which express themselves in stealing. Hopefully, education in values as well as psychotherapeutic services will be available to all the children. Group meetings can also be helpful in dealing with these issues as exemplified in the following recording of a cottage meeting with a group of delinquent-oriented adolescents led by a child care supervisor and therapist:

Burt said that he would like to talk about stealing in the cottage. Johnnie echoed this by telling the boys that we had originally started the group meetings because there was a lot of stealing going on. Then things improved but now they are getting worse and something has to be done about it. Burt said that this morning, a lot of his clothing and other items were stolen. Phil said that some of his cigarettes were taken. Howard began waving his arms wildly saying, "In this damn cottage, there's a lot of stealing." Billy was incensed saying that he used to steal but stopped. He feels that something has to be done about the guilty ones. Niles suggested that locks should be put on the doors and locked. Phil felt that he would rather tell the cottage parents first and suggest to them that when all the boys are out of the cottage, they should search the lockers for the stolen items. Only a few felt they should use force against the offenders. Jim suggested mandatory punishment for those who stole, but Niles said that he wasn't sure it would solve the problem.

Donald was the chief spokesman for that faction of the group which placed the major emphasis upon an external framework of rigid control. He insisted that this structure was necessary, and that he would not regard the problem as solved unless controls were established. Billy, who had also supported the principle of an external framework and severe punishments, thought that each cottage should establish for itself a system of laws based upon the needs of its own group, with clear definitions as to what would constitute stealing and what would be the consequences if boys transgressed. Barry, whose focus was upon his own personal need, said that he would beat up any boy who he caught stealing from him. Many of the other boys stressed the need for staff coverage throughout the day, even when they were in school, when there are persistent thefts.

Mr. B. (the therapist) wondered why some kids steal. Niles gave the example of a boy who stole clothing because his parents could not provide them. Jim said that he knew a boy who stole things he did not need. "Maybe he was neurotic." "Well," replied Dan, "if there are such kids in the cottage, they should get to work on it with their therapists." Izzy added (and we thought he was talking about himself) that he knew a boy who would go out and steal following a fight with his mother. "He did it just to hurt her." Niles then said that since some of the children here have come with problems in relation to stealing, there ought to be greater tolerance for this in boys, because this is the central problem. Barry replied that he feels that he has as much tolerance as the next fellow, but that there is only so much of it that he can take. This opened up discussion among the group as to how much tolerance boys in treatment should have for one another's problems.

Mr. B. pointed out to the group that in their discussion of the problem, the major emphasis was upon the use of external controls for the handling of this problem. He conceded that stealing was wrong, that it constituted a problem about which something had to be done. However, he wanted to know whether they saw external restraints as being the sole solution to this kind of problem. Danny said that some had already given samples of neurotic or reactive stealing and that those kids should be in treatment. But consequences are also necessary. Maybe they as a group should punish the offenders.

Mr. B. had misgivings about this and discussed authorized aggression with examples—kangaroo courts, lynch mobs—and talked about mob hostility against a person who is an offender against the community. Sometimes a group will use severe punitiveness because of their own hostility which they cannot express alone, but in the group, they are more easily able to do it and this is especially easy if it deals with a situation which is socially disapproved. He also commented that this is one of the reasons that we do not condone kangaroo courts, that our youngsters have difficulties themselves and they cannot be judges.

Billy said that he can understand that there are some boys who have severe problems. They have frustrations and they take it out either by stealing or other things. One of the solutions that he sees is to get them interested in positive things—for example, hobbies—and giving them interesting programs to get them to use their energy for good rather than bad things.

Mr. A. introduced the issue of values and expectations. The boys were here to develop controls through living in a cottage where expectations are upheld— that is, kids should not be hurt, not be stolen from, or so on. This expectation is not inconsistent with Barry's point that there is a limit to tolerance of acts that hurt others. There is really no one in the cottage who is so sick that he doesn't know what he is doing or who has no capacity to control inner urges. If that were so, he should be in a hospital or a closed setting.

Perhaps our discussions here and the examination of a problem like stealing which we are talking about will help. The boys should continue discussing it among themselves and with their cottage staff. Jim then suggested that Mr. A. go to the cottage and hold a meeting with the cottage parents to discuss practical measures to take to stop the stealing in the group. He responded that he felt that the cottage parents were competent and interested people, and that the boys and they meet together to discuss solutions to stealing. He did, however, offer to meet with the cottage parents afterwards and work out ways and means of implementing whatever sound decisions might be made between the cottage parents and the group.

Disciplinary action may also become part of the preventive process. When there is a stealing incident and the culprit is identified beyond a reasonable doubt, disciplinary action is necessary. This may include return of the stolen objects or money, restitution through replacement if the object is no longer available, and some degree of deprivation to reinforce the ethical lesson. A child who steals in neighborhood stores or on shopping trips should be required to return the items to the store, personally if feasible, and accompanied by a staff member, if possible his child care worker. A community problem may be created if a youngster steals a car or burglarizes a neighborhood home. He should not be protected from legal action. In these cases, staff, including the child care worker, participate in the proceedings in order to interpret his action to the court and, if at all feasible, to request that he be returned for continued treatment.

A child care worker understandably has strong feelings about children in his group who steal. However, theft cannot be considered a personal affront, nor a failure on his part. Stealing is but one aspect of children's disturbance and must be dealt with constructively as any other symptomatic behavior.

RUNAWAYS

Institutions have a variety of methods for dealing with runaway children upon their return. These range from welcoming them back with sympathetic understanding that there was good reason for the action, offering additional attention to demonstrate that they are loved, issuing warnings of pending punishment for repetition, to ordering them to undergo severe deprivation in special isolation rooms or "discipline" cottages. The benign approach, often practiced in small residential treatment centers, may not be acceptable nor applicable in large, heterogeneous institutions or rehabilitation centers for adolescent delinquents where there is administrative concern that to treat a runaway lightly may make other children feel that running away "pays off." Large institutions with low staff ratio may also institute harsh deterrents out of concern for the children's safety.

Deprivation of privileges, such as home visits and recreational activities or additional work assignments, are prevalent methods of dealing with returned runaway children. When they are automatically imposed by edict, the results are not necessarily effective. Such consequence may deter some children but not all. In one institution with a high ratio of runaways, the usual methods were ineffective until another approach was instituted to parallel it. A Runaway Board of Review, consisting of the top administrative personnel from child care, school, and clinic, was instituted. It met with each child following his return. The child had an opportunity to present his reasons for running away and to hear staff reaction. The seriousness of his act was emphasized, but disciplinary action was left to the unit administrator. A dramatic reduction in the number of runaways resulted, principally because the children viewed this conference as an expression of concern on the part of the staff. Isolation, excessive or frequently meaningless work activity, extensive deprivation of home visits and leisure-time activities seem to be undesirable. These punishments tend to focus the child's attention on what he considers the unfair consequences imposed upon him rather than his own actions which caused it. Feelings of hostility are projected on staff, and feelings of rejection are enhanced.

Emphasis should be on prevention. Running-away may be caused by peer pressure, home-sickness, a lack of news or disturbing news from home, a frustrating home visit or an upsetting parental visit, conflicts within the child or within the group living situation. The following situation is not characteristic of the usual types of run-aways when a child either runs away from something unpleasant or runs to something which might give him a sense of satisfaction. This runaway is a consequence of a dilemma experienced by a girl regarding leaving the institution.

When Mary was returned to the cottage following her runaway, she was sulky, didn't want to talk to the workers or to the other girls, and asked if she could go to bed. Mrs. Simms said "Mary, it's only 7 p.m. If you want to go to bed, it's all right. Won't you have some evening snacks first?" "Thanks, no," and Mary went to bed. "I don't understand Mary's actions," said Miss Williams. "She was doing so well here. In fact, she was to leave for home next month. So she runs off and instead of going home, she goes to the East Village, hideout of her former cronies. Why didn't she run home instead?" "It is puzzling. I'll talk to her tomorrow morning," said Mrs. Sims.

Next morning, Mary was the first girl to be up, and when she came down-stairs, Mrs. Sims was in the kitchen. She said to Mary, "Would you join me in a cup of coffee before I go upstairs to wake the girls?" Mary agreed, and Mrs. Simms said, "You seem cheerful today in contrast to last night. I want you to know I'm glad that you are back. We were worried about you and also wondered whether we had done anything wrong." "No," Mary assured her. "You and Miss Williams have been very nice to me; so have the girls. I can't fully understand what happened but I do know that I suddenly became anxious when my social worker told me that I would be leaving within a month." "But I thought you wanted to go home," exclaimed Mrs. Simms. "I thought I did," replied Mary. "But last weekend, during my home visit, my mother and I started bickering again and my father stood by, saying nothing. Maybe this started me worrying about the future. I guess I got frightened. It seemed that neither I nor my mother were ready to live together. I know I should have talked this over with Miss Jay or you, but I was ashamed. As the anxiety built up, I thought of running away to give myself a chance to think things over. The only place I knew I'd be welcome was with my former friends. So I went there, but I didn't like it after a day or two because I don't like their lifestyles. I want to finish high school and go to college. So I'd like to stay here another semester, prepare myself educationally as well as emotionally. Then I think I'll be ready to leave." "You're welcome to stay," said Mrs. Simms. "I suggest you talk about this with Miss Jay."

Child care workers are situated in a good position to perceive the behavior which is the precursor of running away. A child may seem restless, show anxiety following receipt of mail from his family or a friend, or be upset following a parental visit. When anxiety is evident, the child care worker might comment on the child's worried appearance and suggest talking about the cause or arranging for the child to see his caseworker. Where the precipitating factor in running away is a severe frustrating experience, such as rejection by peers or adults, failure in sport or school activities, abuse by peers or staff, or guilt or fear following the commission of a delinquent act, discussion would have to be supplemented by examination of the situation which caused the action and determination of appropriate interventions. Running away caused by inducements from another child or a peer group to join them or caused by unsettled conditions in cottage or the institution have to be treated differently. Discussion with the children involved may be suitable in the first case; staff evaluation of conditions in the cottage or irritants in the overall program may be essential in the latter case.

Running away is not a constructive way for a child to cope with frustrating situations. The rationale that occasional running away might be good for an inhibited child because it demonstrates assertiveness is faulty. There are more therapeutic and safer ways to help a child handle his conflicts. When a child absconds, he exposes himself to danger. He may have an accident, or he may engage in behavior which is delinquent and harmful to himself and to others, or he may be exploited by adults. Girls have frequently been "picked up" by men who exploited them sexually. Time away from the residence also interrupts continuity of treatment.

The child care worker may have to administer the imposed punishment, but his attitude toward the child must be one of continued acceptance and not of anger for the inconvenience caused or a desire for retribution. Understanding of the runaway should be conveyed, but the act cannot be approved or condoned.

Group discussion can be fruitful in exposing children's thinking and feelings about running away, and can serve to educate them about its hazards. The following excerpt from a group meeting following a multiple runaway was conducted by a child care supervisor (the author) and a therapist in an older boys' cottage.

Several of the boys began the meeting by telling us how pleased they are about their new cottage parents. They enumerated some of the good qualities which were just the opposite of the negative qualities they had listed when they criticized their former cottage parents.

We saw here an opportunity to introduce the question of running away and to raise the question that if the cottage parents were so good, how could they explain that several of the boys had run away the previous week? There was almost immediate response that it had nothing to do with the cottage parents. Those who had run away were "jerks" and that they just didn't want to have anything to do with them. We remarked that it might be good to discuss why children ran away. Jim opened the discussion by saying that tensions were often built up and one had to run away from them. Phil immediately counteracted by saying that this was "a lot of baloney." He had never run. Anyway, it's only running away from oneself. Jim explained that he never really had a good reason to run away but simply had to do it and then find a rationale for it. Donny seemed quite uncomfortable and wanted to stop the discussion. He said running away is a personal problem and therefore there was no point discussing it in a group. Earlier in his stay, he had run away and got into severe difficulty during the escapades. Fred felt that when there were ambivalent feelings about one's family, and resentment about placement, one was compelled to get away — simply to walk around the streets feeling a little "free" and have time to think. However, at the same time, he added that it wasn't very comfortable being a runaway because one was quite insecure about being called "fugitive." Steve agreed. John said that he had run away twice but every time this had set him back in treatment. In fact, when one runs away, there is a danger one might get hurt. The consensus seemed to be that running away was not advisable but was often necessary. Dave said that sometimes boys run impulsively or because others had run before and it was sort of catching.

When Mr. B., co-leader, asked the group what they thought our objections were, the boys gave no clear answer and asked us to tell them. We did, reiterating that it interfered with treatment, was risky because many of the boys had poor impulse control. When they ran away, they could do things which might hurt them and others. The boys agreed. When we mentioned that running away may also be a manifestation of immaturity and incapacity to face one's problems rather than escape them, Burt went over to the window and turned his back to us, Fred took out his lighter and lit pieces of paper in the ash tray and Larry asked to be excused because he wanted to go to the bathroom. When we said that there was nothing to be ashamed of for not having as yet reached maturity, Burt returned to his seat, Fred put out the fire, and Larry relaxed.

SEXUAL BEHAVIOR

Sexual behavior includes a broad range of actions, such as language, gestures, exhibitionism, perversion, individual and group masturbation, homosexuality, and heterosexuality. Viewed from a developmental point of view, it encompasses the life span of an individual. In contrast to other types of behavior, including aggression, sexual behavior in children seems to evoke a great deal of adult anxiety and concern.

Pleasure and curiosity seem to be the motivating forces in children's behavior which is considered sexual. So-called sexual behavior is expressed in earliest childhood. Because myelinization of the nervous system (protective sheathing of the nerve fibers) is not complete during the early months of infancy, body areas rich in nerve endings, like the mouth and genitals, are highly sensitive to touch. When the infant discovers that contact with these areas is pleasurable, he tends to perpetuate it. Thus thumb-sucking, and, later on, genital manipulation becomes homoerotic sources of pleasure. Our culture accepts thumb-sucking as normal in infancy. Genital manipulation is discouraged.

When thumb-sucking persists into the second year or beyond, it evokes concern, verbal disapproval, shaming, and, not infrequently, physical intervention such as coating the thumb with a bitter solution to discourage the child from this activity. The reaction to genital manipulation, now given the status of masturbation, is reacted to with even greater concern and, not infrequently, destructive and punitive reactions by parents. These may range from threats of dire consequences such as illness and body weakness, to physical punishment, evocation of "burning in the fires of hell" in afterlife, and even castration threats. Parental reactions to such sexual behavior have important emotional consequences and contribute to the child's attitude regarding sexuality.

The child care worker is frequently faced with children's sexual behavior which, among emotionally disturbed children, is generally exaggerated in form. It may include verbal, homoerotic, homosexual, or heterosexual behavior. It may be persistent, aggressive, or provocative in expression, depending on the nature and degree of the child's disturbance. The worker's therapeutic effectiveness in handling this behavior depends on how he feels about it, which in turn depends on his attitudes regarding sexuality and the extent of knowledge he has about the subject. The manner of handling such behavior should be adjusted to the type of child who expresses it. Thus the psychotic child who has poor judgment of reality and little impulse control is less likely to be responsive to "intellectual" discussion regarding his behavior than the child who is fully aware of reality and has sufficient inner controls to modify his behavior following a talk with his worker.

Thumb-Sucking

There is no research evidence that confirms that thumb-sucking or masturbation is physically harmful. However, if such behavior persists and is pervasive, it justifies concern because it is symptomatic of difficulties. It may be indicative of conflict regarding sexuality/social relationships. The child who persists in sucking his thumb is generally an insecure, emotionally deprived child. When he finds greater security in relationship with others, and in activities, whether creative or in sports, it is most likely that thumb-sucking will cease because it will no longer be his major source of comfort and pleasure. This will take time, adult patience, and support. He will also need protection from ridicule from his own peers as a consequence of this immature behavior.

Masturbation

Unlike thumb-sucking, which is generally associated with immaturity rather than sexuality and which is generally rare beyond early childhood years, masturbation is definitely associated with sexuality and, consequently, evokes a great deal of adult concern.

Most, if not all, children masturbate occasionally. Most workers do not consider it a problem and tend to ignore it. However, if they find that a child is masturbating excessively or in public areas—in the living room while watching television, during meal times, or if there are reports that he does this in the classroom—it requires attention either through direct intervention or by involving clinical personnel, or both. The worker can deal with this constructively by calling the behavior to the child's attention and explaining to him that it is inappropriate in public. The child's therapist can explore further the meaning of this persistent behavior and the sources which motivate it. Knowledge of the fantasies accompanying masturbation can be helpful for therapeutic planning and intervention. Mutual masturbation or group masturbation is not infrequent among older children and adolescents. It evokes concern because it may be associated with a belief that if continued, it may develop into homosexuality. For the most part, this type of behavior is transitory or experimental among preadolescents and adolescents. When witnessed, it should be discouraged by the adult through verbal disapproval or separation of the individuals involved.

Aggression and Sexuality

There is no question about immediate and firm intervention in cases of sexual exploitation of one child by another. If one child is forced by another into masturbation, fellatio, or any form of sexuality, intervention must be swift and decisive. These are physical and forced assaults from which a child must be protected. Both disciplinary action as well as psychotherapeutic intervention should follow.

Sexual aggression is an extreme expression of children's association of sex with aggression. Among disturbed children this fusion results in exaggerated expressive behavior. For example, lewd language and physical gestures may be used to offend peers as well as staff. Outbursts of anger may be accompanied by profanity or sexual references. Sexual gestures or verbal sexual insults may also be utilized to attract attention, to provoke shock. In addition, exhibitionism or sexual teasing may be used by either boys or girls as seductive maneuvers toward child care workers or other adults of the opposite sex. Exhibitionism should be handled expeditiously, conveying to the child or children that it is socially unacceptable, that it infringes on the rights of other people, and can be upsetting to peers as well as adults. The worker has the opportunity to educate children in social propriety by conveying that sexual expression is a private affair and should not be exhibited in public. He should encourage the child to discuss it with his social worker or therapist so that he can understand the underlying motivation. This may serve to help the child disentangle his distortions of sexual expression as an aspect of aggression.

A child whose life experience has resulted in misconceiving sexuality as aggression may reenact it in play or interpersonal relationships. In play therapy children frequently express their perception of parental sexual activity in terms of aggressive or even assaultive acts by the father on the mother. Others reenact it interpersonally. For example, one day a child care worker had to intervene in a fight between Virginia, a ten-year-old, and her roommate. It was serious,

with screaming, hitting, and hair-pulling. After the children were separated, Virginia was scolded because she was generally the initiator
of fights. When asked why she was fighting this time, she insisted,
"We're not fighting. We were practicing for marriage!" The worker
was shocked and saddened by such a distorted view of marriage.
Apparently Virginia had not witnessed expressions of tenderness between her parents. In families where physical violence is a prevalent
mode of expressing anger, hostility, or resolving arguments, a child
grows up with the notion that this is the way all people act (Gardner
1973: 141).

The children may also exhibit their curiosity about sex or their
conflict about it by an interest in pornographic literature and pictures. This may be of concern to the worker because of its possible
impact on the other children, and could be handled in the same way
as situations involving exhibitionism.

Profane Language

Use of profane language is a common occurrence. Most children and
adults have at one time or another used swear words or sexually
tinged expressions impulsively or as a reaction to a frustrating situation. Since disturbed children have a lower frustration tolerance, it
should not be surprising that they may resort to such expression
more frequently. A child who persists in doing so should be told that
it is annoying, disrespectful to oneself and others, and unacceptable
as a mode of expression.

Children who have grown up in families or neighborhoods where
profanity is widely used tend to perpetuate such communication patterns. They will require help through reeducation and identification
with other people who use more socially acceptable means of expression. Some younger children who use sexualized phrases may not be
aware of their meaning or inappropriateness. For example, Vivian,
aged nine, used the phrase "fuck you" persistently. It distressed her
child care workers when she responded with this phrase to their
"Hello," "Goodnight," or a request to do something. One young
worker was particularly infuriated because she perceived it as a hostile, provocative challenge. When it was suggested that this may not
be the case, she reacted more calmly to Vivian, talked with her about
it, explaining that it was not an appropriate response to a greeting

or request, and that its usage was to her disadvantage because it annoyed others. Vivian responded favorably, and the phrase gradually faded from her communication.

Excessive use of such sexualized phrases by older boys and girls may represent their immature way of dealing with disturbing situations and interpersonal conflicts. This explanation might be suggested to them along with some appropriate ways of dealing verbally with others. If it persists, they should be dealt with firmly, preferably in calm tones to minimize the secondary satisfaction they may derive from getting their worker upset or making him "lose his cool." It should be made clear that such language will not be tolerated and if it persists, disciplinary action would be taken.

Teen-age language styles change frequently. It may be helpful for child care workers to be familiar with current usage of profane phraseology. For example, Comer and Poussaint (1975: 308) point out that the term "motherfucker" which only a few years ago was considered among black youths as an extremely insulting provocation which triggered serious fights, has undergone a transformation in meaning. It is now used by many as a "term of endearment and respect." If a child care worker finds it offensive he should say so and suggest more socially appropriate alternatives. There are also word games which may get out of hand. For example, the "dozens" is a teasing game in which a group of youths provoke each other by inventing sexualized jingles, frequently involving each other's mothers or sisters as the sexual objects. It is a method of discharging tension, a status-seeking banter, and a way of testing one's "toughness." It has resulted in serious fights when the invectives hurled at each other have gone beyond a participant's tolerance. Child care workers should discourage such games in their groups.

Homosexual Behavior

In residential living overt homosexual behavior can become an unsettling and distressing problem. Even homosexual stimulation evoked by the presence of an effeminate-looking boy in an adolescent boys' cottage can cause anxiety, hostility, and attacks upon the individual who prompts it. This is exemplified in notes from a group meeting recorded by the author.

Howard, a fragile, effeminate-looking intellectual youngster, was admitted on an emergency basis and placed in a cottage with a predominantly aggressive, delinquent-oriented group. It was not the most appropriate choice but the only one where a bed was available. Within a few days there were complaints from Howard that he was being abused and from the other boys that he did not belong in their group. The issue came up when several of the boys began to complain about Howard. He in turn accused some of them of attempting to molest him sexually. Donny said that when he first came to the cottage he was also approached sexually. He had a very hard time, but he took it. Izzy added that during the first night after his arrival, some boys came over and asked him to blow them. He told them to "fuck themselves and leave him alone." They did. But Howard doesn't seem to know how to defend himself. He fights with words. Barry said to Izzy, "What do you want from him? It's the only way he knows how to react. He doesn't even know how to fight." I (the group leader) commented that may be true but I was sure that if anyone approached Bill with sexual advances he would knock them down or give them a black eye. Bill nodded in agreement. Someone said, "But he doesn't fight back." I said that it seems that he fights back in a way that seems to hurt some boys more than black eyes—with "big words." Some responded, "That's right and we don't like it." Howard waved his hands in excitement, insisting that he wasn't going to take any of this stuff. He was not going to be called a "fag."

Izzy turned to me and said that I had once commented that he seemed to enjoy taunting Howard. He said maybe he does, but actually he's had a tough time too. He isn't so sociable but he tries to live with others. Howard doesn't know how, and doesn't want to. He just cannot get along with him. There is something about Howard that makes him get angry and he wants to hit him. It had become evident to Mr. B., the co-leader, and myself that Howard's effeminate innate mannerisms were stimulating the strong homosexual tendencies in many of the boys and they were becoming panicky about their impulses. We looked at each other and felt that we should face the boys with this. Otherwise, there would be serious difficulties afterwards. This seemed the opportune time. Mr. B. remarked that teenage boys had sexual concerns and it was not unusual to have homosexual thoughts and even desires. Perhaps Howard's presence was stimulating such latent feelings and to protect themselves they wanted him out of their sight. Others might be so angry that they want to hurt him, and a few actually did.

This seemed to make a deep impression. The boys looked at each other. Billy laughed, saying, "Remember when I talked about the pool table and shooting out! The guys started to think immediately in homosexual terms." (Billy somehow had the knack of hitting on the root of many of the problems that the youngsters were struggling with.) This evoked laughter among the group. Donny said that most of them had been faced with something like Howard faced on admission to the cottage, most of it from boys who were kidding about homosexual advances. Howard could not see it as a joke because he takes everything so seriously. Howard screamed back that he wasn't going to take it even if it was kidding. I then turned to Howard and asked him whether there was a possibility that maybe some of the boys didn't mean what they said and that they really were kidding him along. He looked a little puzzled and said "maybe."

I then remarked that perhaps Howard had no previous experience in living with other boys, and maybe it was hard for him now. Perhaps he could try. Howard sat down, saying he would give this some thought. But when Jim said that Howard aggravates them because of his mannerisms, Howard said with strong emotion: "The boys accuse me of having a funny grin on my face. Can I help that I look this way? I seem to smile but never learned to cry, not even when it hurts most." There was a sudden stillness among the group and then Billy jumped up and pointing to Eddie said that he is the kind of guy who stands by and let kids get hurt, doesn't lift a finger to stop others from doing it. He enjoys tormenting Howard and that's why he dislikes him. Eddie cringed.

Donny got up and said that he is only going to speak for himself. From now on he is going to leave Howard alone. He will try to talk to him on his level but if Howard doesn't respond he's just going to freeze him out and not talk to him. Phill said I'm going to try to give this guy a break. Several of the other boys said they would do the same. Billy concluded, "You better."

Homosexuality is a complex phenomenon. There are numerous theories to explain it, including its source in pathological and faulty family identification, hormonal imbalance and arrest in psychosexual development, and homosexual seduction in childhood. Changes in attitude have taken place during the past ten years. There is greater understanding conveyed through the media of communication about homosexuals. Although homosexuality is still considered a legal offense in most states, the statutes are not generally enforced. Recently the psychiatric profession declassified homosexuality as a category of mental disorders. One must guard against the hasty labeling of a child as homosexual. A boy who manifests feminine tendencies, a girl who appears "mannish" or acts tomboyish, a child who shows preference for close association with members of his own sex is not necessarily homosexual. Research has shown that no more than 10 to 15 percent of male homosexuals act or appear effeminate. Our society also differentiates between behavior which is permissible among females and among males. For example, holding hands, physical closeness, or even exchanges of kisses is not considered deviant when it occurs among girls and women. But if boys or men are observed in such activity, they will generally be viewed with suspicion and may be labeled homosexual. In residential settings for emotionally disturbed children, it is not infrequent that a child may get into bed with another. This should not be immediately interpreted as sexual behavior, especially if it occurs among younger children. Rather, it may demonstrate insecurity and a fear of being alone. Two boys associating closely may do so because they fear others or because they are insecure about having more extensive relationships. If they become sexually involved, it is safer not to (mis)judge them as being homosexual. Homosexuality is a justifiable description if the following conditions are in evidence: The individual feels sexual desires and sexual responsiveness to members of his own sex; he tends to establish emotional and sexual attachments with members of his own sex; and he finds gratification of his sexual needs only with a partner of the same sex.

Adolescent boys and girls may participate at one time or another in experimentation with homosexual behavior, but this does not mean that they are, or may become, confirmed homosexuals. It may indicate confusion as well as a search for sexual identity. In this process, they may submit to sexual seduction by a member of the same sex or involve themselves in limited individual or group experimentation.

The following case situation illustrates staff concern about a close relationship between two teenage girls which had homosexual implications.

The workers in Cottage 7 were concerned about the relationship between Ann and Sybil. Mrs. Williams maintained that a developing closeness between the girls might involve them in homosexual activities. Miss James was concerned that they were becoming a subgroup apart from the rest of the cottage.

When they consulted their supervisor, Mrs. Fine, she asked them to be more specific about what they meant when they designated the relationship between the girls as "too close."

Mrs. Williams enumerated—they have been observed to walk around holding hands; during study hour, they study in one room and often close the doors; they have tried to take showers together but have been told not to do so; when Ann was away last weekend on a home visit, Sybil seemed depressed; they have asked permission to change home visiting time so they both could be away at the same time. Regarding Mrs. Fine's questions about their relationship with the other girls, Miss James said that though they spend a lot of time together, they are liked by the other girls because they are friendly, sharing, and generally in a good happy mood. However, their constant involvement in keeping to themselves may antagonize the others. Miss James agreed that Ann and Sybil are quite different since their arrival. Ann had been withdrawn and fearful;

Sybil, sulky and antagonistic. In fact, they seemed good for each other and had made a great deal of progress in school and in the cottage. But is their relationship getting to a point that it may become "unhealthy?"

"What do you mean?" asked Mrs. Fine.

We mean "sexual," said Mrs. Williams. "Why, the other night I found them asleep in Sybil's bed. I woke them and told Ann to go back to her room. Both girls seemed upset about it, but Ann explained she had trouble falling asleep and woke up Sybil. For some reason unknown to her, she felt anxious and when she could not sleep, became frightened. She felt Sybil might be helpful. Sybil added that she suggested that Ann stay with her for a while so that she would get over her anxiety. There was no planned intention to sleep together through the night. But they both fell asleep.

"This seemed like a plausible explanation," added Miss James, "but we got worried anyway and decided to talk with you about this."

Mrs. Fine asked whether they had talked with the girls' social worker. Mrs. Williams informed her that last week they talked with Miss Clark who reassured them that the girls' relationship was not necessary homosexual. At most, it might involve them in some sexual experimentation which is not abnormal because adolescents generally may go through such phases, especially those living in an institution. She pointed out that both girls had been neglected and deprived of wholesome family affection, and the closeness between them could be an expression of mutual dependency needs rather than sexual needs.

"We went along with this explanation," said Miss James. "But last night's incident worries us. Maybe the girls should be separated."

"Such an action might be a shock to both girls," cautioned Mrs. Fine. "And this cannot be done without a formal discussion and decision by the whole interdisciplinary team. You did it well last night. Let's watch the girls behavior and let me know how it affects the other girls. I suggest you talk to Miss Clark again. Maybe Dr. Brown should see both girls. Perhaps their projective tests should be reviewed or given if one of the girls has not been tested to determine whether there are any indications about the girls' sexual tendencies and identifications."

The workers concurred but as they left Mrs. Williams said, "I hope Miss Clark is right for the girls' sakes."

In residential living overt homosexual behavior cannot be condoned because of its threat to group stability. If it involves forced seduction, its consequences on the individual child may be traumatic. It may evoke extreme anxiety among children who may be confused about their own sexuality or have latent homosexual tendencies.

The child care worker can exercise a degree of control over the overt manifestations of homosexuality. The simplest approach, not necessarily the most effective, is to disapprove or stop the overt acting-out immediately. Incidents should be immediately called to the attention of administrative and clinical personnel for therapeutic intervention.

Heterosexual Behavior

In residential settings that serve both male and female adolescents, heterosexual acting-out may become a problem. It is a justified area of concern. Institutions do not function in a vacuum outside of greater society. They reflect societal attitudes towards adolescent sexuality. The community expects conformity to prevailing sexual values of society. Residents, like their peers outside, are subject to the same pressures and contradictions which lead to conflicts, confusion, and sexual acting-out. Among these are contradictory adult teaching or preaching ranging from rigid prohibition to outright permissiveness, peer pressures and seductions, and stimulation via mass communication media such as television, movies, and pornographic literature.

Sexual acting-out may also be an indication of intrapsychic conflicts which are expressed interpersonally in sexual activity. For the most part, young people who require residential treatment have not experienced wholesome family or peer relationships. Consequently, they may have developed distortions, ambivalence, anxiety, and conflict about sexuality. Those who have acted out sexually may attempt to perpetuate such behavior by involving other youngsters. This presents serious difficulties in a coed setting. Both the perpetrator and the follower may need help in overcoming impulsive or defensive sexual tendencies.

The therapeutic environment, consisting of the structure which designates rules of conduct, and the staff representing significant relationships to the young people should provide guidelines for change toward greater emotional health and maturation. Rules concerning appropriate sexual conduct without support from significant persons who represent and monitor them do not guarantee control of unacceptable behavior, and certainly are not very effective in helping the young people internalize constructive values. Rules and guidelines clearly communicated do provide a protection for those who are unable to resolve internal conflicts about sex. They provide a shelter from anxiety for those who are not yet ready to assume responsibility for determining their own standards of sexual behavior. The staff's sensitivity and skills in dealing with the sexual conflicts of youth are of importance. The degree of their conviction about established regulations concerning sexual behavior does not escape the residents. The genuineness of their own value system concerning sexuality is readily perceived by the children, who are influenced more by actual rather than professed values and behavior.

Coed activities require adult superivsion because many of the boys and girls are easily stimulated to act out sexually. Creativity and ingenuity are required in planning dances, outings, and parties. Inconspicuous but alert adult presence is essential to assure that these activities remain pleasant socializing experiences for all children rather than arenas for sexual stimulation and impulsive acting-out. The latter circumstance is illustrated by the following: During a coed party hosted by a girls' cottage, some of the children requested permission to watch a television program. One of the girls, Joan, insisted that all lights be out. Despite some misgivings, staff acceded. During the program, a number of the girls seemed restless and upset. After the party was over, the girls, accused Joan of manipulating staff and her peers to agree to darkness so she could pet with her boy friend. They felt exploited and accused her of spoiling what could have been a very nice party. The recriminations, denials, tears, and shouting resulted in a highly upset group of girls and a distressed staff. It seemed that staff indecisiveness about implementing a supervisory function had turned a pleasant coed party into an unpleasant experience for children and staff. Joan's sexual activity had evoked anxiety in the other girls. All of this could have been avoided if staff had logically refused Joan's request since there was a rule about keeping a TV light on during television-viewing. Someone should have said, "Sorry, Joan, you know the rules. It is not good to watch television in darkness because it is damaging to the eyes." The girls, including Joan, would have had to accept this because they were aware of the established practice, and thus Joan's manipulation and her acting-out, as well as the impact on the group, could have been avoided.

SEX EDUCATION PROGRAM

Child care workers must be well informed and secure about their own attitudes regarding sexuality in order to help the children in this area. They should be an integral part of the comprehensive sex education program involving children as well as staff. One such program in a foster care agency addressed itself first to staff in order to develop their competency in conveying sex information to the children and to enable them to deal more constructively with children's sexual behavior. The first phase of the program consisted of sessions led by medical personnel which presented to staff factual information. This included anatomy, pubescent development in boys and girls, menstruation, pregnancy, abortion, and venereal diseases. A psychiatrist talked with the group about sexual deviation including excessive masturbation, homosexuality, and promiscuity. The second phase focused on staff attitudes and values. These were discussed in small groups, including social workers and child care workers. Examples from daily child care practice were the basis for discussion. Values and personal attitudes were discussed, reaction to children's sexual behavior was examined, and methods of dealing with it worked out. This prepared the staff for the most important phase of the program—conveying sex education to children and dealing with their sexual behavior. The group meetings were held and, at the children's requests, medical personnel joined sessions to present sex information and to answer questions. Subsequently, more of the children were able to bring their questions and concerns to staff, especially to child care workers. The atmosphere of receptivity came across to the children, and they felt more comfortable in talking about these matters with staff.

Child care workers emphasized that the group discussion had made them more aware of their own attitudes regarding sexuality, which was helpful in guiding children toward more constructive values. However, the road to self-awareness was not always an easy one, as exemplified by the following:

During a staff discussion about masturbation, Bill, a young child care worker, expressed a very liberal attitude. He felt that children who masturbated excessively were troubled. When they did so in public they should not be reprimanded as "bad" nor punished. It was best to tell them that their behavior was inappropriate in the presence of others.

When Bill came to the next group discussion, he seemed distressed and asked to speak first. He said that something happened the night before which made him feel ashamed because he had mishandled a child. He had walked into the living room where the children were watching television, and noted that Jimmy was masturbating. His immediate response was to shout at the child, "What the hell do you think you are doing?" Jimmy had cringed at the onslaught. Bill immediately realized that he had acted impulsively and unfairly. He questioned why he had reacted in this manner when the week before he had discussed such a situation entirely from a different point of view. He realized there was still a gap between his intellectual understanding and his deeply ingrained feelings and attitudes. There were still vestiges of his childhood upbringing in a fundamentalist Protestant family where he and his siblings were indoctrinated about sins related to sex. Masturbation was considered a serious transgression which would be severely punished here and in the hereafter. Bill felt that since he is now conscious of the connection between his impulsive reaction to Jimmy and his early indoctrination, he could handle himself differently in the future.

DRUG ABUSE

Many children in residence have been affected by drug abuse, including alcohol, either by exposure in their families or neighborhoods, by actual experimentation, or by extensive usage. Involvement with drugs results from a diversity of influences and motivations—curiosity, a desire to be accepted by peers, defiance or rebelliousness against adult values, a manifestation of inner conflicts, or more serious disturbance.

The extensive use of drugs has deleterious effects upon the physical/psychological wellbeing of the user. Certain drugs create an actual physical dependence (addiction), and painful withdrawal symptoms occur upon discontinuance. A broad range of psychological effects varying from mildly to euphorically pleasant sensations and experiences, to disruptive, extremely anxiety-arousing reactions are possible. Acute panic and profound anxiety leading to psychotic episodes necessitating hospitalization are not uncommon. Reliance on drugs to enable one to "feel good" is an avoidance of responsibility and of facing reality. It may reflect underlying personality disturbance. Pre-adolescents and adolescents who become involved in drug use are more vulnerable to the various harmful influences of drugs than adults because of the unusual stresses associated with this tumultuous early stage of development.

The child care worker is in a crucial position in drug control and prevention programs in the institution. His close proximity to the children enables him to note behavior which may be related to drug usage. He should be sufficiently knowledgeable to recognize drug symptoms and to convey to children the dangers of drug usage. The following are guidelines for identifying drug usage:

Drug Identification and Consequences of Usage
(Taxel 1970)

1. **Glue sniffing**

    Physical symptoms include drunken appearance, dreamy or blank expression, and violent actions.

    Objects associated with usage are tubes of glue, large paper bags, or handkerchiefs.

    If used extensively, there is danger of damage to lung, brain, liver, and death through suffocation or choking.

2. **Marijuana**, is a drug which causes changes in consciousness and perception. It is also known as "pot," "grass," "Mary Jane," "hashish," "reefers," "tea":

    Physical symptoms include drowsiness, wandering mind, enlarged pupils, lack of coordination, craving for sweets, and increased appetite.

    Objects associated with usage include strong odor of burnt leaves, small seeds in pocket lining, cigarette paper, discolored fingers.

Although varied authorities have indicated that excessive use of marijuana may result in psychological dependence and inducement to use more harmful drugs, in lethargy, or some physical damage, this is not as yet clearly confirmed by research findings. Results of studies have not been definitive or consistent and are often contradictory.

3. **Hallucinogens** include **L.S.D.** also known as "acid," "sugar cubes," "tabs"; **D.M.T., S.T.P.**, also known as "serenity," "tranquility," "peace"; and **Mescaline**, also known as "peyote," "mescal beans," "cactus":

    Physical symptoms include severe hallucinations, feelings of detachment, incoherent speech, cold hands and feet, vomiting, hysterical laughing and crying.

    Objects associated with usage include cube sugar with discoloration in center, strong body odor, small tubes of liquid.

    Dangers include suicidal tendencies, unpredictable behavior. Chronic exposure causes brain damage.

4. **Amphetamines**, which stimulate the central nervous system, are also known as "Bennies," "Dexies," "Poppers," "Pep Pills," "Lid Poppers," and "Wake-ups"; and **Methamphetamines** ("Speed," "Dynamite"):

> *Physical symptoms* include aggressive behavior, giggling, silliness, rapid speech, confused thinking, no appetite, extreme fatigue, dry mouth, shakiness, insomnia.
>
> *Objects associated with usage* are pills or capsules of varying colors, chain-smoking.
>
> *Dangers associated with usage* include death from overdose, hallucinations, psychotic episodes.

5. **Cocaine**, a stimulant, also known as "snow," "coke," "flake," "gold dust."

> *Physical symptoms* include hyperactivity, excitability, irritability, talkativeness, dilated pupils, loss of appetite, insomnia and hallucinations.
>
> *Objects associated with usage* include powder resembling epsom salts or snowflakes.
>
> *Dangers associated with usage* include severe depression and nervous exhaustion from large doses, suicidal depression and temporary mental derangement from heavy doses, psychological dependence.

6. **Barbiturates** are depressants that relax the central nervous system. They are also known as "barbs," "blue devils," "yellow jackets," "candy," "phennies," "goof balls," "downs":

> *Physical symptoms* include drowsiness, stupor, dullness, slurred speech, drunken appearance, vomiting.
>
> *Objects associated with usage* are pills or capsules of varying colors.
>
> *Dangers of overdose* include death or unconsciousness from overdose, addiction, convulsions in withdrawal.

7. **Narcotics** are opium derivatives. They include:

> **Heroin**, also known as "horse," "scat," "junk," "snow," "stuff," "Harry," "joy powder":
>
> **Morphine**, "white stuff," "dreamer," "Miss Emma":

Codeine, "schoolboy":

Physical symptoms include stupor, drowsiness, needle marks on body, watery eyes, loss of appetite, blood stain on shirt sleeve, running nose.

Objects associated with usage include needle or hypodermic syringe, cotton, tourniquet-string, rope, belt, burnt bottle caps or spoons, glassine envelopes.

Dangers include death from overdose, addiction, liver and other infections due to unsterile needles.

8. **Cough Medicine containing codeine and opium:**

Physical symptoms include drunken appearance, lack of co-ordination, confusion, excessive itching.

Object associated with usage is an empty bottle of medicine. There are *dangers if used extensively*; the most serious is addiction.

ALCOHOL ABUSE

Alcoholism is a progressive and serious disorder that affects the alcoholic physically, mentally, and socially. Alcohol is one of the more readily available drugs. It is addictive. Ten percent of all adult "social" drinkers, numbering about 10 million men and women, become alcoholics, most commonly after five to ten years of social drinking. Although there are no precise statistics about adolescent drinking, there has been an alarming increase among junior and senior high school students.

Prolonged drinking can enlarge the liver, weaken the heart, damage the nervous, digestive, and endocrine systems, and thus contribute to serious physical and mental illness and a shortened life span. Drinking excessively is particularly dangerous to adolescents because their physical and emotional development is not fully stabilized. They are more apt to lose control of their faculties and reflexes after drinking in excess of their individual capacity which is limited in the first place. When drugs like barbituates or tranquilizers are taken along with alcohol, the consequences are extremely dangerous, and fatalities are not uncommon.

Alcoholism also affects the family and the nation's economy, and contributes to crime and loss of life. It figures strongly in family conflict, juvenile delinquency, and divorce. The cost to the economy is more than 15 billion dollars annually in absenteeism, sick leave, accidents, and wasted materials. Alcohol accounts for half of the homicides and one-third of the suicides, and causes 800,000 automobile crashes and 25,000 traffic deaths annually.

The child care worker should be aware that the youngsters he might caution about drinking will give him valid counterarguments. Among these are that drinking is legal, that its sales are highly promoted by the communications media, that most adults drink, and that most drinkers do not become alcoholics. They may argue that anti-drinking policies of the institution are hypocritical because the adults who formulate such policies and the child care workers who enforce them imbibe alcoholic beverages. The answer is that adults in residential settings are responsible for protecting children from risks to their health, even if there is only a 10 percent probability of drinking causing alcoholism. If alcohol becomes the method of escape from tensions, a substitute for social relationships, and an overall crutch to sustain oneself in reality, then serious consequences are likely to occur. Youngsters in residential treatment may have greater vulnerability because of their emotional problems and weakness of inner controls.

The following excerpt from a group therapy session with a cottage group of adolescent boys illustrates some of the issues about adolescent drinking.

This group session took place a day after a widespread beer-drinking incident in the cottage. The issue was raised by Mr. A., a child care supervisor, who was the group co-leader along with Mr. B., a therapist. Some of the boys responded defensively, maintaining that since drinking is widespread in society, it is unrealistic to expect them to behave differently. "Your rules against drinking are hypocritical," they said.

Mr. B. noted that the institution was for children who suffer from emotional disturbances, which often impair a boy's or girl's judgment as to what constitutes proper or safe behavior. Their capacity to exercise sound judgment, to make decisions as to appropriate and even safe behavior, and their ability to mobilize inner strengths to act upon these decisions, involve greater problems for them than one encounters in the general community. Therefore, intoxicants, which impair one's judgment or one's capacity to mobilize inner strengths to act, are risky. One glass of beer, under certain circumstances, could make the difference between behaving safely or dangerously, well or badly, in a way that reflects good contact with reality or distorted contacts with reality.

The response of the group was interesting, in that it appeared that to many of the boys, this was an altogether new concept. A direct confirmation of this feeling came from Tim, a boy whose history reflected the use of alcohol as a means of relieving tension or as a way of anaesthetizing himself against the stress of painful situations. He said that he had gotten into a lot of trouble as a consequence of drinking. Some of the boys said "that drinking made them feel good," implying that the feelings of invulverability associated with intoxication were in some way associated in their minds with grandiosity and power. There was some awareness on their part that the relief from feelings of inferiority, which is often produced by the use of intoxicants, was in some way associated with feelings of invulnerability and grandiosity and could lead to dangerous behavior because of failure on the part of the intoxicated person to perceive dangers realistically. This is exemplified in driving a car. To some people driving a car meant little more than one had the strength of 300 horses under his foot to be used to make himself feel powerful. "But," emphasized Mr. B., "any damn fool can jam his foot down on a gas pedal and when he is drunk he can kill himself and others because he can't control this power adequately." This stimulated a series of association among the boys which gave support to Mr. B's statements. After the meeting both leaders felt that some of the most productive work done with the group had been to set up a kind of standard for greater maturity, in which the individual is given a basis for pride in himself through the adoption of more mature standards of behavior and thought about his actions. There seemed to be a sense of satisfaction in living up to that standard, with the support both of the group and of the adults who represent the values associated with these standards.

Upon discovery of any alcohol or drug usage by an individual child or group of children, or the circulation of drugs in the group, the worker should report immediately to his supervisor. Drug use may raise the level of anxiety in the group as a whole because children may become aware of its use by one or more peers before staff discovers it.

These clues should be followed up. Some children may bring drugs from home visits. The kind of action to be taken regarding an individual child using drugs will be dependent on agency policy. It may range from treatment based on clinical assessment, disciplinary measures, or both, to temporary transfer to a drug treatment facility or removal from care.

Child care workers should be involved in drug education programs. When a drug incident occurs, group discussion about it is called for and should be initiated by the workers.

REFERENCES

Alterman, J. 1973. "Child Care with an Aggressive Child." Unpublished paper, Pleasantville Cottage School, New York.

Comer, J.P., and A.F. Poussaint. 1975. *Black Child Care.* New York: Simon & Schuster.

English, S.O., and G.J. Pearson. 1945. *Emotional Problems of Living.* New York: W.W. Norton.

Freud, A. 1965. *Normality and Pathology in Childhood.* New York: International Universities Press.

Gardner, R.A. 1973. *Understanding Children.* New York: Jason Aronson.

Pierce, C.M. 1967. "Enuresis." In *Comprehensive Textbook of Psychiatry,* edited by A.M. Freedman and H.L. Kaplan, pp. 1380–1383. Baltimore: Williams and Wilkins.

Schaeffer, C.E., and H.E. Millman. 1978. *Therapies for Children.* San Francisco: Jossey–Bass.

Taxel, I. 1970. *Narcotics Identification Guide.* Woodmere, New York.

Treischman, A.E. 1969. "Understanding the Stages of a Temper Tantrum." In *The Other 23 Hours,* edited by A.E. Treischman, J.E. Whittaker, and L.K. Brendtro. Chicago: Aldine.

10 THE RELATIONSHIP NETWORK

The relationship network within group care consists of a number of systems including peer relationships among the children, child–staff interactions, staff relationships, child and staff community contacts, and child–parent and staff–parent relationships.

The child care worker's primary interaction is with individual children, subgroups, the total group, and his child care colleagues in the unit. As a member of an interdisciplinary team, he interacts with a professional group. Administratively, he relates directly to his supervisor and indirectly to other administrative personnel. He is in contact with service personnel, parents, and community resources. In contrast to workers in large institutions located in rural or suburban areas, workers in group homes have many relationships in the community through neighbors, shopping, recreation, and educational and religious services. The intensity of parental contacts will also vary with the location and type of group setting.

The children are similarly involved—with peers, staff, family, and, to some extent, community. The child care worker is drawn into the child's relationship network. The degree of his involvement is determined by agency policy. Thus, in residential treatment programs where the caseworker functions as the "coordinator of treatment," he, rather than the child care worker, becomes the principal aide to the child in his relationships with child care, educational, recreational, and administrative staff as well as his family and community connections. In addition to helping him negotiate these relationships, the caseworker also functions as the child's advocate, an approach which is viewed by some child care workers as limiting to their relationship with children. Some prefer to the Canadian "psychoeducateur" model in which the worker is the coordinator and child advocate, while the caseworker's role is limited to work with the child's family. In the United States, this issue is controversial.

A child care worker's involvement in the child's extended relationships also varies. The worker in community-based group homes located at a distance from the agency's central services, including administration and casework, becomes the principal adult who helps the children negotiate school and neighborhood contacts. If a group home or group residence is located in urban neighborhoods where the children's families reside, the child care workers may be in closer contact with the children's parents than their colleagues in suburban or rural residential settings where parents have to travel relatively far distances to visit. In programs where the caseworker assumes primary responsibility for parental contact, the child care worker's involvement with a child's family is either sparse or indirect.

RELATIONSHIPS WITH INDIVIDUAL CHILDREN

From the moment of arrival, a child finds himself in a planned, controlled environment: a group living situation with a broad range of relationships with peers and adults. He is confronted by unfamiliar interpersonal situations to which he will have to adapt. The prospect evokes uncertainties and anxieties among relatively well-adjusted children, so to the handicapped, disturbed child, it can be frightening and threatening. In extreme cases, there may be regression to earlier, more immature modes of behavior, with troublesome consequences to residential staff (Adler 1971).

The new resident cannot readily divest himself of fixed attitudes and anxieties that have guided his relationships in the past. Lacking basic trust in himself and others, he approaches new relationships with reservations and suspicions. Before he will permit himself to trust adults, he may test them to the limits of their patience.

Many children in group care have not developed sufficient ego strengths to enable them to control inner pressures and tolerate frustration. Like the young child who, in the process of socialization, learns to postpone impulse gratifications by giving in to his parents' demands in order to gain their approval, the child in placement interacts similarly with significant persons in his daily living. This process will have a chance of success if the child is able to establish relationships with adults who represent accepting, caring, and firm, benign authority. We find Brendtro's exposition of relationship applicable here. He states that establishing a relationship with disturbed or maladjusted children consists of three components: increasing the child's communication with the adult, increasing the child's responsiveness to social reinforcement provided by the adult, and increasing the tendency of the child to model the behavior of adults (Brendtro 1969).

Alice and Danny illustrate the influence of significant relationships upon asocial and antisocial youngsters:

Alice at age thirteen and a half looked like a street urchin and acted like one. She did not attend school, associated with undesirable companions, and was not controllable by per parents. Upon admission from family court, she was shabbily dressed in boys' dungarees and shirt, was unkempt, ragged, and dirty. She came from a severely deprived working-class family and grew up in a home sparsely furnished with broken furniture. She was sulky and unfriendly. Unbeknown even to herself, she was endowed with high intelligence, sensitivity, artistic talent, and capacity for relationships. Within a year, she became intrigued by her caseworker and an art teacher who expressed a genuine interest in her. She began to paint and displayed a great talent, wrote highly sensitive poetry, and became seriously involved in therapy. She modified her asocial attitudes and modeled her behavior on the people who had become significant to her. Her life outlook and self-image had changed dramatically by the time she left the institution at the age of seventeen.

Danny, an example of a child reared in a disorganized, economically impoverished family living in a deteriorated neighborhood, had become delinquent at an early age. He was hostile to authority, uninterested in education, and pleasure-oriented. He resisted treatment and soon became a domineering leader in the peer culture. His gradual attachment to the school principal, a physically impressive man who took an interest in Danny and could cope with his persistent provocation without becoming hostile, modified his attitude toward adults. He admired the principal and became devoted to him. He seemed to have found an ideal replacement for his irresponsible delinquent father who had deserted the family years before. As a consequence, he gave up his delinquent lifestyle.

Like Danny, children who are able to establish significant relationships with adults, including their child care workers, tend to develop a capacity to control inner urges, thus helping to curb pleasure-seeking patterns of behavior. Before this stage is achieved, a child will persist in seeking gratification even when it may be harmful to himself and others.

Manipulation

Manipulation is a prevalent technique of children in residential settings. For example, if a child finds that his worker does not grant an inappropriate request, he may approach his caseworker, a supervisor, or an administrator. How this maneuver is dealt with is important because of the implications for the developing relationship between the child and his child care worker. The child should be told that he has to resolve the issue with his worker, consult him before a decision is made, or ask him to review the request. The worker then avoids becoming a tool of manipulation and helps the child focus on their relationship. Respect for the worker's authority strengthens it and conveys to the child the need to work things through with him directly. This circumscribes the child's operational sphere and facilitates the expression and working through of ambivalent feelings evoked by frustration.

Administrative or supervisory staff may be constructively involved with an individual child for treatment reasons. A child care worker, teacher, or caseworker may request a supervisor or administrator to see a child to clarify institutional policy against which he may be reacting or which he may question, to reaffirm standards or expectations, and to deal with disciplinary action that requires administrative intervention. Such use of multiple authority roles in group care can be therapeutically advantageous. It is particularly applicable with acting-out, impulsive adolescents who are generally distrustful of authority (Adler 1971). The child care worker who is confronted by a child's behavioral difficulties has to decide upon appropriate action related both to the child's treatment needs and the developing relationship between himself and the child. To avoid a threat to the relationship, he may prefer to shift disciplinary responsibility temporarily to an administrator. Confronted by a powerful authority figure who may impose limits, including punishment, the child may then turn to the worker, to whom he can express his complaints and hostility against the supervisor. The worker provides the child with an opportunity to discuss the total situation and helps him examine his own role as contributor to the difficulty that resulted in punishment. This places the worker in a more favorable position with the youngster, increasing the child's dependence on him and strengthening their relationship. As the degree of the child's dependence and trust in the worker increases, he is more likely to accept controls from him, eliminating the need for the supervisor's intervention (Adler and Berman 1960).

When a child care worker requests intervention by a supervisor or administrator either because he is fearful or does not care to become involved in a situation where firmness and strength on his part have to be exercised, he faces complications. For example, John, the biggest boy in the cottage, refused to do his cottage chores and defied the new worker's efforts (including demands, pleas, and threats) to cooperate. The worker telephoned the cottage supervisor, insisting that he come to the cottage to help him cope with John. When the supervisor entered the cottage, John turned to the worker, disdainfully called him "chicken," and began to work. John's challenge to the worker's authority was purposive, and the latter failed the test. By calling for intervention of a higher authority before fully exploring other possibilities such as deferment of a head-on confrontation, individual discussion with John, or group involvement in evaluating John's actions, the worker exposed his inexperience as well as his weakness. He left himself open to group resentment and future challenges that might further undermine his authority and therapeutic effectiveness.

The interpersonal transactions between an individual child and his child care worker occur within the context of a group. The adult's actions and reactions are subject to observation and judgment by the other children. If a worker is unfair to a child or openly rejects someone, the others are affected, even his "favorites" who may become uneasy about the permanency of their favored position. His trustworthiness would certainly be put into question.

Observations of a Child's Relationship Capabilities

1. Does he initiate physical or verbal contact with peers and adults? If he does, does he do it appropriately in terms of timing or situation? Is he unreasonable in demanding physical contact, envious of others, overaggressive, whining?
2. Does he avoid physical contact with peers and adults?

3. Does he ever ask for help from workers? If so, is it appropriate or immature? Is it expressed in a crying or whining tone, and is it generally attention-getting?

4. Does he refuse the worker's help?

5. Does he like to help others or does he refuse even when asked?

6. Does he have a "single" friend, many friends, or none at all?

7. Does he try to buy friendships by giving gifts or acting as a flunky to others?

8. Does he enjoy playing with others or is he a loner?

9. Does he tend to dominate in relationship with others, or is he a follower or the scapegoat of the group?

10. Is he able to compromise in controversial situations? Does he tend to argue uncompromisingly, or does he withdraw from an argument?

11. Is he cooperative or highly competitive?

12. Is he able to tolerate frustration? If not, does he try to avoid it? Does he react with anxiety, crying, attack on others, or a temper tantrum?

13. Does he adapt to new situations with ease or avoidance?

14. Does he become easily frightened?

15. Is he easily influenced by peers or adults?

16. How does he relate to group pressure?

17. Does he give evidence of a sense of guilt? When it occurs, does it seem excessive?

18. Is he capable of learning from experience?

19. Can he control aggressive impulses?

20. Is he capable of expressing affection?

21. Can he tolerate a show of affection toward him?

22. Is he sensitive to other people's feelings?

23. How does he react when he makes a mistake or when he fails at something?

24. How does he react to success?

25. Is he able to admit to wrongdoing?

Communication Issues

Child care workers are faced with difficult communication problems in their working relationships with children. The children's verbal statements are not always the complete message. The form, nuances of expression, subtle nonverbal postures and behavior may contain the most significant elements of a communication and reflect his developmental level, family lifestyle, and cultural background.

A specific act or behavior may represent a multiplicity of feelings. For example, a child may refuse to eat because he does not like the food served, he may not be hungry, he may be angry or anxious, or, in the case of a psychotic child, he may be afraid the food will poison him. Similarly, a particular feeling which evokes anxiety may be acted out in a number of different ways. Thus, a child who is afraid of something may react with crying, withdrawal, or by clinging for protection, by avoidance (for instance, is afraid of animals or of being hurt in contact sports) or by stalling during bedtime if he is afraid that something dreadful will happen to him when he falls asleep.

The worker should be able to perceive the totality of a child's communication before a trusting and significant relationship can develop between them. If the worker's responses to a child's messages are perceived as inappropriate, the child may withdraw or become hostile. A capacity to listen, to observe, to understand the child's communication, and to convey this understanding through words is important. The worker's awareness of his own reactions to the child is essential because the child also reacts to the totality of the worker's communication, including nonverbal cues, during a confrontation with a child who is acting out provocatively. If a child's provocation has made the worker feel angry or anxious, it might be more helpful to tell the child the feelings he has evoked instead of reacting physically. Through the worker's expressing his feelings, the child can become more aware of the impact his actions have on others. In the same way, the child should be praised when his actions are constructive, when he expresses concern for others, when he is cooperative, creative, or makes an effort to modify maladaptive patterns of behavior and interaction.

Throughout a child's group living experience, he will judge and test his workers' trustworthiness. If they are firm in guiding him but not authoritarian, that they have an accepting attitude about him and want to help him, then it is likely that the child will permit himself to accept and trust them. A worker will have established a meaningful relationship with a child when communication between them is open and mutually satisfactory, when the child takes direction and strives for the worker's approval, and when he becomes a model for the child to follow.

Since communication in human relationships is "an activity in which one individual engages another in face-to-face encounter to transmit information" (Seabury 1980: 41), the worker should become aware of some of the common problems that may interfere with effective communication between himself and the children.

First of all, the communication process should represent a mutual involvement. Giving a child an order is one way of communicating. If there is enough adult power and pressure to back it up, children will obey because they fear the consequences. It does not, however, represent mutual accord, interaction, and understanding. If giving orders becomes the prevailing method of communication, the child will not be inclined to talk openly and freely to a worker. On the other hand, superficiality on the part of the adult is not appreciated either because it conveys to a child that the worker has no real commitment to a relationship. If a worker's message is ambiguous or contains contradictory elements, it confuses the child further. If the message conveys a sense of indecisiveness or weakness, the child may not respect it. This may encourage manipulations rather than responsiveness based on a meaningful relationship.

The worker has to be careful how he uses certain words as well. For example, "mad" and "angry" are sometimes used interchangeably when dealing with children. A youngster in a residential treatment center or in a psychiatric hospital may misinterpret the reference to his "being mad" (meaning "angry") as saying that he is "crazy." A black youngster may react to a reference like "colored" or "Negro" angrily because he perceives it as an insult or a racial slur. In communicating with minority-group children, one must be knowledgeable about the different connotations of meaning in a given ethnic, racial, or cultural environment. Some children get confused with compound phrases because they cannot process multiple information or instruction. When they do not respond to the worker's multiple message, he may get angry because he interprets it as resistance rather than the child's inability to comprehend what is being conveyed.

A child will be inclined to communicate freely with a worker who is a good listener, conveys respect and interest in his concerns or ideas, and does not impose unilateral solutions. As the worker listens, he should be aware of the nonverbal components of the message, such as the child's tone of voice, his feeling, and his gestures. The worker might ask a question to clarify the overt message or underlying connotation he feels it conveys, such as, "How can I be of help?" or "What do you think about it?" "What would you like to do about it?" This represents "active" listening and conveys empathic understanding.

An interesting and useful approach to improving adult–child communication has been developed by Thomas Gordon. The essence of Gordon's formulations is contained in his "Credo for My Relationships with Youth" (Gordon 1970: 305–306) which outlines the basic principles for a mutually constructive relationship and meaningful open communication between an adult and youth:

1. They should mutually respect and accept each other's individuality.
2. The adult should be committed to listening to the youth's problems and helping him find his own solutions.
3. Youth and adult should communicate freely about behavior which may interfere with their needs, and both should try to modify such behavior.
4. When there is a conflict of needs in the relationship between adult and youth, there should be mutual commitment to resolve it without resorting to power tactics.
5. There should be commitment to a relationship of "mutual respect and affection."

Implementing these guidelines require effort from worker and child, and even if a child care worker is fully committed to realizing them, he may still face difficulties because of the children's personality characteristics as well as structure requirements of the group setting. For example, the impulsive youngster has needs which he strives to satisfy, though they may be destructive to himself and others. Since he has limited inner controls to curb them, outside controls are necessary. It would be contrary to his therapeutic needs to tell him that if the worker's behavior "interferes" with meeting his needs, the worker "will try and modify" *his* behavior.

The same applies to the sociopathic youngster whose need satisfaction is primary and who does not seem to care about the needs of others, and to the borderline or psychotic child whose judgment of reality is poor. One cannot realistically expect that when such children's behavior interferes with the needs of the worker or a requirement of established structure, that they will be able to modify their behavior. These children are not always capable or ready to "search for [a] solution . . . acceptable to both." Consequently, the guidelines of Gordon's credo have to be modified in the case of emotionally disturbed and/or multiply handicapped children. The therapeutic thrust of a group care program is to help the children reach a level of emotional maturity to make it possible for them to participate in a relationship in conformity to Gordon's guidelines. The weight of responsibility for maintaining the attitudes implied in the credo rests on the child care workers and any other adults involved.

Gordon has classified into twelve categories characteristic parental responses to their children's communications. Most of these convey directly and by implication lack of understanding and lack of sensitivity to their children's feelings and concerns. Instead of listening, trying to understand the message, and helping the child find a solution and work through the problem, parents may:

Tell him *what* to do or what he ought to do.

Try to influence him to come to their way of thinking about a problem by intellectualizing, giving information, lecturing, presenting arguments for the solution they deem correct.

Interpret his motives, analyze his thoughts and expressed concerns as they see it.

Divert the child from facing the problem or console him by minimizing its significance to him.

Ridicule or shame him regarding his views or make a negative judgment of him; for example, "You are not thinking straight about the problem."

Warn or threaten him that he better do something in accordance with their views.

Such responses are not helpful because they do not encourage a child to face a problem and seek his own solution. In fact, the result is usually a child's withdrawal from further discussion with a parent, with feelings of disappointment or resentment, anger, or a deflated sense of adequacy. Gordon's "active listening" approach conveys confidence that the child is capable to work out a satisfactory solution. Even in group care situations where the worker may have to explain that the child's need cannot be met because it is contrary to the "rules" of the group, the child might be able to accept the reality more readily if he feels the worker's sympathy for his concerns. Based on this alone, the relationship may be strengthened.

The communication process is quite different in a situation resulting from a problem caused by a childs' behavior which interferes with the worker's or the group's needs. Here, the worker should initiate an active confrontation. Instead of warning, moralizing, shaming, or threatening punishment, the worker points out the difficulties the child is causing to himself and to others. The message should come across clearly and firmly. For example:

1. James has been bullying David. The child worker talks to James about it. "It bothers me when you pick on David. He is smaller than you and can't stand up to your provocation. It's not fair. So cut it out! I trust you can do it if you try. If someone bullied you, you wouldn't like it and neither would I. I would intervene for you as I am doing for David."

2. John has been manipulative with Ann, the new worker. Bill, the senior child care worker, has, with Ann's approval, decided to intervene. "I'm disappointed in you, John, when you take advantage of Ann. You know I don't like manipulators and when you act like one, you are not very likeable. I expect this to stop, and I feel that if you give it some thought and effort, you will do so."

3. Ben, an aggressive, violent-prone adolescent, is causing great concern to the staff. Some are afraid of his explosiveness, and most are angry because he is very difficult to manage. Jim has decided to talk to Ben about his behavior because he believes that the boy is not fully aware of the impact he has on the others. He invites Ben into the cottage office and tells him that he has something on his mind he'd like to share with him. "Ben, I have been thinking for some time about having a talk with you." "What have I done now!" Ben exclaims defensively. "Nothing wrong now. But are you aware how angry you act when we ask you to do your share of the work or call to your attention that you are not following the rules?" Bill replies.

"No one is going to boss me around or bug me," Ben replies, eyes flashing and hands tightening into fists.

"It may seem like that to you. It isn't our intention to 'bug' you," Bill tries to reassure him. "Maybe you are not aware that you react with such fury! Sometime I feel that you are ready to 'kill.' "

"Is this how I come across when I get angry?" Ben asks.

"I feel this way. We try to understand you and certainly want to like you, but you make it difficult. Why do you get so angry with us?"

"I don't know, perhaps because I feel pushed around and that you guys hate me," said Ben.

"Speaking for myself, I can assure you I don't hate you. In fact, I wish I could help you get some control over yourself when you feel I make an unfair demand," said Bill. When Ben did not respond, Bill added that Ben might try to talk about his feelings, rather than "blow his top." All the workers would be glad to listen and help.

"O.K., I'll think about it," said Ben.

In all of the above situations, the workers presented themselves as real people and talked openly and "straight." They seem to be understanding of the children without compromising their expectations or masquing their feelings. When a youngster behaved destructively to others, they indicated clearly that his behavior was not acceptable. In fact, his actions did not make him likeable at the time. Their expectation was, however, that he could modify his behavior.

Another reality is that a worker should not hesitate to communicate to children that adult patience and tolerance has limits. When, for example, a worker is distressed or under severe pressure, his tolerance is weakened. He should then feel free to communicate this to his group with such remarks as "I am not as patient today as usual" or "I've been under a lot of pressure today, so be careful not to push me too far and we'll get along." Children generally appreciate such outspokeness and know when the worker means what he says.

Sometimes the most complex communication problems arise in situations where there is a conflict within the worker–child relationship. Gordon suggests to parents that they and their children commit themselves to resolve such a conflict without ever resorting to the use of power—"to win at the expense of the other losing"—and to strive to search for solutions where "no one will lose, both will win." This no-lose method means a readiness by both parties involved to identify and define the problem causing the conflict; to discuss potential solutions, deciding which one should be worked on; to spell out each one's responsibilities for implementing the agreed-upon action; and subsequently to evaluate the resolution is success or failure. If either the adult or the child is the sole victor, the situation can be destructive. The adult can win by sheer force of his authority and power to impose punishment, but the child may be made to conform to the adult's demands at a cost to the adult–child relationship and the child's mature growth. If the child is permitted to win because the adult does not wish to take the trouble to work through the issues or prefers to avoid a clash, the consequences are the same but for other reasons.

For example, if the child is permitted to win because the worker wants to avoid a confrontation, the relationship suffers because the child is made aware of the worker's weakness or indifference or lack of caring. It may strengthen a child's sense of grandiosity that he can get what he wants. He may then try to act like the spoiled child who learns how to get his way by resorting to temper tantrums or manipulation. The child does not learn to curb impulsivity and learn self-discipline or to face reality. The adult's lack of forcefulness to stop a child from wrongdoing may also convey that the adult does not care for him.

In the case of the alternative resolution of the conflict in favor of a worker who has his way by force of his power to impose his will or a solution, the child may become resentful or hostile. He may resort to destructive or deviant methods in future relationships with the worker, such as: avoidance, lying, blaming others, or manipulating; he may give in and become submissive and overconforming; or he may withdraw from relationships with adults.

Gordon's no-lose method suggested for parents as well as to teachers in community-based schools is a commendable approach for a child care worker to try to follow. The degree of success achieved will depend on a child's capacity to participate in the process as well as the quality of the worker–child relationship, something that is constantly tested in problem-solving situations. Throughout the day, the worker is called upon to intervene in crises generated by misunderstandings, provocations, arguments, fights among children and by individual children, or group acting-out behavior. The following situations exemplify constructive handling by the workers and delineate the principles involved in a problem-solving process:

Johnny complained to Miss Davis, his worker, that Ben had punched him. Ben claimed that he hit Johnny because he insulted his mother. Johnny then accused Ben of "picking" on him "all the time." Ben said that Johnny "provokes and, therefore, deserves what he gets." Miss Davis was aware of Johnny's provocative tendencies, had talked with him about it, and had informed his caseworker who was discussing it in therapy sessions with him. She decided that Ben's tendencies to strike out physically at other children required immediate attention. She told both boys that their behavior was troubling her and she wanted to help both of them. She had decided to deal with Ben first. Johnny left saying "O.K., but make him stop punching me!"

Miss Davis had taken the first step in the problem-solving process by *assessing the problem, deciding on priorities and a course of action.* The next step involved helping Ben modify his behavior. *Goals* and *tasks* to achieve them had to be devised by mutual agreement.

To motivate him, Miss Davis encouraged Ben to talk about his attitude toward Johnny, his feelings that Johnny provokes him, and his anger which is expressed by hitting. At first, Ben reacted defensively, saying Johnny is a "pesty kid" and "deserves what he gets." However, when Miss Davis asked specific questions like "Tell me what happened. How did you feel when Johnny referred to your mother in insulting terms?," Ben clarified the facts as well as his feelings; he would get angry and strike out. She assured Ben she would follow up on Johnny's or any other child's provocation, but she felt that it would be better for Ben and everyone else if he could talk first instead of striking out physically. Ben agreed he had a "temper." To Miss Davis' question, "What do you want to do about changing it?," Ben replied, "I don't know." Miss Davis then suggested a brainstorming exercise—to say whatever solution came into his mind. Ben was intrigued and offered a number of suggestions, among them to ignore Johnny, to tell Miss Davis when Johnny provokes him, to challenge him to a fight if he insults him, to get a friend of his to beat him up, etc. Miss Davis thought that the first two seemed preferable, and Ben agreed. "What about your temper?" she inquired. Ben said he could attempt to control it but that it would be difficult. Maybe he should "think" before he "hits"—or maybe "count to ten." "That would be good," said Miss Davis. "Maybe you and I can talk about it sometimes. Would you perhaps like to talk to Dr. Green about it?" Ben selected two approaches—if he feels provoked by Johnny or some other boy, he'll come to tell Miss Davis or Mr. Jones if she is not around. He will also talk to Dr. Green if she can arrange an appointment.

The final step in the process was *evaluation.* Miss Davis and Ben agreed that they would periodically (every five days) review his behavior toward Johnny. Ben would also keep a written record of incidents which he considered "provocations" and what he did about it. Miss Davis offered to intervene with Johnny to help him control his provocation. She would also arrange an appointment for Ben to see Dr. Green.

A similar approach is applicable to group situations. For example:

The boys who had the responsibility for preparing snacks and cleaning up the kitchen complained to the workers that they could not work efficiently because some of their peers interfered by coming into the kitchen, distracting them, and in general "messing" things up. The workers agreed that snack time had periodically deteriorated to "chaos" time, characterized by noise in the kitchen, grabbing food, dumping plates in the sink, and so on. A decision was made to convene a group meeting to discuss the matter.

At the meeting, Mr. C., the senior child care worker, introduced the issue and called for comments from the group. There was a heated reaction, dominated by complaints about the quality of the snacks, delays in serving, and the mess that was left. Feelings were also expressed about the noise and grabbing of food. Mr. C. asked, "What do you want to do about it?" After some discussion, the consensus was to make snack time a relaxed, pleasant time.

The next step was to outline the strategies to achieve it. The following were agreed upon: Staff would try to get more diversified snacks. A worker would supervise preparation of snacks and cleanup. A specific time (8 p.m.) was set for serving the food; one-half hour for preparation and one-half hour for cleanup. The kitchen would be off limits to all except those who were involved in the work. Evaluation was built into the process by designating a weekly review of snack-time behavior.

In summary, communication is the key to relationship-building and the means to sustain it. If there is mutuality, both worker and child derive emotional satisfaction from it, and it contributes to the child's emotional and social growth which is the goal of group care.

REFERENCES

Adler, J. 1971. "Interpersonal Relationships in Residential Treatment Centers for Disturbed Children." *Child Welfare* 50, no. 4: 208–217.

Adler, J., and I. Berman. 1960. "Ego–Superego Dynamics in Residential Treatment of Disturbed Adolescents." Paper presented at the 37th Annual Meeting of the American Orthopsychiatric Association. Mimeo.

Brendtro, L.K. 1969. "Establishing Relationship Beachheads." In *The Other 23 Hours*, edited by A.E. Treischman, J.K. Whittaker, and L.K. Brendtro. Chicago: Aldine.

Gordon, T. 1970. *Parent Effectiveness Training.* New York: Plume.

Seabury, B.A. 1980. "Communication Problems in Social Work Practice." *Social Work* 25, no. 1: 40–44.

11 RELATIONSHIP WITH THE GROUP

Residential treatment is based on the assumption that the emotionally disturbed or multiply handicapped child requires coordinated therapeutic services, including group care, because he cannot be helped by outpatient or day treatment services. Consequently, "referral to residential treatment is a 'last resort'—an escape from the untenable situation in which the child finds himself" (Mayer, Richman, and Balcerzak 1977: 76), while living with his family, relatives, or in a foster home.

It does not follow that group living is good for all children requiring residential treatment. It may be very burdensome to the child who is fearful of others, who does not have sufficient ego strength to cope with the requirements of group living. Similarly, the highly impulsive and aggressive or violence-prone youngster poses serious difficulties in group care. The impulse-ridden child tends to upset the environment constantly; the aggressive, delinquent youngster tends to perpetuate a delinquent lifestyle and to dominate his peers for purposes of his own power needs, which are contrary to the therapeutic objectives of the residential setting (Polsky 1962). The violent represent a serious physical threat to peers and staff.

Since group care units frequently consist of children in all of these categories—the fearful, withdrawn and asocial, as well as the physically acting-out and antisocial, they represent difficult management problems for child care workers who, jointly with their colleagues, must devise methods to facilitate group living for all of the children.

The residential living unit plays a crucial role in the growth and maturation of its children. Like the (wholesome) family, it strives to provide nurture and care, a sense of security in oneself, and trust in others, adult guidance, and identification with socially and ethically sound values. Unlike the family, where the sense of belonging stems from biological roots, and family cohesiveness is based on emotional ties, the residential group has to strive to develop both feelings. They cannot be imposed by adult authority or a delinquent peer code. Adult authority may succeed in creating a superficially cohesive group based on conformity to authoritarian adult control, a peer code representing a sense of "we-ness" enforced by the power of indigenous leaders, and a pecking order of social organization (Adler 1979). Both these forms of group organizations may make child care worker's life and tasks more comfortable, but they are destructive. In the first, children obey the feared adults; in the second, staff delegates authority to indigenous leaders at a price that benefits only those leaders. Both are contrary to therapeutic objectives of residential treatment (Polsky 1962).

Workers must be cautious about enlisting the help of the "natural" group leader in managing the group. Such help, when offered, generally has a hidden price tag. For example, the following situation illustrates the consequences of turning over management responsibility to a youngster regarding cottage cleanup:

"I am very pleased with the way you have managed to put the cottage in order in such a short period of time," said Mr. Smith to Mr. and Mrs. Albert who had moved into the cottage a month ago. "You have a rough group of boys who in the past gave their child care workers a hard time. Your place looks neat and orderly."

"Bill knows how to get the boys to cooperate," said Mrs. Albert.

"In fact, we had trouble during the first week, and Bill had to make a fuss to the point of threatening deprivation if the boys did not keep the place clean. The biggest problem has always been Saturday morning cottage cleanup, but things have straightened out since Johnny volunteered to help us. He has kept his word, and we've been pleased about his efficiency in this respect. It frees us to do other necessary chores like going shopping, seeing the housekeeper, and so on. We can even leave the kids alone, and things are done when we get back."

"I know Johnny well," remarked Mr. Smith. "Are you sure he doesn't use strong-arm methods to get the boys to do their jobs?"

"I hadn't thought of this," said Mr. Albert. "I hadn't seen any evidence, but I'll be glad to look into this."

Following this conference, Mr. Albert made an effort to talk with some of the boys, individually and in small groups, about the house chores, especially Saturday morning cleanup. The older boys said they didn't mind doing the work, but the younger ones were strangely unresponsive. Mr. Albert was puzzled and, after consulting his wife, decided to talk to some of the other child care workers. While visiting the adjoining cottage, they mentioned it to Mrs. Williams who was a person of many years' experience in the institution. She smiled, saying, "You have not been around here long enough to be skeptical about boys like Johnny. My kids tell me that Johnny and his cronies are using strong-arm tactics to get the younger boys to do all the heavy work. Anyone who refuses gets roughed up."

"I better get to work on this matter," said Mr. Albert.

"That's a good idea, Jim," said Mrs. Albert. We do not want to be unfair to the children and certainly we don't want them to be exploited."

DYNAMICS OF GROUP LIVING

The group is a dynamic entity. Each interaction among the children and between children and staff generates new interactions. The worker must be constantly aware of the dynamic balances and imbalances within his group. A crisis for an individual child has an effect on the whole group. When a child has to be hospitalized, the rest of the group becomes anxious. When a member of the group is involved in serious delinquency, the group is affected. Continuous evaluation of the group, both as a unit and as a composite of many different individuals who are interacting in a complexity of relationships, is essential.

Adaptation to residential group living presents adjustment problems for all children. It is difficult for the more seriously disturbed. By his very presence, a child who acts bizarre poses a threat to the group as a whole or to individual members because he may arouse latent anxieties that are turned against him in the form of hostile and aggressive acts. The socially immature, physically unattractive girl, placed in a sexually oriented teenage girls' group, evokes annoyance and rejection; the effeminate-looking, intellectual boy placed in an aggressively oriented boys' group seems to be a threat to the others' tenuous sense of security. The girl as well as the boy are likely to become objects of derision and end up as abused, ridiculed scapegoats.

Every child tends to reenact his conflicts and accustomed patterns of behavior. The delinquent youngster will strive to perpetuate his tendencies within the cottage group by recruiting others to join him in antisocial acts. If a boy with sadistic tendencies is placed in the same room with one who has masochistic traits, it is likely that both will tend to reinforce their pathological needs in their relationship and may even join forces to attack others. An important task here is to estimate whether the relationship between two or more children is based on common disturbances or common strengths. When the latter is the case, the relationship is a wholesome one and should be encouraged. If it is the former, the relationship should be discouraged. In some cases, separation into different rooms or even transfer may be required. A group should not be overbalanced with large numbers of children manifesting severe disturbances. It should have a number of children with sufficient ego strengths and positive value orientations to represent a nucleus of wholesome leadership which will enhance and motivate others to follow positive staff and peer values. This is particularly important in preadolescent and adolescent groups. Unless counteracted by adult control, significant relationships, and constructive programming, there is a tendency for the informal cottage culture to be dominated by gang leadership, a gang code, and a pecking order of social organization.

INFORMAL GROUP CULTURE

Adler and Berman (1960: 218) describe such an adolescent cottage group:

> There were few constructive goals within the group and energy was dissipated in destructive pursuits and in the maintenance of a delinquent hierarchy against adult authority. Interpersonal relationships in the peer group were strongly authoritarian with the "strong man" and his lieutenants dominating the group. This clique bullied the weaker youngsters. There was little, if any, respect for the autonomy of the individual. A minimum of democratic processes operated. The group's values were anti-intellectual. Boys who showed a tendency towards scholastic achievement were ridiculed and those who attempted to move toward more constructive social values faced group disapproval. Thus, the group's mores and behavior tended to counteract the therapeutic purposes of the institution.

It is valuable for the child care worker to be aware of the natural leaders, the manipulators, the instigators, and the scapegoats in their groups as well as understanding the composition and characteristics of the various subgroups of cliques. One way to increase this understanding is to learn how the children relate to each other in terms of friendship patterns. In one method involving sociograms, children are asked to rank their peers on a scale from 1–15 regarding role and status in the group (whom they respect most or least, whom they consider most popular, whom they would like as a roommate or as a playmate during leisure-time activities.) The children have to be reassured that their choices will be confidential and that the staff motive for asking for this information is to facilitate grouping for activities on the basis of preferences. Sociograms could then be charted, giving information regarding status hierarchy in the group. The most favored, the rejects or isolates, the leaders and the scapegoats, could then be identified.

Knowledge of the informal group culture and the unwritten group code is important but not easily achieved. It requires sensitive observation and good relationships with the children. The expectations and practices of the group do not generally conform to established rules and therapeutic objectives. The degree of difference between them may be an index of the effectiveness of the therapeutic program. It may also serve to formulate intervention techniques to help the children modify an antitherapeutic or destructive code of expectations and behavior.

A key factor in the informal group culture is peer leadership. If it is constructive, it should be supported and given encouragement. Delinquent leadership that exploits the weak and dominates the group through a pecking order organization and strong-armed methods must be controlled and its abuses curbed. (If it is tolerated by active support of the leader and his henchmen or indirectly by staff passivity, a delinquent gang-type organization is perpetuated because it is interpreted by the children as staff-approved.) This requires staff consistency in attitude, and joint action is essential to control domination by delinquent leadership. Differences among staff results in dilemmas among those who are concerned, as exemplified by the following situations:

During his first week in Cottage 10 (an adolescent group), Don Wilcox observed that Charley, the strongest boy, enjoyed a privileged status. He seemed to be influential with several of the child care workers and catered to by his peers. For example, although Don never saw him clean his room, his bed was always neatly made and the room he shared with two other boys orderly. He had the best seat in front of the T.V. and choice of programs during T.V. time. During meals, Charley had first choice of food dished out by one of the boys and extra desserts. On one occasion, when a dessert was not passed to him, Charley looked at his buddy, Tim, who then turned to Johnny, saying: "Hey jerk, didn't you forget something?" Frightened, Johnny passed his dish of ice cream to Charley. Don had also noted that the boy who brings the food tray served Charley first.

When Don shared his observations with Bill, his more experienced coworker, the latter dismissed it by saying, "It's not a big deal. This is a cottage custom that does little harm."

"But it's not fair to the other kids! Charley's acting like a dictator. He bosses the kids. They do his chores. When they sit down to watch a T.V. program, the best seat seems to belong to Charley. No one dares to sit in it, even when he's out of the room. Don't you think that the kids look to us to correct such abuses?"

"Don't be naive," said Bill. "It's good to have Charley on our side. If we made a fuss about these minor items, we could expect lots of trouble in the cottage. Don't you think that this is a good cottage to work in? Things seem to run smoothly, don't they?"

"I've noticed that the first day I started to work here. Things are comfortable here for us, but is it good for the kids?" Don wondered.

Such conditions are not "good for kids," as demonstrated by Polsky's research (1962). A gang structure in a group care setting is harmful to all concerned—the philosophy of the agency, objectives of the program, the authority of staff, relationship between the children, and the child care workers. It is contrary to the needs of the children who are victims of peer domination and the maturational needs of the exploiters. Individually, committed workers like Don Wilcox cannot modify an existing delinquent-dominated group culture. They need encouragement and backing by colleagues, supervisors, and administrators.

STATUS IN THE GROUP

Most children in care, like their peers in the community, strive to be accepted by the status group. To do so, a child may become a "follower" or even a "flunky" of the aggressive in-group which dominates group life. According to Mayer (1958: 43), the child care worker "has to help each of the followers to recognize that they have a right to be themselves. He has to support them in developing enough security to express their individuality in word and action even if it differs from expectations of group leaders or adults." He may be able to achieve this by providing opportunities for them to demonstrate leadership qualities, talents, or skills which will enhance their status in the group.

The child who is withdrawn or isolated avoids relationship in the group. It takes time and requires patience to help him overcome his misgivings and suspicions. The other children who may resent the isolate also need help to understand that his isolation is not due to dislike of them but to his own problems.

The scapegoat who evokes hostile attitudes and at times physical abuse needs protection from attack. His peers will have to be worked with to help them understand that he is being exploited as a result of their own hangups. Group discussion can be helpful in such situations. This was dramatically illustrated in a cottage meeting with an adolescent, delinquent-oriented group of boys. The group was talking about their attitude and behavior toward Fred, a weak, physically inadequate, effeminate youngster who had recently been admitted to the cottage. At one point John said: "When someone gets frustrated for some reason, the first thing he does is to seek out a weaker boy to vent his anger. At the moment, it's Fred who is the target for today." The worker asked whether this was a "mature" way of handling one's angry feelings. There was much discussion, and at the end of the session, Alan suggested that they continue talking in order to find a better way of coping with their feelings than projecting them at Fred. Fred, like many children who achieve the scapegoat status in a group, may actually be unconsciously provoking antagonistic attitudes and even physical attack. This requires intervention by both child care workers and therapists.

GROUP COHESIVENESS

As indicated, the worker's relationship with an individual child evolves and is sustained within the framework of group life. He has to individualize within the context of group living. This is not easily achieved because individual and group needs do not always harmonize. Every child care worker, at one time or another, experiences conflict about individualization versus group needs, and individualizing versus group controls. The group should be the medium for each child's growth and development. This is achievable only when through the efforts of the child care workers, the milieu represents an atmosphere of acceptance, warmth, and sensitivity to the children's needs as individuals and as a group; provides a sense of security for all the children; and encourages child participation in issues of group living. The degree of a group's effectiveness in meeting this primary objective of enhancing children's healthy development may be measured by the following criteria:

1. **The quality of communication within the group.** Is the group climate conducive to open and free expression of feelings and opinions without fear or threat of retaliation by adult or peer leadership? Is there an open, two-way flow of communication between children and staff rather than one-sided authoritarian orders from adults to the children or from a delinquent group leadership to the rest of the group?

2. **A balance between individualization and group needs.** Overemphasis of group needs, especially those involving "control" to the detriment of individual children's needs, stifles individual growth. Carrying individualization to extremes contributes to dissension and conflict within the group.

3. **Degree of child involvement in planning management, decision-making, and evaluation group tasks.** Do the children have an opportunity to participate in discussion regarding the above processes, or is life directed primarily by adult authority through imposed rules and regulations?

4. **Degree and quality of group cohesiveness.** Is there a genuine cohesiveness, based on a sense of security of belonging in the group, feelings of satisfaction from joint tasks and daily social interaction, respect for each child's individuality and mutual support among children and staff? Or is it cohesiveness due to a (delinquent) gang structure or pseudo-cohesiveness as a consequence of adult authoritarian leadership? This type of group cohesiveness or the lack of a sense of "groupness" among children and staff is not constructive.

The interactions among children and staff represent the dynamism of group living. These group dynamics involve forces which bind the group together and reinforce a sense of cohesiveness. They also generate pressures that contribute to dissension and conflict within the group. It is important for a child care worker to observe and become knowledgeable about the dynamics of his group: How do the children relate to each other? Who are the leaders, followers, or scapegoats? How do members of the child care team relate to each other and to the children? Is there a consistency in their approach to the children? How does each worker exercise authority? Is there a consistency in leadership styles?

Understanding of group process and development of skills to guide the collective energy of the group into constructive channels of expression, activity, and relationships enhances the child care worker's efforts to aid the maturational growth of all of the children in his group. It provides group support rather than opposition; it generates the potentials of self-help among the group for the benefit of each individual member. Group cohesiveness based on constructive social values can develop through processes involving children and staff. Adults must take the initiative and maintain the momentum of guiding the "group process," defined as the "ongoing nature of interpersonal relationships" (Yalom 1970: 109). One method involves regularly scheduled group meetings which help children become accustomed to talking together, to feel more comfortable with each other, and to mobilize group energies in the service of individual growth and enriching group experience. It encourages the self-help potential of the group to contribute to each member's growth.

TYPES OF GROUP MEETINGS

Whittaker (1979: 117–22) classifies groups in relation to purpose — management of daily living groups, program activity groups, problem-oriented groups, and transition groups.

The **Daily management group**, consisting of all the children and child care workers, meets to work out common concerns of staff and children around major tasks and routines of the day. In group homes and group residences, the housekeeper and cook also participate. The major emphasis is on planning, scheduling, and evaluating work responsibilities, sharing information, and arbitrating minor disputes.

Activity groups may involve all or part of the group to teach basic physical and social skills or to provide special activities for children who have specific interests, talents, and hobbies.

Transition groups are organized around discharge planning. This includes discussion regarding feelings of separation, preparation for return to family, neighborhood, and community schools. Some of these groups may continue meeting after discharge to discuss adaptation to community living.

The problem-oriented discussion group may involve all of the children or a subgroup led by one or more staff who have clinical skills and understanding of group dynamics. Such a group should meet at least once a week. It is designed to explore feelings, develop behavioral alternatives, and provide group support and encouragement as well as criticism (Whittaker 1979: 118). This type of group is the major treatment modality in Positive Peer Culture programs.

Another type of group meeting which Fant calls "small, spontaneous interview group," involves subgroups in the cottage convened to discuss destructive acting-out. "These groups, or more appropriately, cliques, bring out various behavior patterns directed at themselves, their worker, another child or another subgroup. The worker in the cottage, whenever possible, should isolate the subgroup and non-punitively highlight their behavior, helping them see the implications of what they have been doing or how they are using each other in the group." (Fant 1971: 79).

This type of meeting applies Fritz Redl's life-space interview concept to a group (Redl 1966: 35–67). The life-space interview deals with crisis situations and is built around a child's direct life experience in connection with a crisis issue, which then becomes the interview focus. It is most effective when conducted by a person who is "perceived by the child as part of his natural habitat of life-space, and with some pretty clear role and power in his daily living. The child care worker is such a person. In a crisis situation, his immediate availability is assured, representing support at a time of severe emotional stress and offering understanding at a point of greatest receptivity.

GROUP PROCESS

According to Yalom (1970: 231), "There are mass forces operating in groups which broadly influence their course of development and which provide us with a crude but nevertheless useful scheme of developmental phases." On the basis of observational studies of sensitivity and therapy groups, three developmental phases have been identified—*orientation, conflict,* and *development of cohesiveness* (Yalom 1970: 231–254). These stages will be discussed in relation to groups in child care settings.

Orientation

During this initial phase the emphasis is on clarifying objectives and establishing ground rules. The worker should suggest the time and frequency of meetings for the group's consideration and outline requirements such as mandatory attendance for all and behavior conducive to orderly discussion.

The child care worker who plans to involve his children in group discussion sessions should be clear about his objectives. To begin with, the meetings should be task-oriented, related to either an activity of interest to the children or to resolving situations which are causing problems and tensions in the group. If the objectives are not clear, if the suggested tasks are objectionable or beyond their children's capacities, they will not be well received. The topic should be presented in clear and concise terms. For example, the worker might say: "Let us plan a day outing for next week. A number of possible places are available to us. We have to decide which of these activities the group prefers, what food and equipment we'll need to take with us, and who should be assigned responsibilities for various aspects of the outing. We'll need volunteers for the food, equipment, and activity planning committees." If the issue is a problem about chores, the worker might begin with: "Let's review how well we did with getting our cottage chores done this week and then we will plan for next week. Each of you will have a chance to express your opinion, and each can make suggestions about how we can do the work most efficiently."

The style of leadership will vary, depending on the group. Younger, immature children or severely disturbed adolescents will require greater initiative and activity on the part of the leader and a tighter structure of rules. The worker may have to prepare a specific agenda, allocate time limits, and spell out ground rules. Lambert (1977: 25–26) suggests "simple rules, such as one child speaking at a time, no yelling, everyone remaining in his seat. . . . A typical agenda should organize the content into concrete items such as chores, gripes, and planning . . . the meeting must conclude with a sense of accomplishment. . . . " Meetings with a group of verbal, more mature adolescents can have greater flexibility in agenda content, leader control, and ground rules.

Preparation is very important. This includes prior consultation with supervisors, colleagues on the child care team, and indigenous leaders of the group, scheduling, and physical arrangements. For example: Complications arose when a worker met with his group of mildly retarded youngsters in one of the bedrooms. The boys who sat on the beds tended to doze off during the sessions. After the meetings were moved to a larger room with chairs arranged in a circle, this difficulty was overcome. In a girl's cottage group, the meetings scheduled a half hour before dinnertime were disrupted by restlessness because the girls were anxious to get ready to go to the dining hall. In a group home, meetings were scheduled during the time of a favorite television program. Resistance was severe until the time was rescheduled.

In all groups this stage is characterized by verbal and nonverbal expression of anxiety and insecurity on the part of the membership, communication difficulties, and a focus on the leader for direction and decision-making. There is primary concern for oneself rather than group goals ("What's in it for me?"). Under the best of circumstances, the worker should not expect an enthusiastic response from his group initially. The contrary is more likely. Even in therapy groups, where the membership is voluntary and motivated, there is anxiety as well as overt resistance, which is expressed by questioning, defensiveness, silences, and overdependence on the leader. In residential groups, the first meeting may be marked by lack of responsiveness, silences from the more passive inhibited children, and vociferous objection, manipulative tactics, or physical disruption by the more aggressive youngsters.

In time, if the meetings are well structured, goals clearly defined, and participation by all encouraged by a firm, benign, confident adult leader, resistance will tend to diminish and productive work will be achieved. Task-oriented groups are not "group therapy" groups, though they do have therapeutic implication for each individual as well as for the group as a whole. Eventually the group becomes ready to discuss other matters, including relationships within the group. It cannot be emphasized sufficiently that the group discussion process will have to be nurtured by the child care worker(s) leading the group. At the beginning, he may have to be more active in initiating discussion, asking for or giving information. As the group develops, more and more of this should come from the children.

Once goals are set, tasks are specific, and work assignments made, the worker becomes the coordinator of the group effort.

Phase of Conflict

During this stage, the group becomes involved with issues of conflict, dominance, and power. There is competition for control of the group. Indigenous leaders may attempt to perpetuate their power by challenging the worker, initiating gripes, and unrealistic demands. They may succeed initially because the other children fear their power of retaliation. If the group process evolves successfully, there is likely to be a shift in the peer relationship structure (Adler and Berman 1960). Intragroup rivalries are expressed, and scapegoating of individuals takes place.

As the adult leader, the worker can expect to become an object of expressed hostility. This is prevalent in group care settings because the adult represents more than personal adult authority. He may be viewed as the "agent" of administration. At such times, he should then expect a stream of demands which he is in no position to gratify. Consequently, he may be accused of hypocrisy, of paying only lip service to democratic process, of expressing concern for the group that is professed and not real, or told he has "no guts" because he is a lackey of the administration. Then there is displaced hostility. During the course of a day, a worker may serve as a target of individual children's displaced emotions, and he must develop self-awareness as well as self-control to avoid hostile counterreactions (Adler 1973). It is even more difficult to face the kind of group hostility and collective displacement of irrationality which the child care worker may confront in these formal group sessions. It takes a great deal of strength, security, and self-awareness not to react defensively. If the worker can accept that this is a testing period for him, consciously or unconsciously staged by an individual child or part of the group, if he "keeps his cool" during this period of turmoil, he gains respect and may gradually gain allies within the peer group against those who attempt to sabotage the sessions.

Fant states that a basic requirement in group care meetings is that "freedom of expression must be encouraged, with cottage staff interceding only at those points where they feel that the excitement and stimulation emanating from the discussion will cause the group to suffer from overwhelming quiet, anxiety, fear or despair" (Fant 1971: 78). This implies controlled passivity and watchful neutrality. If the worker's manner is authoritarian, he may succeed in having an orderly conforming group of children who will do as he wishes; there will be no vital group process, no individual growth, and no development of a genuine sense of constructive group cohesiveness. If the worker is completely passive, and represents a laissez-faire leadership, he may face a chaotic group situation. The worker has to aim at a balance that avoids repressive conformity and the risk of uncontrolled, impulsive, and regressive behavior. His leadership style and actions should convey to the children the feeling that he is in control of the situation and capable of assuring each of them the opportunity to express himself freely, without fear of emotional retaliation from peers or himself. When the inevitable scapegoating occurs, the worker's handling of the aggressor(s) and the victims is a "moment of trial" for him, with the peer group acting as jury and judge of his strength and fairness and competence. The scapegoat must be protected from group abuse.

Group discussion can be enhanced by the leader's sensitivity to developing tensions and skill in reducing them so that they do not explode into destructive behavior. He encourages the timid by asking for their opinions. He mediates differences among individuals, encourages verbalization of feelings about an issue, discourages aggressive and hostile acting-out. He sometimes interprets and clarifies a child's confused statements, thus helping individuals to understand one another better. When discussion is stymied, he might say, "Let's see where everyone stands," or he may summarize the content. A sense of humor is helpful in diluting intense, potentially explosive situations. In all phases of a group's existence, expression of resistance is inevitable, particularly in the conflict phase. It will be expressed in a variety of ways, such as:

1. Hostile or aggressive verbalization or mannerisms, including criticism, attack, ridicule of an individual, or physically disruptive behavior.
2. Diversionary behaviors, such as "horsing around," squabbling between two or more members, "joking," and so on, which attempt to divert the group's attention from the group's deliberation.
3. Attempts to take over group leadership from the adult leader.

4. Attempts to win others over to support one's point of view through flattery or by threats.
5. Interruption.
6. Attempts to get special privileges.

The leader must not react emotionally, hostilely, or sarcastically to any expressions of resistance. At an appropriate moment, he might call attention to these manifestations, try to help those who display disruptive actions to become more aware of what they are doing and why, and to realize that their interference is of no help to anyone, including themselves. In time, individual children will support the worker in calling attention to resistance, taking the initiative to remind the disrupter(s) that established ground rules are being violated and the group's work is being hampered.

Development of Cohesiveness

Following the tumultuous conflict phase, the group begins to express a desire for intergroup harmony. Although individual differences continue to be voiced, they are secondary to the developing sense of group cohesiveness. Willingness to listen, to think through disagreements, and to work together toward the achievement of mutually planned group tasks occurs. Discussion deals with individual and group problems, maladaptive behavior which is harmful to harmonious group life, and suggestions for change. This seems to indicate a greater awareness of socially acceptable values and understanding of the therapeutic objectives of the residence, which is also carried over to varying degrees in other aspects of group life.

The relationship between child care workers and the group is strengthened significantly in the course of this process. There is less ambivalence toward adult authority, greater respect, and inclination to accept the worker's values. During this phase, the worker as group leader has the opportunity to introduce an "educational" component into the group sessions by presenting to the group, when appropriate, his own thinking about social issues and values.

Experience with adolescent groups (Adler and Berman 1960) indicated that when a group reaches a more mature level and raises questions of concern to them on subjects such as drugs, sex, delinquent behavior, and abortion, the leaders need not hesitate to explain and share knowledge and attitudes regarding acceptable values and standards of behavior. The boys and girls involved in these groups became more receptive because they had developed a greater sense of trust and confidence in the leaders and could, therefore, permit themselves to hear what was being said. Eventually, they were intrigued by the possibility of trying the social standards their group leaders represented; many of the youngsters seemed to be gratified by the adoption of more mature standards of perceiving, thinking, and behaving. The change was probably in large part due to the experience of participating in the group process. Wolins (1974: 27) states: "Participation, then, is a critical matter in any social system that intends to promote growth, propel members in the direction of common values and have its norms win out, after a change in setting."

Reference has been made to a single leader. This doesn't exclude dual or multiple leadership, depending on the number of child care workers working simultaneously with a group. Multiple leadership requires common objectives, coordinated effort, mutual respect, and similarity in attitudes and values. The leaders must demonstrate to the group that adults can work together in harmony. If they are not "in tune," the group will tend to test them, attempt to split them for manipulative purposes. For many of the children who have experienced adult disharmony and conflict within their own families, neighborhood, or school, it will confirm the generalization that the child care workers are like the other adults and cannot be trusted but can be controlled or manipulated. When changes in group leadership take place because of staff turnover, new workers will require preparation, training, and close supervision in order to participate as group discussion leaders. They should start as observers and gradually increase active participation as leaders. Changes in staff, like changes in the child population, require discussion by the group because they involve separation. Separation has to be worked through because it reactivates the pain and trauma of separation from family and friends which all the children have experienced.

Continuation of group meetings with a group that has achieved a sense of cohesiveness has validity. Maintenance of such stability is essential for perpetuating a therapeutic milieu. It facilitates the adjustment of new members as the population of the group changes. The newcomer is expected to adapt to standards of behavior supported by the peer group as well as staff. Some may initially attempt to disrupt this pattern, but they are unlikely to succeed because the peer group exerts a powerful force in promoting values. There are, of course, situations where a youngster can't adapt because of the severity of his illness and has to be transferred to a more structured protective setting. Such an event is an appropriate subject for group discussion.

Regardless of the theoretical orientation or methodology practiced in a particular group care setting, group activity involving children and staff in group discussion, joint planning, collective effort, and evaluation can further the therapeutic objectives of the program.

PRIVACY

It is important for a child to be by himself, to be able to think, read, work, or play in privacy. This is difficult in group living because of physical limitations of space or requirements regarding accountability. The latter refers to programs where the child care workers are held responsible for knowing at all times the whereabouts of every child. Accountability is important for safety and, when interpreted as such, conveys to children adult concern and caring. However, when used as a rationale for adult control or when it is based on suspicion and lack of confidence in children's capabilities to be alone without getting into mischief, it is neither helpful nor therapeutic. As much as possible, opportunities should be provided for a child to be by himself in his own room, or in a corner in a common room, or outside the cottage. Occasional informal checks by the workers should meet accountability requirements. A period of each day should be scheduled as "free time" to allow children to pursue individual activities of interest to them.

ETHNIC AND RELIGIOUS DIFFERENCES

Cultural, ethnic, and religious diversity are also important in group living. Each child's heritage and identity deserve respect and attention. When the population of an institution is heterogeneous, as most are today, the total program should take into consideration the varied identities among the children. The religious education program provides classes and services for each major religious group. Religious holidays are given recognition so that each religious group can celebrate according to its customs. Food should reflect cultural diversity, not only to meet the tastes of a particular group but also to acquaint the other children with a variety of foods. Above all, staff attitudes should reflect tolerance and respect for all differences. The benefits derived go beyond a responsibility to provide reinforcement of the children's cultural, ethnic, and religious identities; they reflect pluralism in democratic living. The entire population is enriched by education in diversity and the practice of tolerance.

Cultural diversity can also have a direct impact on cottage living. To quote Steinfeld (1975),

> More than any other factor, the quality of institutional life and group care is determined by the way the children treat one another. Therefore, the major task of all staff is enabling children to live together in peace. This requires acceptable outlets for aggression and frustration, opportunities for learning, growth and achievement of self-esteem. All this leads to an acceptance of difference or the assurance that the unique or even provocative aspects of an individual are no personal threat, but in fact a source of fascination. The behavior, race, language, religion, home background of one's roommate or classmate, however different, are not fearful. I have found that the religious and cultural diversity of children offers a special opportunity to communicate these concepts of respect for difference, and so transform fear and hatred of one's peers to creative group living.

Oversensitivity, insecurity, and uncertainty about dealing with ethnic differences may at times immobilize a child care worker. Burns (1971: 93) states:

> There is no magic that can prevent confusion, conflict and anxiety around racial situations at this time. However, there are some points to be made: All workers, no matter what their classification, need constantly to look at and try to face their true attitudes and biases. Black workers as well as white workers have problems in working with black children.

Burns recounts an experience with one of his workers, who was white, who had difficulty in handling a small group of black children. He was not setting required limits because he was worried that he would be judged unfair by black children and black staff. Burns told him, "Forget that these children are black and treat them as you would treat other children who have similar problems." To treat these children differently, Burns felt, was to be overly permissive and to "practice discrimination in reverse" (Burns 1971: 92).

In summary, the group is the focus of the child care worker's tasks; the welfare of the individual child is his primary concern. According to LeMay (1974: 37), "The group, while being the unit of work, is not an end in itself. It is a therapeutic tool." The group becomes the medium for each child's growth and development, achievable only when through the efforts of the child care workers the cottage or group home milieu emanates an atmosphere of acceptance, warmth, and sensitivity to the children's needs as individuals and as a group. The home should provide a sense of security for all the children and encourage their participation in issues of group living.

REFERENCES

Adler J. 1979. "The Child Care Worker's Leadership in Group Process." *Child Care Quarterly* 8, no. 3: 196–205.

_____. 1973. "The Child Care Counsellor as Target of Transferred Behavior." *Child Care Quarterly* (July) 2, no. 2: 98–106.

Adler J., and I. Berman. 1960. "Multiple Leadership in Group Treatment of Delinquent Adolescents." *The International Journal of Group Psychotherapy* 19, no. 2: 213–226.

_____. 1960. "Ego–Superego Dynamics in Residential Treatment of Disturbed Adolescents." Paper presented at the 37th Annual Meeting of the American Orthopsychiatric Association. Mimeo.

Burns, C.E. 1971. "White Staff, Black Children: Is There a Problem?" *Child Welfare* 50, no. 2: 90–96.

Fant, R.S. 1971. "Use of Groups in Residential Treatment." In *Healing Through Living*, edited by M.F. Mayer and A. Blum, pp. 72–93. Springfield, Ill.: Charles C. Thomas.

Lambert, P. 1977. *The ABC's of Child Care Work in Residential Care*, The Linden Hill Manual. New York: Child Welfare League of America.

LeMay, M. 1974. *Functions of the Specialized "Educateur" for Maladjusted Youth.* English translation by V. Jarvis. Brewster, N.Y.: Green Chimneys School. Mimeo.

Mayer, M.F. 1958. *A Guide for Child Care Workers.* New York: Child Welfare League of America.

Mayer, M.F.; L.H. Richman; and E.A. Balcerzak. 1977. *Group Care of Children.* New York: Child Welfare League of America.

Polsky, H. 1962. *Cottage Six: The Social System of Delinquent Boys in Residential Treatment.* New York: Russell Sage Foundation.

Redl, F. 1966. *When We Deal with Children.* New York: Free Press.

Steinfeld, P. 1975. "Relevance of Residential Treatment." Paper presented at the National Conference of Jewish Communal Service, Grossinger's, New York. Mimeo.

Whittaker, J.K. 1979. *Caring for Troubled Children.* San Francisco: Jossey–Bass.

Wolins, M. 1974. "Some Theoretical Observations on Group Care." In *Successful Group Care*, edited by M. Wolins, pp. 7–35. Chicago: Aldine.

Yalom, I.D. 1970. *The Theory and Practice of Group Psychotherapy*. New York: Basic Books.

12 RELATIONSHIP WITH PARENTS

A child's emotional difficulties cannot be viewed apart from his family. To understand the children, one must know their families. To treat the children effectively, one must work with their families. There has been a tendency in foster care to isolate the child from his family. Although this does not necessarily represent a conscious attempt by foster care agencies to exclude the children's families, it is reflected in practice by insufficient involvement of parents after a child's placement. It may, therefore, be considered as an act of "omission" rather than of "commission." Perhaps this is due to a deeply rooted societal attitude which is unsympathetic to parents who cannot adequately care for their children and have to depend on public assistance to maintain their children in foster care or residential treatment. Child welfare workers do not seem exempt from such attitudes despite social work's commitment to the humanistic ethic of social responsibility for those who cannot be economically self-sufficient. This vestige of social Darwinism is also reflected in foster care practice in the form of a lingering "rescue fantasy" that children need to be protected and "saved" from their inadequate parents. However, the vast majority of children do not wish to be rescued from their families. If we are to expedite a child's return home, parents must be involved in the process. Since most children's problems are family-related, the treatment effort must involve their families, as the trend is increasingly doing. However, an advocacy position like Whittaker's, to advance parents to "full and equal partners in the helping process" (1979: 137–54), is still far from realization.

The degree of interaction between child care workers and parents depends on the established policies of a particular setting. A friendly relationship is encouraged. When parents visit, they should be made to feel welcome, and the worker should make himself available to them for discussion of any questions or issues of interest. When appropriate, parents should be referred for future discussions with caseworkers or administrative staff.

PARENTAL REACTION TO PLACEMENT

Parental problems account for most placements of children in foster care. This is particularly true of children designated as dependent or neglected who are in placement in foster homes, group homes, group residences, and general institutions. On the other hand, the major reasons for placement in institutions for the mentally retarded, or in residential treatment centers for emotionally disturbed children, are considered to be within the children themselves (Bernstein, Snider, and Meezan 1975: 11). A clear dichotomy cannot be made between a child's and his parents' problems because both interrelate and contribute to the circumstances which may eventually lead to a decision to place the child in placement.

Understanding of a child's background, including family experience, school, and neighborhood relationships, is helpful to the child care worker. This information should be available to him through the child's caseworker. It is particularly important because by his role he approximates a parental figure; further, many of the children in residential treatment project distorted images of parenthood upon their child care workers. If, through his expressed attitudes and behavior, a child care worker resembles the child's actual parent with whom he was in conflict, it is more likely that the child will try to replicate his accustomed destructive relationship patterns in his relationship with the worker. Group care of children involves also having sensitive and complex relationships with parents. The way parents feel about placing their child has important implications for the course of his adjustment. Parents who were unable to manage a child may feel guilty about their failure. They handle this guilt in a variety of ways.

Some try to alleviate it by viewing the residence as the "perfect" place, so that they will feel better about placing their child. Such parents are pleasant to child care workers. Others may make up for their guilt feelings by overindulging their children during visits, helping them violate regulations, giving them extra money, and collaborating with them in their attempt to perpetuate pathological patterns of behavior. Still others need to maintain the delusion that their child alone is responsible for his failings and that no one can succeed with him. They tend to look for difficulties in the child's adjustment in the institution and negate his progress in order to convince themselves that he cannot be helped by anyone. They may disparage the institution and its staff to the child; in this way they attempt to sabotage his efforts to adapt and to benefit from treatment. Such parents seem to have a stake in perpetuating their child's emotional disturbance.

Some parents whose children were committed through the courts against their wishes may not be cooperative. The most difficult are those who will complain to administration about residential staff, send complaints to the city and state agencies, and collect grievances in order to prove that their child should not be in placement. A child care worker, irritated by such parents, may understandably wish they would take their child home. While this would remove a taxing experience for staff, it would harmful to the child. This is exemplified by the following incident.

"I can't take another Sunday like yesterday," complained John to his supervisor.

"Is it the Stone family again?" asked Mr. Thomas.

"Yes," responded John wearily. "Every time they visit, they cause dissension, influence Danny to be sassy to us, and distress other parents, some of whom just leave the living room when they arrive because they can't tolerate their behavior. Most of the parents are fine and we enjoy their visits because it gives us an opportunity to get to know them and to talk about the children's adjustment. The Stone family, on the other hand, come in with a chip on their shoulders and, as soon as they enter, begin to complain about the food, about Danny's schoolwork, about our supposed negative attitudes toward the children, and the poor administration of the institution. Sunday was the limit because they accused me of having hit Danny. This was absolutely not true. We had had a run-in with Danny on Thursday and when I threatened him with consequences if he did not leave the other kids alone, he threatened to tell his father on me.

Well, he certainly told a lie, and when I confronted him about this, Danny said he did not say that I had hit him, just simply threatened him. His father warned me that if I ever hit Danny, he would take me to court. Mrs. Stone constantly investigates the state of the kitchen, and one time, she went up to the boys' rooms to check whether everything was in order. Sometimes I would like to physically throw them out of the cottage but I've controlled myself. How long will this go on? If they carry on this way, I don't think we will be able to do anything with Danny. Perhaps he should be transferred out of our cottage. Maybe we should take up on Mrs. Stone's frequent threats that she will take Danny out of the institution."

"The Stones can be pretty rough sometimes," sympathized Mr. Thomas. "They are both very disturbed people. Mr. Stone has been hospitalized a number of times. Despite their threats, they really don't want Danny at home because they can't manage him. It would be quite easy for us to have Danny out of here but it would not do him any good. We've tried to restrict visiting by Mr. and Mrs. Stone. We've even petitioned the court, and the judge told Mr. and Mrs. Stone to behave themselves, but apparently they are unable to comply. I appreciate the difficulties they are causing and I think you have done well to control your actions to their provocations. Don't talk to them too much and if they press you, suggest that they see the administrative person on duty. Whenever I'm on Sunday duty, I'll be glad to talk to them."

"I suppose it's the best we can do," said John. "But it's really unfair to all of us, including Danny."

The above exemplifies extreme parental reaction and possibly displaced emotions which are difficult to cope with. It also represents intense parental distress which merits sensitivity, understanding, and a helping effort. Families like the Stones may be difficult to involve in a cooperative working relationship. They cannot and should not be ignored or discarded. Some parents may hesitate or be fearful of becoming involved, and a few may actively resist or reject an agency's effort to work with them. However, all deserve a reaching-out to make them feel wanted and needed in a mutual effort to help them and their children.

HOME VISITS

Families are involved through casework services with parents, home visits by the children, and visiting by parents. Home visits provide an opportunity for children to be with their families during weekends or holidays. These reunions are discussed and the interactions examined in casework sessions with parents and children separately and, when feasible, in joint sessions including the child, his parents, and siblings. Home visits can also be used by the child to evaluate changes in attitudes toward parents and former friends in the neighborhood. Regularly scheduled visits should be encouraged, although they should be planned carefully according to the child's needs and the family's capacity to cope with his presence. It is important that the child's caseworker be aware of the way the child makes use of the home visits and how he and his family spend time at home. Misuse of home visits by children, or neglect or abuse of children during home visits, should be discussed with the child and his parents; a decision is then made as to whether the home visits should be suspended, reduced in frequency, or eliminated.

PARENT VISITING

In most settings, visiting by parents generally takes place on weekends when the professional staff does not work. In certain institutions a caseworker is on duty during parent visiting time to permit discussions of their children's adjustment and progress. The degree of interaction between child care workers and parents depends on the established policies of a particular setting. A friendly relationship is encouraged in most places.

Observations by the worker of the interaction between a child and his parents is important and should be recorded or reported to caseworkers. The following are suggested guidelines.

1. How does the child relate to his visitors? Is he actively hostile, distant, indifferent, or is he happy to see them?
2. What is the effect of the visit on the child? Is he anxious before the visitors arrive? Is he distressed, angry, or happy about the parental visit?
3. Observation regarding a child's reactions before or after home visits is also important. If he is anxious before the visit or distressed after he returns to the institution, this should be reported to the caseworker for further followup.

The worker is also (indirectly) involved with a child's family through the child's home visits, mail, or phone calls. His observations regarding a child's reaction before and following a home visit (as well as during parental visits) or to telephone communication with a member of his family are important. He may have to cope with a child's feelings and displacements following a frustrating contact with his family; he may help allay anxieties, anger, or disappointments generated by such visits. More positively, he can reinforce a child's satisfaction of a gratifying home visit, and then share his observation with members of the group care team.

REFERENCES

Bernstein, B.; D. A. Snider; and W. Meezan. 1975. *A Preliminary Report—Foster Care Needs and Alternatives to Placement.* New York: State Board of Social Welfare.

Whittaker, J. K. 1979. *Caring for Troubled Children.* San Francisco: Jossey-Bass.

13 STAFF RELATIONSHIPS

The child care worker consults with social workers, teachers, and recreational workers. He also has contact with nurses, psychiatrists, psychologists; supervisory and administrative personnel; housekeeping, clerical, and maintenance staff; and the director. The following is a description of the role and function of staff with whom the child care worker may interact in various types of group settings.

THE STAFF

Caseworkers

The caseworker is involved with children from intake through discharge and frequently in aftercare services. He sees the child regularly and is his therapist in many settings; he is in contact with the child's family and, if necessary, community agencies; he is responsible for maintaining the child's case record, for writing reports to cooperating agencies, and for the preparation of required statistical reporting for administrative and research purposes.

Cooperation and continuous interchange of information between child care workers and caseworkers are of utmost importance in the realization of established treatment goals. The caseworker's knowledge of the child's history, his family, and his feelings and attitudes— and the child care worker's observations of the child's

231

functioning — should be freely shared. Child care information of interest to caseworkers include the following:

1. Problems related to physical care such as grooming and overall personal hygiene.
2. Sleep routines, including problems regarding falling asleep or waking.
3. Food idiosyncracies, including food fads, overeating or undereating, and behavior while dining.
4. Use of leisure time, including the child's interests, and his attitude in recreational and play activities.
5. Adaptability to cottage routines.
6. Relationship with cottage staff, particularly his attitude toward them: Does he cling or withdraw, is he hostile, or does he comply passively? Does he tend to manipulate or to be cooperative?
7. Relationship with peers, including his capacity for friendship, leadership role, and acceptability by others.
8. Reactions during parental visits.
9. Reaction to illness and prescribed medication.

Teachers

Generally, children in residential treatment settings have experienced frustration and partial or complete failure in community schools. Consequently, they come to view education with reservations. They have misgivings about their learning capacities and preconceived stereotypes about teachers. There is apt to be little contact between child care workers and teachers if the children attend off-ground school. Where education takes place within the institution, communication between them is facilitated. Interchange of information with teachers and involvement in the child's education process convey to children that their child care workers are interested in their learning.

Medical

Child care workers are involved with the medical services through scheduled sick-call at the infirmary, emergencies, preventive medicine, and accidents. They are generally first to become aware of a child's complaints about not feeling well; they bring him to the infirmary for examination and treatment; they may dispense medication.

Psychiatrists

The psychiatrist usually functions as a consultant to staff. He sees individual children for diagnostic purposes or, in crisis situations, prescribes medication and, when necessary, arranges for psychiatric hospitalization. As a member of the residential treatment team, he participates in treatment planning and evaluation conferences. He is also involved in staff training and may carry some treatment cases.

Psychologists

Psychologists are responsible for psychological testing for psychodiagnostic purposes and may also function as therapists and consultants.

Recreation Workers

The number and type of recreation specialists depend on the size and scope of the institution's program. When recreation is provided by a separate department, child care workers may be involved in consulting recreation staff regarding their children's functioning. They are responsible for supervising children's movements to scheduled activities and for orienting activity group leaders to an individual child's needs, attitudes, and behavior in group situations. In turn, recreation leaders should inform child care workers of a child's functioning in activities, development skills, relationship to other children, and anxieties evoked by certain activities. They can also be helpful as resource persons in planning leisure-time cottage activities.

Religious Workers

The religious program, comprising religious education and services, provides opportunities for continuity of children's religious identification. Child care workers accompany children to religious services. Consultation with the religious workers regarding children's religious attitudes can be helpful.

Other Personnel

The child care worker also has occasion to deal with institutional personnel not directly involved in the treatment of children, such as housekeepers, dining room and kitchen staff, office and maintenance workers.

Volunteers

Volunteers serve in residential treatment in a number of capacities, including teacher assistants, tutors, recreation specialists or aides, and companions to children. The volunteer "is an adult who stands somewhere between a parent person and a peer and represents a bridge between adult and peer relationships" (Hirschfield and Starr 1971: 98).

In terms of leisure-time activities, the volunteer assigned to a child provides essential relationships and social activities on grounds or outside the institution on a regular continuing basis. In the case of "Big Brothers" and "Big Sisters," the child has opportunities to spend time in their homes which, by selection, represent harmonious family living.

Child care workers are (or should be) consulted about the assignment of a child to a volunteer. Knowing their children intimately, they can be helpful in the selection of one appropriate to a particular child's personality and needs, as well as his readiness to participate in a relationship with a friendly, interested adult other than his relatives or staff. The relationship between volunteer and child care worker is friendly and noncompetitive. It is generally not as intensive or as extensive as that between the volunteer and the child's caseworker, who generally supervises the volunteer's activities. The volunteer should be given recognition for his contribution to a child's treatment, and the child care workers can, by their attitude, convey appreciation when the volunteer visits the cottage.

CHILD CARE SUPERVISION[a]

The child care supervisor is responsible for the professional development, monitoring, and evaluation of his workers. He orients them to the philosophy and practice of group care of children. In his educa-

a. The scope of child care supervision is outlined in Appendix II.

tional capacity, he helps the worker develop knowledge, skills, and attitudes relative to his role and functions. Administratively, he sets standards and expectations which he monitors to assist the worker to maintain a high level of competency. In his supportive role, he is sensitive to the emotional stress generated by crises and work pressures. The effective supervisor provides a supervisory climate and relationship that nurtures in his workers a sense of gratification in their work, professional growth, and a feeling that they play a significant role in helping the children in their care. These expectations are not unrealistic. When they are not achieved, strains in the worker–supervisor relationship may develop. Without a sense of mutual respect and trust, openness in supervisory conferences is hindered and skepticism of supervision flourishes. In such a climate, workers, particularly those new at the job, may find themselves in a dilemma about consulting their supervisor, as the following incident illustrates:

"You seem troubled about something, Don," commented John, as he and Don were relaxing in the children's staff rooms after hours.

"I didn't realize that it shows," replied Don. "I'm concerned about Billy. He seems to resent my authority. He is the tough guy in the cottage, and he bullies the younger kids. When I ask him to do his chores, he is resentful and is far from cooperative. What gets me most are his snide remarks and defiant attitude."

"Perhaps he is testing you since you are young and relatively new on the job," said John. "Maybe you have to show him that you are the 'boss' in the cottage."

"You may be right," replied Don. "We could have a confrontation. If I had to rough him up, I could easily do so, but I don't believe in hitting kids. However, there are times when Billy gets me so angry! I don't know when he'll drive me to lose control of myself. . . . so I often feel on edge."

"Why don't you take Billy aside and tell him what he is doing to you? He may not even be aware of what he is doing and doesn't realize he may be pressing you too far. If I recall correctly, he's not too bright," said John.

"Maybe you are right. I should have done this earlier," said Don. "But I have also been thinking about consulting my supervisor. But I'm conflicted. Mr. Daniels may be able to help me deal with Billy and my own reactions to him. But then I'm concerned he'll think I can't handle my boys."

"I wouldn't do it if I were in your place. There is the risk he'll begin to wonder about your capabilities. If your talk with Billy doesn't bring results, he may need a little roughing-up to get him to respect you," said John.

"But in our orientation session, we were urged to consult our supervisor if we had problems with the kids! And as for roughing kids up, I'd rather not be in child care work if I have to resort to strong-arm methods," Don exclaimed.

"Suit yourself. I've been in this work longer than you; I think I know better," replied John.

After Don left the staff room, he was still worried. "Maybe John is right. Maybe I should not bring this problem to Mr. Daniels. But if I don't and there is a blowup with Billy, won't I be worse off?"

John may have been well-meaning but not helpful to Don. He has injected doubt and distrust of a supervisor and has misguided a young, thoughtful, and concerned worker. A sense of trust is essential for openness in communicating, for frankness in expressing feelings, and for confidence that one will be listened to with sympathy. In such an atmosphere, situations can be discussed objectively, errors examined without fear, and with a sense of comfort gained that one can learn from mistakes.

Generally, child care workers meet with their supervisors for regularly scheduled individual or group conferences and, as needed, for special and emergency situations. As much as is possible, supervisory conferences should be based on an agenda prepared by the worker. If one is submitted in advance, it is helpful to the supervisor because he can prepare for it ahead of time. Phone calls and other such interruptions should be kept at a minimum. Problem-solving is the major focus of a supervisory conference. According to Fant and Ross (1979: 638), the problem-solving approach assumes that:

> once the problem is clearly identified, the worker can be helped to think through various productive responses. This approach points out to the worker that problems in child care do not have stock answers, but rather there is a continuum ranging from ineffective responses on the one end, to productive responses on the other. The supervisor helps the worker: 1) to state the goal; 2) to identify the problem; 3) to break down the problem and define the parts; 4) to develop a plan of action for each part of the problem; 5) to anticipate pros and cons of each plan of action; 6) to develop a system of feedback to monitor the intervention; and 7) to evaluate outcomes and make adjustments.

The following is a suggested outline for evaluating interactions between worker and children. It may be used to evaluate situations with a group as well as with individuals.

1. Describe the incident.
2. What action did you take?
3. What was the outcome? On the child, on the group (if other children were involved or witnessed the incident)?

Analysis of the Incident

1. What do you think made the child act as he did? (What is your interpretation of his behavior—its motive and objective?)
2. What was your feeling toward the child at the time of the incident?
3. What were the reasons for the action you took? (What did you try to achieve?)
4. Were there alternative actions you could have taken?
5. How did you feel after it was over?
6. How did the child act toward you after the incident?
7. If other children observed the situation, how did they react to the child and to you?
8. If another worker was on duty with you and observed the incident, what was his reaction?
9. If the incident was a crisis situation or had consequences which were distressing, do you now think it could have been foreseen and the crisis prevented? How?

Evaluation conferences are also held periodically to assess work performance. According to Mayer (1958: 160–161), these should cover a wide range of subjects, including the worker's relationship with individual children, the group and his co-workers, his management and organizational capabilities in the cottage, and his ability to function within the administrative structure of the agency. They should convey to the worker his strengths and the progress he has made, as well as weaknesses and areas requiring improvement.

Written evaluations are essential personnel practice requirements. The first evaluation covers the probationary period (generally six months). Subsequent evaluations are written periodically, varying from twelve to eighteen months. Whether an evaluation is in narrative form, a checklist, or combination of both, it should succinctly cover the following:

1. Worker's understanding and commitment to agency's philosophy, policies, and practices.
2. Degree of conformity to administrative requirements—attendance, punctuality, adherence to work schedule, personal appearance, degree of responsibility.

3. Level of knowledge, skills, motivation, and capacity to learn.

4. Capacity for self-awareness and empathy for others. Capacity for relationships.

5. Capacity for relationships with:

    (a) *children* — capacity to communicate with the children and to evoke responsiveness from them; to what extent do they respond to his guidance and demands? To what extent does he serve as a potential model for them?

    (b) *fellow workers* (child care teams) — degree of cooperativeness, coping with disagreements, degree of respect he evokes from others, and so on.

    (c) *members of interdisciplinary team* — caseworkers, teachers, and so on.

6. Leadership qualities within children's group, in work team.

7. Capacity to assess a child's functioning in group, set goals and formulation of service or treatment plans for individual children and the group as a whole.

8. Functioning in crisis situation.

9. Uses of one's authority with children, handling of disciplinary problems.

10. Use of supervision (attitudes toward supervision, how he prepares and functions in supervisory conferences).

11. Attitudes and performance in *recording* requirements.

12. Summary of areas of strengths and weaknesses.

13. Areas requiring further work, suggestions and expectations for the ensuing evaluation period.

INTEGRATION

The quality of the relationships among the staff affects its therapeutic effectiveness. Ideally, the various disciplines represented on the team function as an integrated whole for planning and evaluation of treatment objectives. The obstacles to interdisciplinary integration may range from organizational structure of the institution, differential status levels among the staff, differential working conditions, to personality factors. These may block channels of communication and generate tensions which become impediments to the development of a sense of team cohesiveness and purpose.

Successful teamwork requires the following (Lemay 1976):

1. A common treatment orientation among the members of the team.
2. A commitment to common treatment objectives.
3. Clear definition of diagnostic and treatment goals.
4. Consistency of approach based on common understanding of a child and his needs.
5. Mutuality of understanding and genuine respect for each other's skills and contribution to the treatment effort.
6. A sense of professional identity as a member of the working team.
7. Ongoing interaction and collaboration.
8. Readiness to face and resolve disagreements.

These qualities can be developed when there is a commitment to close collaboration and administrative supports. The organizational structure of a residential setting is a determinant factor. A comparison of three organizational models—The departmental, team, and psychoeducateur—will serve to illustrate this.

The Departmental Model

Staff is organized in separate departments of child care, education, medical, psychiatry and psychology, social work (the last three may comprise the "clinic" or clinical department), and recreation. Although interaction among the various disciplines is encouraged and planning and evaluation conferences on individual children may include representation from all of the disciplines working with the child, each discipline functions as a separate entity with the clinical as the dominating and directing influence. The departmental separateness and professional status hierarchy may impede the development of a sense of team cohesiveness. It tends to generate tension and misunderstanding among the members of the team, resulting in inconsistencies in dealing with children and in implementing treatment planning. The child care worker is particularly affected. He frequently feels inferior in status to his "professional" colleagues.

This model, prevalent in large residential programs, has undergone modification to facilitate team functioning. Many institutions have been divided administratively into quasi-independent units serving forty to fifty children each, while maintaining their departmental structure. There are weekly unit meetings, generally including the clinical and child care staff. All planning and evaluation conferences take place within the structure of the unit.

The Team Model

This model eliminates separate departments. The basic administrative unit consists of all the staff working with a particular group of children. All members of the team participate and are equal in the decision-making process. Regularly scheduled weekly team meetings are given the highest priority. Administrative problems are shared, inconsistencies and staff conflict resolved, policy discussed, individual and group treatment plans formulated, and crisis situations reviewed. This model, according to Garner (1977), is operating successfully in a number of American public and voluntary residential treatment programs in the Midwest and the South.

The Psychoeducateur Model

This model, developed in Montreal, is a radical departure from those desired above. The key person is the psychoeducateur, a new type of professional who incorporates a number of roles including child care, education, recreation, and counseling. He becomes the most significant person in the child's life, integrating all aspects of treatment. This requires a highly competent, educated, and trained individual. All activities take place in the living unit. For example, in Boscoville, a residential treatment center for adolescent boys near Montreal, a team of five psychoeducateurs are responsible for weekly coverage of a group of sixteen boys. Each worker has total responsibility for three or four boys whom he sees individually in counseling sessions. In addition, each one, when on duty, works with the group as their teacher, recreation worker, and group counselor. The psychoeducateur consults with social workers who see the boys' parents and with psychologists and psychiatrists as needed. He facilitates a youngster's integration into community life when he is ready for discharge.

The psychoeducateur model circumscribes the child's relationship network, thus reducing the scope of transference and countertransference possibilities and manipulation. It enhances identification with staff and value incorporation. The wholeness of the child is more readily maintained because parts of him are not portioned out to various specialists—caseworker, child care worker, teacher, and recreation worker.

This model is attractive to child care workers in the United States because it represents a high degree of professionalism, and material and personal benefits, and to administrators because it tends to be more efficient and perhaps less costly than the multidisciplinary models. However, the psychoeducateur is not a child care worker but a composite of four disciplines. The development of such a professional is costly, requiring a commitment by government to fund training programs analogous to the existing *École de Psychoeducation* at the University of Montreal. In the United States, we have just entered an initial and financially modest phase of government support through Title XX funds for the training of child care workers. We must also overcome deeply ingrained, historically determined attitudes regarding the child care worker's role in group care. Because jobs might be eliminated, the psychoeducateur model may pose a threat to the teaching and social work professions; however, this should not exclude efforts to develop it in the United States.

Realistically, therefore, the current emphasis is on improved interdisciplinary integration in existing models. The team model represents highly promising possibilities. Much can also be done in the departmental model.

TREATMENT PLANNING

Planning a child's treatment begins at intake with an initial assessment of his needs and the formulation of long-term objectives. When he is accepted for a particular group care program, an admission statement should be prepared and made available to staff. It should contain a brief description of the child's social functioning, emotional and physical problems which may affect his daily care, educational abilities, skills and other positive attributes, the living unit to which he is assigned (cottage, group home, and so on) and reason for the selection, caseworker assignment, school program, and initial strategies to be used by staff of the various disciplines in caring for the child related to the problems he presents at admission. These plans are generally tentative since knowledge of the child is incomplete. Direct observation during the initial period of residence by staff directly involved with him (caseworkers, child care workers, teachers, recreational workers) and psychological, psychiatric examinations contribute to a more precise assessment of his needs. The input of each discipline contributes to the formulation of a more comprehensive treatment plan which should be made between thirty and forty-five days following admission. It should include:

1. Long-term goals such as projected length of residence and discharge objectives (return to family, adoption, independent living, or long-term care) as well as specification of problem areas in relation to the child and his family which will require attention and services.

2. Short-term goals within group living, the educational and recreational programs, casework and psychotherapy, targeted for a three- to six-month period.

3. Service plan directed at behavior which requires immediate attention. These may include aggression or withdrawal, habit disorders like enuresis, phobic reactions, learning problems, and so on. This is particularly important in relation to classroom or group life because a child's problematic behavior affects not only his functioning but other children's as well.

The initial evaluation conference aims at a more specific assessment of the child and family and provides the basis for developing a service plan which outlines the treatment process. Goals to be achieved are identified, as are services which all members of the interdisciplinary team will provide in working toward achieving time-targeted treatment goals. A treatment goal should communicate to those working with the child or family results which are to be achieved. It may specify a behavioral change for the child such as control of temper tantrums, stealing, enuresis, lessening of specific fears, or improvement in learning or social skills. It may aim at changes in feelings and attitudes toward oneself, peers, learning, toward authority figures and family members; for a family, improved marital relationships, parental acceptance of the child's handicap, or more consistency during home visits. The target date is the anticipated date when a specific goal is to be achieved. It should not be viewed as an absolute since it may change with circumstances. Basically the target date is when the specified goal will be evaluated (for example, three months for a short-term goal). At that time, the delineated services which have been provided will also be assessed and modified if necessary.

The child care worker's contribution to the initial conference is a statement of the team's observations of the child's reaction to placement, his strengths and difficulties in adapting to the various group living routines and expectations, his interaction with peer and staff, and specifics of problematic behavior. These comprise the child care assessment. This part is followed by suggestions regarding goals in group living and strategies to deal with target behaviors. The final decision regarding goals and intervention techniques will be determined by consensus of the interdisciplinary team. Followup conference will evaluate progress, modify strategies and goals as necessary until the final discharge conference.

When it is not possible for all members of the child care team to be present at a planning conference, the team should meet to review goals and proposed intervention strategies in order to apply them consistently or to allocate various responsibilities to different numbers. For example, one worker may be more suitable or feel more comfortable in dealing with specific techniques.

As indicated, the evaluation conference deliberations should include the formulation of guidelines and specifics of child care management strategies. Precise solutions may not always be possible. What is essential is that the child care workers come away with a clearer understanding of the behavior that they have to face in daily living with the child, and realistic guidelines which may help them cope with the problems. Diffused guidelines and unclear or unrealistic strategies, expressed sympathy without the provision of additional supports to deal with a highly disruptive child, is neither helpful nor appreciated by child care workers. In such cases, they may feel that their input of information, questions they raise, or suggestions they propose to deal with the problem are not given sufficient consideration by the more professional members of the team.

The following situation illustrates child care worker's dilemma in implementing recommendations of professional staff which they consider unrealistic.

Ann and Jean came to the evaluation and planning conference on Mary, determined to convey to the professional members of the team that they could no longer cope with her unless they had additional help in the cottage and more specific guidelines to deal with her. Her presence was disrupting cottage life, and hurting staff and the other kids.

They hoped they would get to this issue quickly, but as usual, a lot of time was devoted to reports by the caseworker, psychologist, psychiatrist, and educational counselor. Both of them reported their misgivings about Mary. For three months they have been trying to cope with her temper outbursts, defiance, threats, and the bullying of the younger girls. She required more attention than all the other kids combined, which was not fair to the other children. The prescribed medication has not made much of a difference. "Maybe she needs to be in an older group where she would not hurt others because she would be afraid of the bigger girls," suggested Ann.

Mary's social worker, Mrs. Fowler, felt she was not mature enough for an older group. She explained that Mary's current family situation was very upsetting to her. Her mother was still in the psychiatric hospital, and her father's alcoholism was no help. During her last home visit, he was drunk and hit her. Perhaps home visits should be curtailed. Mary now talked more freely about her parents, but she was still very upset by them. She may be displacing her feelings toward them unto the child care staff. The school report confirmed Mary's disruptive behavior in class, although, it also indicated her potential to do well academically. Dr. Barnard, the psychiatrist, sympathized with the child care worker's struggle. An increase in dosage of the medication might diminish Mary's anxiety and reduce her aggressiveness. He urged Ann and Jean to continue their efforts. Mary needed the structure of their cottage; she could not cope with older girls. It would take more time for her to become less fearful of relationships with others and to develop greater inner controls to cope with her hostile impulses.

"But how can we deal with her outbursts, defiance, and abuse of other children? She punched little Jane yesterday!" exclaimed Jean.

"Keep trying," suggested Dr. Barnard. "With increased medication and an additional weekly therapy session, which I recommend, things might take a turn for the better."

Mrs. Fowler added that she knew how difficult it had been for the child care staff, but it was essential that they continue working with her.

Mr. Flint, unit supervisor who chaired the meeting, added that they all realized the strain Mary's behavior imposed on the child care staff. "Do the best you can. We'll try to give you all the support we can." Dr. Barnard's recommendations would be implemented; "Let's hope things will soon change for the better. If not, we will meet again to reevaluate the situation," he concluded. After the meeting Jean said, "We sure get a lot of sympathy but little help."

Ann wondered, "Should we have been more persistent about getting more specific guidelines to deal with Mary? Should we have asked for additional staff coverage to cope with Mary's need for attention? Finally, should we have insisted that Mary should be transferred to another cottage because we are at the 'end of our rope' in coping with her?"

"It would have been useless. They seem determined to keep Mary where she is, and so we have to carry on and suffer!" Jean said bitterly.

"They don't know what to do with her either . . . she can't be discharged, so we're stuck with her," Ann said.

"Maybe they'll be more convinced that we are right when there is another serious blowup and some kid gets hurt," Jean exclaimed.

Input by clinical members of the team about diagnostic classification, explanation of etiology of a disorder, and a generalized approach to helping a child overcome his difficulties is not sufficient for the child care workers who live with and have to manage the disruptive behaviors. They need to get a more specific response to the following question: "Given a specific behavior disorder of the child, what specific remedy or therapeutic technique can best be applied?" (Schaeffer and Millman 1978: 1).

The guidelines and management strategies the child care workers and their team colleagues formulate in the interdisciplinary deliberations give direction to the child care worker's therapeutic role. When recorded in the child care record, the plan should enhance consistency in carrying it out by the various child care workers comprising the group care team. As part of the child's record, it represents accountability within the overall treatment plan.

The following case example is illustrative of interdisciplinary case conference planning. It includes recorded initial evaluation and discharge planning conferences. The focus is on planning.

I. INITIAL PLANNING CONFERENCE

September 25, 1977.

I. Description of Child

Tim C., a white, Protestant child, age 10, was admitted on September 2, 1976, from his home on Family Court on a Neglect Petition.

II. Family Composition

Tim is an only child of a divorced family. Mother, Ann nee Williamson, age 33, has been hospitalized several times (most recently on September 8, 1977, with diagnosis of Manic Depressive Psychoses.) She was unemployed, receiving supplementary public assistance to supplement Mr. C.'s monthly contribution of $150. Mr. C., age 35, is a construction worker, earning $15,000 annually, and seems to be an interested parent. He initiated divorce proceedings on grounds of his wife's infidelity and obtained the divorce three years ago. However, mother had custody of Tim. He also instituted a neglect petition, maintaining that Tim was neglected and abused by his mother. Tim is fearful of his mother and fond of his father, who hopes to take care of him when he remarries within a year's time. Father is now dating a young childless divorcee who seems to get along well with Tim. Father is not active in community or church affairs.

Reasons for Referral. Tim is an attractive, undernourished, anxious child who was left alone in the apartment by his emotionally unstable mother. He did not play much with other children, and had no close friends. His school performance was satisfactory, but he attended irregularly. He was enuretic and had nightmares.

III. Current Psychiatric Diagnosis

Court examination diagnosis is *Adjustment Reaction to Childhood.*

IV. Psychological Data

School testing indicates average intelligence — I.Q. 105.

V. Current Status

Child. Tim is considered an immature, anxious child who keeps to himself, avoids group games, is fearful of relating to peers and staff. He is teased by his cottage peers because of his bedwetting. He reacts with crying and pleading to go home to his father. He is no problem in school, but is behind two years in reading and arithmetic. In sessions with his caseworker, he seems depressed, complains the other children pick on him, but he likes his male child caseworkers.

Family. Caseworkers reported one contact with father, who is pleased that Tim is with us. He could not have tolerated a foster family placement. He visits Tim every Sunday. Mother has not been seen.

VI. Treatment Planning

Long-term Objectives.   Father has expressed an interest in having Tim with him after he remarries. If this occurs within a year and he also is given custody, this may be a sound plan. Caseworker will see father twice a month, and joint sessions to include his future wife is recommended. All disciplines will work to prepare Tim's return to the community. This will include development of social skills in the cottage, recreation skills in program, and individual casework sessions on a weekly basis.

Short-term Goals.   Review will take place within three months to evaluate progress in above planning in school, group care, and casework services. The service plan will include the following:

1. Sensitive handling to help Tim become more secure with adults and peers. His need for distance in social relationship should be respected, and he may require protection from other children who annoy him. Regarding his enuresis, he should be asked if he would like to be awakened at night; when he wets he

should be asked to strip his bed the following morning, change pajamas, and shower. Recreationally, he should be helped to develop sports and game skills, since he is well coordinated. Psychiatric and psychological examinations are recommended.

2. No medication is deemed necessary at this point.

3. Weekly Sunday visiting by father, except when Tim visits him. Tim will visit father every other Saturday. Father will pick him up Saturday 9 a.m. and return him on Sunday afternoon. There will be no visiting by mother since she is still hospitalized. Father refuses to take Tim to visit his mother at the hospital and Tim has not expressed a desire to do so.

I. EVALUATION CONFERENCE

January 5, 1978.

I. Current Status

Child. In cottage life, Tim seems more comfortable with peers and staff. He has begun to participate in group games and cottage sports. He eats with his fingers and gorges his food. Some of the boys tease him about this and his bedwetting, which continues to occur from three to five times weekly. Paternal visits are satisfactory.

School. Tim is doing well in school. He has raised his reading and math level by one year, and takes books out of the library. He likes his art class, and his teacher considers him talented. He has a nice voice and likes to sing. In the recreation program, he prefers arts and crafts and library club.

Casework. Tim has begun to be more verbal. He expresses satisfaction with placement, is less homesick, but looks forward to visiting with his father. Enuresis is still his greatest concern. He expresses regret that his mother is still ill in the hospital but he does not wish to see her. His drawings are less depressed in color—in his landscapes, a sun is shining over the horizon. Father is seen biweekly. He is pleased with Tim's adjustment. His girlfriend seems like a mature woman. She will resign her clerical job after they are married, since she wants to be at home when Tim returns. He has asked Family Court for Tim's custody. Staff strategies have been successful except for continued enuresis.

II. Clinical Diagnosis

Tim was examined on November 15, 1976. Diagnosis is *Adjustment Reaction to Childhood*, with enuresis as the major habit disorder. Psychological testing results indicate above-average potential (verbal I. Q., 110; performance I. Q., 100). Projectives confirm psychiatric opinion that Tim is an emotionally deprived child, still immature with a favorable prognosis.

III. Treatment Planning

Long-term Objective.   No change.

Short-term Objectives and Service Plan.   In cottage life, continue to help him develop his physical and social skills. There should be greater firmness regarding poor eating habits. He should be discouraged from piling up his plate with food and should be guided to use utensils. He should be reassured that he will get a second helping of food if he continues to be hungry. Greater activity by child care workers in relation to enuresis, to supplement medication. Intake of liquids should be discouraged before bedtime. If enuresis persists, behavior modification program should be instituted in consultation with psychiatric consultant.

Educationally, school will emphasize improving basic skills to at least grade level performance. His artistic interests will be encouraged.

Casework will focus on coordinating Tim's total adjustment, and when father's remarriage plans are certain, to Tim's preparation for discharge. Mother should be visited at the hospital, if this can be worked out, to apprise her of Tim's adjustment and future planning.

I. DISCHARGE PLANNING CONFERENCE

June 15, 1978.

I. Current Status

Tim C.'s father had recently remarried and had obtained custody. Mother was discharged from the hospital in May and was residing in a half-way house. She agreed that Tim would be better off living with his father. She expressed a desire to visit with him when she is able to do so.

Tim had continued to use the program well. He was now more outgoing, and had friends in the cottage. Enuresis is now infrequent. He had responded well to the behavior modification program and to the medication. At school, he was on grade level in basic skills. In the fall, he will be enrolled in fifth grade in his neighborhood school, which has a good program. Caseworker and father will arrange a membership in the local "Y," which has a good recreation and club program. Father and stepmother are eager for Tim's return.

II. Psychiatric Evaluation

Tim was re-examined on June 10th. He had matured a great deal; a psychiatric diagnosis was not warranted. Prognosis seemed favorable in view of caseworker's report on the adequacy of the paternal home and prospective school.

Discharge Plan.   Tim will be discharged to his father on June 30th. Care will continue on suspended payment for ninety days, subject to extension. Caseworker will visit home in July and will make sure that school transfer in September will go through without complications. She will also be available to father and Tim if they deem it necessary.

Tim may face adjustment problems in relation to living in his new home and may require some sessions, individually and jointly, with father and stepmother. Similarly, he may require attention during the initial school adjustment period. If there are problems in relation to his mother, or reactivation of symptoms, consideration should be given to referral to outpatient treatment.

PLANNING FOR A GROUP CARE UNIT

Planning for the whole group takes into consideration the children's needs, their sex, age, and level of social development, their capabilities and potential. It is different for a group of younger children than for an adolescent group, for boys or girls, or a coed group. The degree of structure the children require is also important and, as indicated in the section on group discussion methods, should include the children's participation in evolving group goals, in planning, executing, and evaluating programmed leisure-time, work, and social activities. Both staff and children should be familiar with group expectations, values, goals, and program.

Crisis situations in a group may require modification of plans or development of new strategies to cope with disruptions in day-to-day living. These may be precipitated by serious behavior difficulties on the part of individual children, runaways, delinquent acts, or instabilities related to staff. Clinical supervisory and administrative staff would generally become involved in such intervention planning.

The Child Care Team

The quality of interpersonal interaction among the child care workers in a group care unit influences the quality of its milieu. Development of a sense of trust among individuals and a sense of team cohesiveness are essential. Supervisory leadership and administrative support contribute to its evolvement and maintenance. Opportunities for the whole group to meet periodically, including time-overlap between shifts of workers, should be provided because they enhance communication and staff consistency. Group supervision and team training sessions are also helpful. The following statement by a child care worker (Myrtle Dryer of Childville), expresses this eloquently:

> Working with my co-workers has helped me tremendously to overcome many obstacles. We are able to challenge one another without getting angry.

Sharing our knowledge in staff meetings has given me the opportunity to improve my mind, provide insight and self-esteem. I feel confident when my co-workers make decisions without my presence. I am able to accept cricicism without becoming defensive. I recognize the importance of the different personalities in staff and what sort of influence they have on each child's dynamics.

REFERENCES

Fant, R.S., and A.L. Ross. 1979. "Supervision of Child Care Staff." *Child Welfare* 58, no. 10: 627-641.

Garner, H.G. 1977. "A Trip Through Bedlam and Beyond." *Child Care Quarterly* 6, no. 3: 167-179.

Hirschfield, E. and Starr, J. 1971. "The Contribution of the Volunteer to the Program of a Children's Institution." In *Healing Through Living*, edited by M.F. Mayer and A. Blum, pp. 94-108. Springfield, Ill.: Charles C. Thomas.

LeMay, M. 1976. "Treatment of Emotionally Disabled Children: A Multidisciplinary Approach." Paper presented at the Armand Esph Symposium, Westchester Division of New York Hospital.

Mayer, M.F. 1958. *A Guide for Child Care Workers.* New York: Child Welfare League of America.

Schaeffer, C.E., and H.E. Millman. 1978. *Therapies for Children.* San Francisco: Jossey-Bass.

14 COMMUNITY RELATIONSHIPS

Group care facilities, particularly the larger general institutions and residential treatment centers located outside of urban centers, function as self-contained communities for children and staff in residence. Situated at a distance from the children's neighborhoods, they tend to isolate children from the realities of community living. The disruption of this linkage turns out to be disadvantageous to children after they are discharged from care. The importance of maintaining close connections with community has been confirmed by a number of studies, among them Allerhand, Weber, and Haug (1966) and Wolins (1974). Their findings indicate that the process of linkage and preparation of a child and community for his return and aftercare services are crucial determinants of his adaptation to community living. The additional costs of staff time are compensated by the gains for the child and family as well as the agency. Viewed as an investment, the costly expenditure of money and effort during the child's residence has a better chance of success. It is less likely to be lost by (negative) forces and pressures that confront the child after discharge. The agency's involvement in the community serves an educational function as well. Its consequence is likely to be greater understanding and acceptance of the agency by the community.

Community-based group care programs are an integral part of their neighborhoods and surrounding community. The children attend neighborhood schools, use community recreational facilities, shop in

251

local stores, and interact with neighborhood residents. The child care workers are also involved in the community. Through shopping, community center activities, contacts with school, the police, service and maintenance people, they serve as representatives of the agency and advocates for the children. It is important to maintain a positive image of the program to overcome deeply ingrained fears and prejudices of neighbors who are anxious about its impact on their children and property. Outreach on the part of the agency and staff is essential. As the neighborhood becomes familiar with the program, the residents and staff, through visiting or joint activities, the misconceptions may slowly change toward understanding and even cooperation.

GROUP HOMES

The most numerous of the community-based group care facilities are the group homes. Since their inception, they have served as halfway houses for older children who could not return to their families following residence in institutions for neglected and dependent children. During the past ten years, group homes have expanded dramatically as alternatives to institutional care for the emotionally disturbed, developmentally disabled, the physically handicapped, and juvenile offenders. They are also appropriate for adolescents who cannot be treated as long as they live at home. A period of separation for the youngster from the family arena of conflict in a community-based group home can be a constructive experience for child and family. The group home, offering a therapeutic milieu for the resident and clinical services, enables him, his parents, and other family members to work on their communication problems and relationship conflicts separately and jointly. The goal for both is family reunion as soon as possible whenever this is feasible (Rosenthal, Harrison, and Harrington 1979).

Although the basic concepts, principles, and child care practices apply in group homes, there are functional differences which separate them from the larger group residences, institutions, and residential treatment centers. Hirschbach (1973) has enumerated six principles of group home care:

1. Group home care should be used only for children who require placement and who can accept the necessity for it. Unless they

are willing to participate in the program, they will not profit from it or will quickly be out of it.

2. A group home represents a community-based environment. It has to maintain good community relations; the children should feel part of it and use its educational, cultural, and recreational programs as fully and extensively as possible.

3. It should provide a living experience in a homogeneous, viable group of peers. A child should be able to form close peer and staff relationships at his own pace in accordance with his capabilities and encouragement and guidance by staff. The group composition is most important. As much as possible, it must be balanced in terms of children's strengths and pathology. Too many acting-out or destructive individuals can harm a group; too many depressed, withdrawn, unstable children may hinder healthy group development. Either extreme may be overwhelming to the child care staff.

4. The child care staff are the key people in group home programs. Unlike their colleagues in group residences and institutions, they are more isolated geographically and cannot depend on immediate assistance in time of crisis. They must cope on their own. Consequently, they should have supervision which is *intensive, dynamic* (help in developing independent functioning), and *supportive* (recognition and support).

5. The group home program must harmonize a therapeutic milieu that provides the children constructive peer–group relationship, adult guidance and identification, and clinical services which are geared to help each child work through problems of his past, present, and future.

6. Group home care is appropriate for a diversity of children's problems. Children's individual and group needs determine the goals and substance of the program.

Since group home child care staff are required to function quite independently, it is essential that they develop competency in a number of areas, several of which are unique to group home practices:

1. To a greater degree than child care workers in large residential settings, the group home worker has to be familiar with budgeting and efficient administration of funds allocated by the agency for run-

ning the household. His supervisor should explain the preparation of operational budget: how much allocated for food, children's spending money, clothing, and other expenditures, and how to present it for agency consideration. Through exploratory visits in neighborhood stores, he is able to learn where shopping is most economical. Planning of menus in terms of nutrition, taste, and cost is important. Information on nutrition should be available, either through an agency resource consultant or through literature. Inexpensive pamphlets are available through the Superintendent of Documents, U.S. Government Printing Office, Washington, D.C. 20400. The children should be familiarized with the financial resources available to the home so that they can be realistic about the economic problems entailed in running their household, and also learn about budgeting their own money, especially if they are working. The group home worker serves as a teacher as well as a model in this respect.

2. Group home workers supervise the children's task responsibilities within the home. During group meetings, problems related to house chores are discussed. There should be a daily schedule which may be posted on the bulletin board. Changes in schedule or flexibility in its application should be preceded by joint discussions between children and staff.

3. Group home living is close and intimate. There is little privacy for staff living with the children. During scheduled working hours, the group home worker is more at anchor in the home than the child care worker in an institution. Even the rooms that are their private domain are no haven from interruptions by children, even on off-duty days. The very closeness of living generates conflict which must be dealt with constructively through individual discussions, life-space interview techniques, and regularly scheduled house meetings. Teaching of household skills, value modeling, guidance, and dealing with social relationships in the house and community are all part of the group home worker's responsibilities.

4. Despite the fact that the group home worker has to rely on his own resources through much of his working day, he cannot be expected to assume all of the group care responsibilities entailed in the operation of a group home. Like all of residential care, group home treatment is an interdisciplinary endeavor and collective responsibility. No individual can do the necessary job 'single-handedly.' Agencies therefore provide casework, consultant services, and

other central services and supervision. Equally important as open communication between staff and children is the quality of the working relationship among staff members involved in a group home program. The team of group home workers must be tuned into each other as working partners and to the group home structure and program so that a consistency of values and expectations is to be conveyed to the children. They need to feel secure in their supervisory relationships, administrative support, and in their relationships with professionals such as caseworkers and consulting psychiatrists. They need to feel confident that they can talk about their concerns and work frustrations freely, that their input to the formulation of treatment goals is taken seriously. They need encouragement to consult but also to make independent decisions in crisis situations or during critical incidents when there is neither sufficient time or availability of interdisciplinary consultation. Finally, realistic consideration must be given to the weight and scope of the group home worker's responsibilities. Overworked staff, even the most dedicated and experienced, cannot do a good job. The burn-out rate among group home child care workers is high. It is the responsibility of administration to keep this at a minimum by providing adequate working conditions, administrative support, supervisory guidance, and staff development opportunities.

5. Because the group home workers are in a more isolated situation and have fewer professional resources available to them than child care workers in other group care settings, they need to develop a sense of independence and competency in carrying out treatment goals for the individual child, and in developing and maintaining a sense of group cohesiveness of the peer–staff group. It is essential that through supervision and staff training, they develop communication, counseling, and group discussion skills to help the children cope with the realities and problems of group and community living.

6. Group homes serving an adolescent population serve as a bridge to community living either by return to family or independent living. This milieu emphasizes development of responsibility, initiative, and decision-making capabilities. It is crucial for child care workers to help the residents assume increasing responsibility for self-care, household chores, involvement in planning recreational activities outside of the home, budgeting of income, and learning to shop economically; to do this, they must be exposed to situations where they

have to make sound choices to buy needed items with a fixed amount of money. Increased social demands on the youngsters through exposure to community living situations are essential.

7. The residents benefit from relationships within the community. The group home worker can help children by familiarizing himself with neighbors, school and recreational, religious, and medical resources of the neighborhood; by becoming acquainted with local merchants and police; and by introducing the children into community activities that are appropriate to individual as well as group needs. The group home workers and the children become public relations agents for the group home. The manner of their involvement and comportment will influence their acceptance and status in the community.

REFERENCES

Allerhand, M.; R. Weber; and M. Haug. 1966. *Adaptation and Adaptability.* New York: Child Welfare League of America.

Hirschbach, E. 1973. "Structure and Program in Group Home Care." In *Group Homes for Children and Youth — Report on Group Home Conference.* New York: Federation of Protestant Agencies of New York.

Rosenthal, S.B.; C.G. Harrison; and W.A. Harrington. 1979. *The Direct Care Worker in the Group Home.* Chapel Hill, N.C.: The Residential Training Program, University of North Carolina.

Wolins, M. 1974. "Some Theoretical Observations on Group Care." In *Successful Group Care,* edited by M. Wolins, p. 7-35. Chicago: Aldine.

15 PROGRAM EVALUATION

Effective planning in group care requires periodic assessment of program components. In addition, public accountability requirements mandated by legislative bodies who fund foster care programs and governmental agencies that monitor them cannot be met without periodic evaluation. Evaluation is related to program objectives and studies the relationship between goals and service delivery.

In group care, a number of disciplines is involved, each one becoming a participant in the overall assessment endeavor. First, they examine its functioning and, second, they are partners in studying the program as a whole. Collectively, they are all concerned about factors which require program adaptations: for example, changes in the clientele referred for care. Among these may be a shift to older, more aggressive youngsters, the multiply handicapped, and more seriously disturbed emotionally. An adjustment in existing structure, education, and treatment modalities may be required as well as financing. A general framework of good practice provides a basis for comparing expectations and actual achievement. For example, there is general agreement about the nature and purposes of the "therapeutic milieu." The events of daily living become the context for teaching competence in essential life skills. A child's capabilities are reinforced and extended, and his problems worked with. The children

257

should be provided with corrective experiences through planned and structured living, interpersonal relationships with staff and peers, special education, and leisure-time activities. It seems that this is particularly important to keep in mind in evaluating the child care component. The following sections suggest pertinent areas for study.

THE QUALITY OF CHILD CARE

The child care worker's fundamental asset is himself. The basics of child care—knowledge and skill—can be taught. How this is learned and translated into daily practice is determined by the worker's personality. The hiring process assesses the worker's potential; the supervisory process confirms it; training enhances it. Principal considerations should be the worker's capacity for relationships, self-awareness, values, adaptability, and commitment. There must be a readiness to learn to communicate with the children at their level of development and understanding, firmness in representing established structure, and skill in carrying out treatment plans. Children will not respect or relate significantly, communicate willingly, meet demands nor model the worker's behavior and values unless they are convinced of his genuine interest in them and strength and firmness of his guidance.

The Worker's Style

If it is autocratic, there may be group control and individual conformity because of punitive consequences; if it is laissez-faire, it represents either lack of concern for the children or fear of them. Both of these leadership styles are destructive and ineffective in a therapeutic milieu. They also serve as negative models for new workers who enter the field of child care with enthusiasm and a commitment to help children.

Degree of Consistency

Staff consistency in attitude, values, and behavior of staff, particularly among the child care team, is essential. Inconsistency contributes to child confusion, encourages manipulations, and generates staff conflict. Consistency must be encouraged and monitored by supervisory staff. Staff on different shifts should be given time to meet to communicate information about children and to evaluate to what extent the members of the team are functioning consistently with the group as a whole and with individual children in accordance with formulated treatment plans.

The Child-Worker Relationship

Children entering placement are wary of relationships, particularly with adults. Their sense of trust is not well developed and will, therefore, require sensitive nurturing. Child care workers are potentially the most significant adults in the children's residential experience. Through their role and functions, they most directly meet children's dependency and control needs. The degree of significance attained by a worker for a particular child will depend on *how* the nurture and guidance is conveyed. The quality of the relationship can be interfered with by factors beyond the personal control of the individual child care worker. For example, a low staff-child ratio, providing inadequate coverage, can limit time and effort available to individual children who require a great deal of attention. Inconsistency or strife among members of the child care team may put a serious strain on child-staff relationships. In residential treatment centers, interference with the child care worker's authority or dilution of his involvement in out-of-cottage programs (school, recreation, family visits, and so on) affects it detrimentally.

Child care staff time should be structured to maximize worker-children involvement. Workers on duty generally share responsibilities for management of daily routines, recording, administrative details, and interdisciplinary team functions. In addition, each worker might be assigned to work more directly with three or four children (depending on the size of the cottage group). He would act as liaison for these children with their teachers and caseworker(s), monitor and assist with their homework, help with skill development in work and leisure-time activities, and assume a major role in crisis intervention and disciplinary matters. Time should be alloted during scheduled work hours to meet once a week for a talking session with the children individually. These sessions are not suggested as a substitute for casework contacts or psychotherapy sessions. Consultation to help the worker increase his therapeutic skills in individual sessions should be available through the caseworker assigned to the group.

These suggested broader responsibilities could strengthen the child care worker's significance to the children. They would (initially) circumscribe a child's relationship to an advocate and benign authority who meets dependency needs, frustrates destructive impulse expression, and, through a close relationship, provides a source for positive identification and ultimate individuation. Supervision and in-service training would have to support this more intensive worker–child relationship.

Definition and Monitoring of Expectations

Behavioral expectations, group routines, and individual responsibilities should be clearly defined for the children. Positive reinforcement should actively support achievement. Visual aids such as charting of individual progress in achieving mutually agreed-upon goals should be considered. Use of contract techniques might also be helpful.

THE QUALITY OF GROUP LIFE

The interpersonal interactions within the group represent its dynamism and may generate pressures which contribute to dissension and conflict in group living. They also represent a potential for developing a strong sense of group cohesiveness. Understanding group process and development of group leadership skills are essential prerequisites for guiding the collective energy of a group into constructive channels of expression and evoking its sense of mutuality and self-help potential. Such training should be available to child care staff. The quality of group life may be assessed by:

1. The quality of communication within the group.
2. The balance between individualization and group management needs.
3. The degree of child involvement in planning, management, and evaluation of group living tasks.
4. The sense of group cohesiveness.

Child Care Recording

Recording is essential for effective assessment, planning, management, and evaluation of treatment goals and services.

Team Work

"Treatment" is a collective effort. Interdisciplinary integration, its essential ingredient, is achieved through informal ongoing communication among members of the team and through periodic evaluation conferences. The child care workers' involvement is vital for assessment, planning, implementation, and evaluation. It may be evaluated by examining the scope and quality of his communication with members of the other disciplines, the quality of his team relationship, and degree of participation during the interdisciplinary conferences.

Staff Stability

Staff continuity and stability is particularly important in group care to counteract the children's previous experiences. Disruption in their relationships with staff reactivates separation traumas, reinforces distrust, and interferes with the establishment of close relationships with significant adults. One should expect that this corrosive element would be controlled by assuring continuity and stability among child care staff. Unfortunately, this is not the case. Discontinuity is rampant because of high rates of turnover—as much as 200 percent annually in some group home settings for aggression-prone adolescents.

Although unsatisfactory working conditions and low pay scales contribute to turnover, it seems overshadowed by job-related stress factors (Reed 1977). These also affect staff stability which frequently culminates in the long-known but only recently studied burn-out phenomenon (Freudenberger 1977; Mattingly 1977). Burn-out, according to Freudenberger (1977), includes a diversity of attitudes and behavior expressed on the job, in one's personal life, and physical well-being. Some convey inflexibility and rigidity in thinking, resistance to change or innovation, intellectualization and distancing from emotional involvement with the children, suspiciousness of fellow workers and administration, and withdrawal. There may also be avoidance of work responsibilities, lack of interest in the job, and a sense of helplessness and hopelessness about the children. Absenteeism due to physical symptoms, an increasing sense of apathy, fatigue, and depression are the more serious manifestations.

Staff turnover is costly to agencies. It is harmful to emotionally deprived children who require continuity in their relationship with significant adults. Staff burn-out may be even more critical because of its consequences for agency, children, and staff. At best, such a worker's effectiveness is marginal and productivity minimal. Generally, it is destructive to children because the worker's behavior may reinforce children's pre-placement experiences with uncaring or hostile adults or feed misconceptions of adult reliability and trustworthiness. Such workers may not follow through on treatment plans or may interfere with their implementation. They may be a burden to co-workers and misdirect or discourage new workers' enthusiasm and commitment.

Since burn-out and staff turnover are widespread, evaluation must address itself to determining its scope, causation, and solution. As much as possible, job-related stress factors must be reduced, if not eliminated, by identifying and modifying those factors in agency policy and practice that contribute to staff discontinuity and instability. Freudenberg (1977: 95), suggests that an agency may alleviate staff burn-out by establishing more effective channels of communication between administrative and child care staff in order to diminish the sense of isolation they so often experience. This would give them a greater sense of belonging and participation in the overall agency objectives, achievements, and tribulations. Ongoing supervision and in-service training are essential for developing knowledge, skills, self-awareness, and competency in coping with crises. The live-in worker should have living accommodations that protect his privacy during off hours and a work schedule that does not unduly restrict his personal life. Factors such as work overload due to understaffing, role overload when a worker is expected to assume multiple roles which are beyond his capacities, ambiguities in expectations, and lack of supervisory support must be corrected before they trigger the burn-out process.

To cope effectively with the children's inexhaustible demands and projections, staff require support as well as opportunities for replenishment of their inner resources. This can best be accomplished when the worker functions in a mutually caring and trusting milieu, where support is available when needed, where initiative and creativity is encouraged, professional development opportunities provided, and a climate for open discussion of differences and expression of opinion is present.

Suppression of feelings of anxiety associated with work-related stress is destructive. Workers should be encouraged to discuss this with their supervisors and co-workers. This may prevent a buildup of debilitating anxiety, a drift into a sense of helplessness and isolation. It also calls attention to working conditions that are destructive to workers' and children's well-being. It is an agency's responsibility to correct conditions that generate excessive stress resulting in worker's physical and emotional exhaustion. Educational programs leading to professionalization of child care and agency policies and practices which recognize and treat child care workers as professionals (including material benefits enjoyed by other professionals) can contribute to a marked reduction in the high rate of turnover and burnout among child workers.

REFERENCES

Freudenberger, H.J. 1977. "Burn-out: Occupational Hazard of the Child Care Worker." *Child Care Quarterly* 6, no. 2: 90–99.

Mattingly, M.A. 1977. "Sources of Stress and Burn-out in Professional Child Care." *Child Care Quarterly* 6, no. 2: 127–137.

Reed, M.J. 1977. "Stress in Live-in Child Care." *Child Care Quarterly* 6, no. 2: 114–120.

INSTRUCTIONAL GUIDE

16 METHODOLOGY

Experiential learning is the instructional method emphasized in this guide. It involves topical questions raised by the instructor for discussion by the trainees, analysis of case situations, and structured exercises. The purpose of the topical questions is not only to stimulate thinking about the content under consideration but to relate it to the daily practice experience of the trainee. The case examples involve the group in disciplined case analysis and problem-solving; the structured exercises aim at promoting interpersonal communication, self-awareness, and attitudinal change. Our experience in supervision and education of child care workers in in-service training, as well as in classroom instruction, has convinced us that this approach is preferable in adult education and especially in child care work where the trainees are involved in actual practice. They are able to draw on their own experience to enrich and integrate what is being taught formally.

The instructional guide represents a framework for teaching an introductory course for child care practitioners. The suggested exercises follow the sequence of Part I and are specific to its content. The instructor selects the format for each session. He may choose to lecture part of the time, focus on group discussion around questions he raises for the group's consideration, suggest structured exercises such as role-playing, analysis of case situations, or a combination of some or all of the above. An exposition of role-playing and case analysis follows this introduction for instructors who may not be fully familiar with these techniques.

In-service training seminars should also include a session, perhaps presented by the director of the institution, orienting workers to agency history, philosophy, and policy. Copies of written policy and procedures or a manual containing them should also be distributed. The instructor should be familiar with policy and practice because course content must be related to the specifics of the agency. In addition, there should be a presentation of the treatment orientation, preferably given by the chief clinician (psychiatrist or psychologist), since the child care worker's method, if not the substance of his tasks, will be affected by the particular theoretical framework of the treatment program.

Where the course is given in an educational (academic) setting, it should include a lecture and assigned readings on major psychoanalytic and social learning theories, including behavior modification techniques since these represent the current, major theoretical orientation of residential treatment programs.

Flexibility on the part of the instructor in using the guide is advisable. He may wish to be selective in his choice of topics, deleting some or adding others. He should, however, provide the trainees with a course agenda and indicate the objectives and methodology for the course sessions. The trainees will then have a framework of expectations. Furthermore, they may have suggestions for enriching the course content. Participation in planning their educational experience may enhance their investment in it.

STRUCTURED EXERCISES

Structured exercises enable participants to focus on selective aspects of a learning situation. Through involvement with others in exercises representative of his actual work experience, the child care worker has an opportunity to learn by reenacting a particular role, by examining and solving a problem situation. As an observer, he sees others in action and shares his ideas with them during the feedback phase of the exercise.

The instructor designs or selects illustrative exercises, like the ones suggested in this guide, in accordance with his objectives and the subject under discussion. The objective may be increasing self-awareness, learning communication skills, enhancing powers of observation, solving problems, interviewing in a crisis, and others. All of these are important in strengthening a child care worker's effectiveness.

A structured exercise generally involves a small number of participants. For example, in role-playing there are usually a limited number of actors; the rest of the group functions as observers. In the small-committee activity the group is divided into smaller sections who work independently on the exercises in separate locations and then come together to hear a report from each committee's recorder which the group can discuss. In "brainstorming" exercises everyone participates in offering ideas or suggestions, with the instructor acting as recorder, classifier, and guide in the group's selection of the most relevant and pertinent suggestions for resolving the problem under consideration.

Since structured exercises are time-consuming, the instructor should specify the amount of time to be used for each phase, including time for the total group's discussion during feedback. Instruction for participants should be in written form. If an exercise requires responses, index cards should be distributed. The instructor's role varies with the type of exercise. In role-playing he is generally part of the observer group; in small-group activity, he circulates among the groups, listening and observing the process. This helps him in the final phase where he may act as interpretor of the action or the person who sums up.

The feedback phase is most important. It provides an opportunity for each participant to reexamine the process, to share and evaluate the information generated by the exercise, to reinforce his powers of observation, learned skills, and expanded self-awareness.

BRAINSTORMING

This is a technique for problem-solving and decision-making and a procedure for generating ideas in a group. It enables participants to respond freely and creatively without anxiety of being judged. It is especially effective in getting a discussion started, and it may be particularly helpful to those who hesitate to express themselves.

The technique involves the following:

1. The statement of the issue or problem under consideration is written down on the blackboard.

2. The group is advised about the brainstorming rules which in essence involve *spontaneity*—"say anything that comes to mind," emphasize quantity responses, and disregard discussion or evaluation of the quality of a suggestion. All of the responses are written down.

3. A time limit is set for the suggestion phase.

4. The list is then reviewed to eliminate those that seem inappropriate.

5. Similar suggestions are grouped into categories.

6. A final selection is made through group consensus of suggestions they feel are most pertinent.

7. The best suggestion and their application to the situation or to the solution are then discussed. Some of them may then be enacted in role-playing exercises.

Role-Playing

Role-playing is a spontaneous acting-out of a controversial or conflict situation, generally involving two participants. A sketch of the event and a profile of the character of each of the actors are the only specifics given to the actors and the observers. The objective is to help participants and the observers to experience what it might feel like to be in a particular situation.

The procedure is as follows:

> Volunteers are called for to act out a situation. Each one is given a copy of the statement describing the event and a character sketch of the person he or she represents. The former includes what is going on, whom it involves, when and where it takes place. The latter describes the type of person, his particular viewpoints, motivation for his actions, and his state of mind. Participants are given a maximum of five to ten minutes to prepare for the role-playing. The observers are asked to listen and watch carefully.

During the discussion following the role-playing, the instructor focuses on the feelings experienced by the actors and by the others as they observed. The role-players may be asked the following:

1. How did you feel in this situation?
2. What was it like to be the particular person you represented?
3. How did you feel about the way you were treated by the other person in this situation?

The observers are asked to focus on:

1. What they heard.
2. The underlying meaning of what they heard and saw and in particular on the nonverbal expression.
3. The feelings expressed by each actor.
4. In what ways the situation could be handled differently.
5. Any interpersonal problems in communicating, and how both actors should work it out.

The following are examples that could be role-played in relation to the issue of authority:

Situation A: It is Saturday morning cleanup time. Jim, the child care worker who is new to the cottage, is supervising the boys' work but is also working himself. Suddenly he hears the television in the living room which is not supposed to be on during cleanup time. Upon investigation he finds Tim sprawled out in an easy chair watching a program. Before confronting him, he checks the bathroom which was Tim's responsibility and finds that it's only half-finished. He walks into the living room, shuts the television set, and faces Tim.

Character sketches: Jim, a young man of 21, of slight build, has high standards for himself and others, is a highly ethical person, and gets upset easily by direct or indirect violations of rules or manipulations.

Tim, age 15, is a tall, husky boy who is one of the leaders in the group, a troublemaker, a bully, and suspected to be behind many difficulties that occur in the cottage.

Situation B: It is 10: p.m. in the younger girls' cottage. Mary and Jane are just finishing their work. Mary comes running down the steps and relates excitedly to Jane, her co-worker, that she had found two of the girls in the same bed. She had separated them and scolded them.

Character sketches: Mary, a middle-aged woman, is a stickler for rules, suspicious of the children, and is easily upset when they behave unacceptably to her.

Jane, also middle-aged, is more thoughtful, flexible, tolerant, and experienced than Mary.

DISCUSSION TOPICS

Discussion provides an opportunity for people to exchange ideas, to learn from another's knowledge and experience. Even though the topic may be framed in terms of a question, the instructor should indicate that the purpose is not simply to ask the group to respond to the question. The expectation is that it would stimulate the members to become involved in examining the issues, to exchange ideas, elaborate on one another's comments, share experiences illustrative of the topic or question, and debate the ideas it generates. The instructor should stimulate comments from others to questions addressed to him and in general try to get as many people involved as possible. He may turn to others to ask, "What do you think?" He can serve as a stimulator by raising a question, by pointing out alternatives that the group may not have considered, by offering additional points of information or pointing out inconsistencies or contradictions which have been expressed, and by eliciting participation from those who do not speak up. If the discussion gets off the track, he can bring it back to the issue at hand.

Since time is a factor, the instructor might select to set a limit at the beginning. The discussion should terminate with a summation and restatement of the discussion's concepts and goals.

Case Analyses

A number of case examples followed by questions for discussion have been included in the guide for use as an additional or alternate teaching aide. By analyzing the issues and discussion of actions that could be taken to solve the problems they illustrate, the trainee learns to apply the same principles in his daily practice. We have found that this exercise stimulates child care workers to present similar situations from their work experience. Copies of the cases should be distributed in advance to save time and make the material available to everyone during the discussion.

Class Assignments

In addition to reading, we suggest two written assignments. The first is observation of a child, the group, and self during a daily activity such as waking, mealtime, work, play, and so on, in accordance with the observation questions at the end of these topics in Part I. The second is analysis of a crisis situation in accordance with the outline in the section on child care supervision.

The purpose of these assignments is to sensitize the trainee to objective observation. This should enhance his capacity to assess a child's handicaps as well as his strengths, to understand his developmental needs, and contribute to the formulation of therapeutic intervention strategies.

EVALUATION

Evaluation provides the instructor with feedback from his trainees about the effectiveness of his teaching methods and objectives. The instructor's observation of a trainee's reactions and responsiveness to the teaching, the degree of his participation in class discussion and structured exercises, and his performance on written assignments represent evaluation measures of the individual trainee. The more formal evaluation procedures apply to the course as a whole. They are useful but may be time-consuming for the trainees who fill them out and for the instructor who collates this feedback information. For example, a pre-test and post-test questionnaire for evaluating whether the trainees have added to their knowledge base, developed additional skills, and increased their self-awareness would have to be quite lengthy.

A more modest effort with objectives limited to evaluation of teaching method and scope of subject matter may be preferable. A simple questionnaire distributed to the trainees at the completion of a topic would make it possible for the trainees to participate in an ongoing process of evaluation and provide the instructor with guidelines for making changes in his instructional plan and teaching method.

The following is a sample questionnaire that the instructor may choose to use as is or with modifications.

1. Did the sessions adequately cover the subject matter?

   Yes _____   No _____

   If the answer is no, indicate what you feel was not sufficiently covered.

   _____

   _____

2. What approach did you like most or least?

Liked Most	*Liked Least*	*Which do you prefer?*
Lecture _____	Lecture _____	Lecture _____
Case analysis ____	Case analysis ____	Case analysis ____
Role-playing ____	Role-playing ____	Role-playing ____
Group discussions ____	Group discussions ____	Group discussions ____

3. Which of the methods was most helpful in increasing your—

	Knowledge	*Skills*	*Self-Awareness*
Lecture	____	____	____
Case Analysis	____	____	____
Role-Playing	____	____	____
Group Discussion	____	____	____

4. Please suggest any changes in method of presentation, additions, or deletions of content which you feel would improve this course (or seminar).

_____

_____

_____

_____

A more comprehensive evaluation method can serve the dual purpose of appraising the instructor of the effectiveness of his teaching and providing the trainees with an ongoing measure of their learning. This method involves the utilization of a series of pre- and post-test questionnaires which the instructor could either prepare for each of the topics covered in the course or he could use the practice review questions which follow the topical exercises.

The pre-test would be introduced at the beginning session and the post-test questionnaire answered at the end of the session, marking the completion of the topic. The trainees should be reassured that the pre-test questionnaire is not a formal test but an opportunity for them to assess the scope of their understanding of a particular topic. They should be told, therefore, that they should respond to the questions in terms of what they feel is correct and not be concerned whether they *are* correct. Also, they will have an opportunity to respond to the same questionnaire when the topic is completed. When correct answers are provided by the instructor, the trainees can then compare their responses on both questionnaires.

The following brief questionnaire given at the conclusion of an introductory seminar in in-service training programs for new child care workers and introductory courses in academic programs may also be useful as an evaluation instrument.

I am asking your help in evaluating the child care seminar (or course) you have just completed so that we may learn more about its effectiveness and need for revision. Please answer the questions below as fully as you can. Your name is not requested on this questionnaire and your answers will be tabulated with those of other members in the program. In no case will you be personally identified in the analysis of the data.

Thank you for your help.

Questions 1–6 can be answered by checking the appropriate box for *A Great Deal, Some,* or *None.*

	A Great Deal	*Some*	*None*
1. Did you acquire new information about child care you did not know before?	____	____	____
2. Did you acquire more understanding of the children you work with?	____	____	____
3. Do you feel that you have a better understanding of your reactions to children's acting-out?	____	____	____
4. Do you feel more comfortable in working with:			
a) the children	____	____	____
b) with other staff	____	____	____
5. Do you feel more able to talk with youngsters about the problems they present?	____	____	____
6. Do you feel more comfortable in discussing problems with your supervisor?	____	____	____

7. Check which parts of the seminar were the *most* useful to you:

1. Child development ____
2. Concepts of child care ____
3. Tasks of the child care worker (from waking to bedtime) ____
4. Dealing with problematic behavior ____
5. Discipline ____
6. Relationships ____
7. Treatment planning ____

8. Check which parts of the seminar were the *least* useful:

1. Child development ____
2. Concepts of child care ____

   3. Tasks of the child care worker (from waking to bedtime)   ——

   4. Dealing with problematic behavior   ——

   5. Discipline   ——

   6. Relationships   ——

   7. Treatment planning   ——

9. Was this seminar generally helpful to you?   Very helpful   ——

                                              Somewhat helpful   ——

                                            Not helpful   ——

COMMENTS

a) Please make any suggestions that might improve this type of course or or seminar. _____

_____

_____

_____

b) Would you be interested in additional seminars?   Yes   ——

                                                                           No   ——

If *yes*, what subjects?

_____

_____

_____

17 INSTRUCTIONAL CONTENT AND PRACTICE REVIEW EXERCISES

THE CHILDREN

In order to get the group involved in this subject, the instructor asks them to enumerate what they consider to be basic needs of children in care. He lists their responses on a blackboard and then suggests they be ranked in order of importance (1 for the most important, and so on). This may stimulate a lively discussion and serve to sensitize the trainees to the whole issue of unmet needs experienced by the children they work with. The instructor might reinforce the above exercise by reviewing what are generally considered to be children's basic needs—physical care, affection, belonging, guidance, a sense of achievement, and so on.

Discussion Topics

1. Why is it important for child care workers to be familiar with the life history of their children?

2. How will this help them understand a child's (difficult or troublesome) behavior?

3. Most of the children coming into group care have not developed a sense of trust in others. How can a child care worker begin to help the child establish it in relation to others as well as in himself?

4. What are some of the developmental lags or deviations from the "normal" you have observed among the children in your group?

5. How do you know when a child is anxious? What are the behavioral clues?

6. How should we deal with a child who —
   a. Seems chronically anxious?
   b. Easily becomes anxious?
   c. Reacts with anxiety to particular situations?

7. List the various ways that anger may be expressed.

8. How do you react to a child who does not seem to have a sense of guilt? Give examples.

9. What is the consequence of a sense of excessive guilt? How may it be expressed behaviorally?

10. What are some of the problems in communicating with an intellectually retarded child?

11. What should one be aware of in dealing with —
   a. Teenagers in general?
   b. The hostile, aggressive adolescent?
   c. The violence-prone youngster?
   d. The withdrawn adolescent?

12. What is meant by "corrective socialization" in relation to the "atypical" child (generally diagnosed as childhood schizophrenic?)

CHILD DEVELOPMENT

Practice Review Exercises

1. List five basic needs of childhood.

2. Name Erik Erikson's five developmental stages from infancy through adolescence.

3. List the major conflicts of adolescence.

4. Indicate which of the following are *True* or *False:*

	True	*False*
a. Many children in group care are impulsive, distrustful, show poor judgment, and think concretely.	___	___
b. Disturbed children tend to express excessive degrees of anger and anxiety.	___	___
c. Children in group care generally have experienced emotional deprivation.	___	___

    d. Children in group care are dull intellectually.   ——   ——

    e. Children in group care lack in development
of conscience.   ——   ——

    f. Knowing a child's background helps to under-
stand his inappropriate behavior.   ——   ——

    g. The aggressive youngster may be also an
insecure youngster.   ——   ——

5. Check which of the following applies to the mildly intellectually retarded child:

    a. He is insecure.

    b. He does not know how to play like "normal" children.

    c. He cannot learn at school.

    d. He has poor judgment.

    e. Communication with him should be in simple, concrete terms.

    f. Because of perceptual problems and/or organic factors, he may not understand what the worker is trying to convey to him.

    g. If he does not follow through correctly what he has been asked to do, it's because he does not want to.

6. What are some of the common characteristics of the aggressive, violent-prone youngster who is in group care because of delinquent activity?

18 CONCEPTS
Discussion Topics and Practice Review Exercises

SEPARATION

Discussion Topics

1. Describe the behaviors that may be indicative of a child's reactions to being placed and how you have dealt with them.

2. How do you go about orienting a new child to your cottage group? Do you involve the other children in this process?

3. Do you believe that one of the youngsters in a cottage should be assigned to orient a newcomer? Why or why not? If yes, how should he be selected and prepared for it?

4. With reference to the case example given in Part I:

   a. Could Jim's anxiety about leaving have been anticipated? If Jim had misgivings about leaving, is it not possible that he would have shown it in some changes in his behavior which the workers could have observed?

   b. How can a child care worker help a youngster deal with the anxiety about going home?

   c. How long before a youngster is scheduled to leave should one begin to help him prepare for it? What specific issues should be considered, and what steps should be taken to help him build a bridge from residential setting to community living?

d. As Billy's child care worker, what would you do to deal with Billy's request to go home?

e. Would you accept his reasoning or would you suspect that he was beginning to panic about leaving his family? If this is so, how would you deal with this anxiety?

f. Would you urge him to stay on because he could be helped here?

g. Would you enlist other staff, such as social workers and psychiatrists, to deal with Billy's anxiety and threats?

STRUCTURE

Discussion Topics

1. Why is structure important in:
   a. Family living?
   b. School?
   c. Sports or games?
   d. Residential treatment?
   e. Cottage living?
2. State reasons why structured living may be resisted by children in placement.
3. Which is preferable, and why?
   a. Discuss with the children the reasons for existing rules and regulations.
   b. Post rules on the bulletin board without followup discussions.
   c. Post them along with a warning that they had "better conform to them."
4. Should exceptions ever be made to existing rules? If yes, under what circumstances?
5. If a worker disagrees with an existing rule, what should he do?
   a. Disregard it?
   b. Voice his opposition to it?
   c. Try to have it changed? How?
   d. Who should be involved in the process of changing established rules?
6. Should children be consulted about changing the following:
   a. House procedures? Explain.
   b. Overall institutional policy? If not, why?

7. What effect might a worker's failure to enforce a known institutional rule have on the children in his care?

AUTHORITY

Discussion Topics

1. Distinguish between benign and despotic authority.

2. Jim, the new child care worker, will be your working partner in a cottage group of aggressive delinquent-oriented boys. He grew up in a household where the father was rigidly authoritarian. His mother tried to protect the children from her husband's unreasonable standards and demands. Jim feared but did not respect his father. He did not openly defy his authority, but as much as he could get away with, he violated his father's rules. He left college in his sophomore year and enlisted in the Marine Corps. He had trouble with sargeants who were authoritarian.

    a. Can you anticipate any problems that Jim may have with the boys? The other child care workers in the cottage? Administration?

    b. If Jim were assigned to a cottage group of younger, severely disturbed children, many of whom are immature, impulsive, and whose sense of reality is poor, what problems could one anticipate? Why do these children need structure and adult direction?

3. Joan, a young inexperienced child care worker who is a college graduate, grew up in a family where there was little structure and minimal parental direction. As a child she spent the summers in a progressive, unstructured, but highly creative summer camp. She majored in psychology and after college graduation was briefly associated with a young people's commune.

    a. What problems can one anticipate if she works in a cottage group of adolescent, aggression-prone girls?

    b. In a cottage of younger children similar to Jim's?

Role-Play

The class is divided into three groups representing a group care situation consisting of a child care worker and his group of teenage boys.

1. *The Situation*:   The administration has asked the cottage groups to participate in a variety show during Easter school recess. The child

workers are asked to meet with their children to work out a presentation—musical, skits, and so forth.

2. *Character Sketch*: Each of the groups consists of two child care workers and the children. The workers represent autocratic, laissez-faire, and democratic types of leadership, respectively. (Either the instructor designates the type of leadership of Group A, B, or C, or he asks for volunteers for each of the three types.) The groups move apart to different parts of the room and reenact the situation. The two child care workers in each of the groups introduce the topic to the "children" in accordance with their leadership styles, and the children respond accordingly. Ten minutes are allotted for the enactment. The instructor circulates among the groups.

After ten minutes, the whole group reconvenes for processing the role-playing. Each group reports on:

1. How each felt in the situation in the role of a child care worker or as child.

2. What was it like to be:

   a. The authoritarian, laissez-faire, or democratic leader?

   b. A child in a group under the staff leadership of the authoritarian, laissez-faire, or democratic worker?

   c. What was achieved in each group?

   d. Which group worked out a plan satisfactory to staff and the children?

EMPHASIS ON HEALTH

Discussion Topics

1. Why is it important to be familiar with a child's capabilities, talents, and learning potential which represent the healthy aspects of his personality?

2. How would you go about finding out a child's capabilities?

3. Do you feel it's important for child care workers to help children develop talents and capabilities? Explain.

4. How would you deal with the following:

   a. Jim, twelve years old, is very insecure in his relationship with his peers. He is not treated nicely by the other boys and is often the group scapegoat. He does not fight back when he is mistreated.

He is fearful of participating in team sports. Jim is intelligent, well-coordinated, has musical and artistic talents. How would you, as his child care worker, go about helping him gain greater acceptance by the group?

b. Mary, age fifteen, is a shy girl, does not like to go to cottage socials, and is frequently criticized by the other girls for being a loner. Though attractive, she is neglectful of her appearance. She has a good singing voice and has artistic talents. How would you, as her child care worker, help Mary become more secure in relation to the other girls and a more active participant in the social life of the cottage?

INDIVIDUALIZATION

Discussion Topics

1. What is your understanding of the term "individualization"?
2. Does "individualizing" mean "favoritism"?
3. How would you counter an accusation by one child that you are "playing favorites" toward another child? For example, that you give special consideration or offering something "extra" to the other child (you are doing this in accordance with an already agreed-upon treatment plan decision.)
4. What would you say to a youngster or a group accusing you or the institution of being "undemocratic" because you don't treat everyone *the same* (they usually mean that not everyone has the same privileges)?
5. List the dilemmas confronting a child care worker regarding individualization in a group setting.
6. Think of examples in your experience with children where you dealt with a number of children differentially, although the event or situation was similar (for instance, mealtime misbehavior or food fads, cottage chores, or waking a child).

IDENTIFICATION

Discussion Topics

1. How can a child care worker help a child form positive identifications?

2. Discuss the importance of an esthetically, pleasant environment in a residence. How would you involve the children in creating and maintaining such an atmosphere?

3. How might a worker use his knowledge of the values which a child has internalized?

4. *Values essential for constructive group living.* Instructor asks the group to list on a slip of paper five values they consider important in group living and to rate them in order of importance from 1–5, number 1 being the most important. After collecting the responses, he writes them on a blackboard in the specified order. Group discussion follows.

5. What are the consequences if the worker does not practice or uphold the values to which he expects the children to adhere?

INTEGRATION

Discussion Topics

1. What, if any, are the obstacles to effective integration?

2. In your experience, how do you feel about the status of the child care worker in the residential team as compared with the social worker, psychiatrist, educator, and administrator?

CONFIDENTIALITY

Discussion Topics

1. Under what circumstances, if any, should a child care worker keep anything confidential from his colleagues when he is asked to do so by a child?

2. How should one respond to the statement, "I want to tell you something but you must promise not to tell anyone"?

3. What would you do in the following situations, assuming that you have made it clear in advance that you could not be bound by a request to keep it confidential:

a. Mary reveals to you that she is pregnant and doesn't know what to do.

b. Don, age seventeen, has received a letter from a friend that his girlfriend is "sleeping around." He is upset and plans to run away so he can confront her about it.

c. Jimmy, age ten, tells you that his roommate has been lighting matches and might set a fire in the cottage.

d. Joan indicates that Ann has been sneaking out of the cottage after bedtime to meet her boyfriend in the woods.

e. Bill confesses he has been taking speed pills.

f. Jack tells you he has had persistent suicidal thoughts.

g. James confides a "rumble" is being planned between the two senior boys' cottages.

h. John is afraid that he will be beaten up tonight following a kangaroo trial.

i. Dave tells you he cheated on his math regents examination.

j. Phyllis confesses she stole a sweater in a neighborhood store.

k. Sam is worried he masturbates every night. He won't consult his caseworker.

l. You have learned from John that Dan is selling marijuana joints.

m. Gail tells you she'll spend her weekend home visit with her boyfriend, even though she is supposed to be at home with her family.

4. On the case cited in Part I:

a. What do you think of the way Mrs. Jones dealt with the question of confidentiality?

b. Mary and David are guilty of a serious breach of discipline. Should they be punished for it despite the fact that Mary has revealed the matter and seems ready to do something about it?

c. Should Mrs. Jones intervene for Mary to ask administration to be lenient about punishing her?

d. Can we assume that Mary and hopefully David have learned from this experience and will be able to control meeting secretly?

e. Mrs. Jones was clear about her own *value* standard regarding Mary's and David's activity. Was it essential to make this point to Mary?

DISCIPLINE

Discussion Topics

1. "A punishment is of no value unless the child learns from it." Explain why you agree or disagree with the above statement.

2. What guidelines should be followed in meting out a punishment so it is effective?

3. Illustrate the term "power struggle. Why should it be avoided? How can it be avoided? Give examples.

4. Should there be fixed punishments for a specific offense, or should the child who commits the offense be considered? In other words, should one "individualize"? Explain and illustrate with examples from your experience.

5. If you have punished a group, describe the situation and the results.

6. How should you, as child care workers, react in the following situations:

a. John and David, both ten years old and of similar build, are fighting.

b. Bill, a bullying-prone fiftteen-year-old, is punching a much smaller boy.

c. While attempting to break up a fight between two older boys, the worker is struck in the face by one of the boys.

d. The worker is threatened with physical force by an eight-year-old. By a seventeen-year-old.

e. During a temper tantrum, Jimmy hits his worker.

f. In a dispute about doing a cottage chore, Don physically attacks the worker with the broom he is holding.

g. Wayne, a violence-prone adolescent who has a history of assaultive behavior, has reacted with an angry outburst against the worker who feels he has made a reasonable request of him. The worker senses his fury and feels fearful that Wayne might attack him.

7. Questions on the case situations illustrating group punishment given in Part I:

a. What are the two main issues in this situation?

b. What is your opinion about Barney's threat to discipline the whole group?

c. Is group punishment unfair, as the boys maintain?

d. Can you think of any circumstances when group punishment is advisable?

e. Do you think the workers are overconcerned about the use of marijuana by the youngsters?

f. Is there some truth about the boys' accusation that adults have a "double standard"? How should a child care worker respond to such a challenge?

8. Differentiate between physical restraint and physical punishment.

9. Are there circumstances when physical punishment should be condoned? If yes, explain.

10. In what situation would you ask administrative staff to become involved in disciplinary action against a child or group of children?

Case Situation

Jim was shocked by Danny's appearance when he arrived at his bedside to wake him. The boy's arms and back were bruised from what appeared to Jim the result of a beating.

"What happened to you?" Jim asked after Danny got out of bed. "Nothing! Leave me alone!" Danny snapped back tearfully.

The other boys seemed unusually quiet, and the only answer he got from them is, "I don't know." Later Jim learned from the neighboring cottage workers that Danny was tried by a kangaroo court the night before. Apparently he was singled out as the one who had revealed to his caseworker that several of the boys were planning to run away. He had also refused to contribute money for it. In consultation with his co-worker Bill and the supervisor, they decided to convene a cottage meeting to talk about kangaroo courts and why they could not be tolerated.

The trainees are asked to help Jim and Bill plan this meeting, keeping the following points in mind:

1. How should they introduce the topic to the group that will probably be hostile and defensive about it?
2. Should they focus on the incident with Danny or the issues involved in a kangaroo court trial? What are they?
3. What are the advantages or disadvantages of group punishment?
4. Can you think of any situation in which it may be justified?

PRACTICE REVIEW EXERCISES

1. Which of the following (a, b, or c) are significant reasons for structure in group care?
    a. Structure serves to curb destructive acting-out and impulsive behavior.
    b. Structure facilitates the child care worker's task of controlling disturbed disturbed children.

c. Structure designates patterns of ordered and planned living for children who have experienced disorder in their lives and consequently were unable to meet demands of reality in school and social relationships.

2. Check following statements as true or false.

   a. Structured living is not good for children's development because it imposes controls on spontaneity and self-expression.

   True_____   False _____

   b. Authority is not constructive to children's growth if it is exercised despotically and punitively.

   True _____   False _____

   c. The worker who is ambivalent about exercising authority will not be effective as an adult authority figure among the children.

   True _____   False ____

3. List the three types of group leadership and their major characteristics.

   a. _____ : _____ _____

   b. _____ : _____ _____

   c. _____ : _____ _____

4. Indicate whether you agree or disagree with the following:

   a. Assessing a child's strengths or personality assets is at least as important as understanding what is wrong with him.

   Agree _____   Disagree _____

   b. Regardless of the seriousness of a child's psychiatric diagnosis, his expressed interests and demonstrated capacities in learning, in play activities, and work represent healthy aspects of his personality.

   Agree _____   Disagree _____

   c. Individualization in group care presents difficulties in managing a group and should therefore be avoided.

   Agree _____   Disagree _____

   d. Excessive individualization is not realistic if it interferes with group living routines and evokes hostile reactions from the group.

   Agree _____   Disagree _____

   e. Individualization implies respect for each child's uniqueness and attentiveness to his (treatment) needs.

   Agree _____   Disagree _____

   f. Tolerance and respect for individual differences by child care staff may help children give up some of their prejudices toward others who have different beliefs.

   Agree _____   Disagree _____

5. Define identification: _____

_____

6. Complete the following sentence:
Cultural, religious and ethnic values and practices are important aspects of a
child's sense of _____

7. List three essential values expectations in group living:

_____

_____

_____

8. Do you agree with the following?
The most effective way to help children adopt adult staff values is through
maintenance of a trusting, caring relationship.

Agree _____   Disagree _____

9. Which of the following approaches regarding group routines is preferable?

a. Discuss with the children the reasons for existing rules and regulations.

b. Post rules on bulletin board without any followup discussion.

c. Post rules and inform the children they had better conform to them or
suffer the (punitive) consequences.

10. The concept of integration in residential group care implies _____
and _____ effort.

11. Circle which of the following can best assure effective team work in the
group living unit.

a. Ongoing and open communication among the child care worker's team.

b. Consistency of approach to the children.

c. A designated senior worker who tells the others how to deal with the
the children.

d. Thorough, specific, written rules and expectations formulated by the
supervisor.

12. Circle which of the following assures the best effectiveness of the interdisciplinary team.

a. Control of children's treatment by the psychiatrist.

b. Joint planning and evaluation by all members.

c. Respect for each member's thinking and contributions to the children's
treatment needs and goal achievement.

13. Check in which of the following situations a worker cannot honor a youngster's request that information should be kept confidential:

a. Mary confides she has fallen in love.

b. Jimmy tells you his roommate is lighting matches at night.

c. Bill confesses he has been taking speed pills.

    d. Jack tells you he has had persistent suicidal thoughts.

    e. John states that he "hates" his teacher.

    f. James confides that a "rumble" is being planned between the two senior boys' cottages.

    g. Jane confides that her roommate plans to sneak out of the cottage tonight.

    h. John is afraid that he will be beaten up tonight following a kangaroo trial.

    i. Dave tells you he cheated on his math regents examination.

    j. Phyllis confesses she stole a sweater in a neighborhood store.

    k. Sam is worried he masturbates every night. He won't consult his caseworker.

    l. You have learned from John that Dan is selling marijuana joints.

    m. Gail tells you she'll spend part of her weekend home visit with her boyfriend.

14. Why is it inadvisable for a worker to agree to keep a child's confidence without first knowing what it is about? _____

_____

15. Distinguish between *discipline* and *punishment*.

Discipline is _____

Punishment is _____

16. Why is discipline necessary in group care? _____

_____

17. Check following statements as *true* or *false*.

    a. Punishment is the only effective method of controlling children's misbehavior.

              True _____   False _____

    b. Punishment of children is destructive and should be outlawed in group care settings.

              True _____   False _____

    c. Without a system of rewards and punishment, child-rearing would be impossible.

              True _____   False _____

    d. Prevention of misbehavior or a conflict situation avoids the need for punishment measures.

              True _____   False _____

    e. Physical punishment is inappropriate as a method of control.

              True _____   False _____

f. There should be no individualization or exceptions made in meeting out a punishment.

True _____   False _____

g. Group punishment is an effective method of keeping order in a group.

True _____   False _____

h. Threat of group punishment is an effective method of forcing a group to expose an offender.

True _____   False _____

i. Trial and punishment by the peer group of individual offenders should be encouraged.

True _____   False _____

18. List three essential guidelines that should be followed before carrying out a punishment.

_____

_____

_____

19. Check which of the following you consider important in preventing disturbing or disruptive behavior and thus minimize the resort to punishment.

a. _____ Established rules of comportment and responsibility should be clearly stated.

b. _____ Call for the intervention of a supervisor or administrator when trouble is threatened.

c. _____ Rules should be consistently interpreted and enforced.

d. _____ Expulsion from the group of the most troublesome children.

e. _____ Adult power and threat of punishment.

f. _____ Give in to children's demands.

g. _____ Regularly scheduled group meetings which involve the children in discussion of issues pertinent to their living situation.

h. _____ Delegating responsibility for controlling the group to the strong-arm peer leadership.

20. Check what action you would take in this and the following situations. Jim and Billy, both age ten, are fighting outside the cottage.

a. _____ Not interfere since they are physically well matched.

b. _____ Break up the fight and punish both for fighting.

c. _____ Break up the fight and talk with them about the cause and help them resolve the conflict.

d. _____ Tell them to stop fighting.

21. David, sixteen years old, is bullying Mike, a weaker and smaller cottage peer.

   a. _____ Hit David to teach him what it feels like being on the receiving end.

   b. _____ Stop David and inquire what the trouble is.

   c. _____ Push David aside, threaten him with punishment if he does it again, and tell Mike to report to you any future abuse by David.

22. During a temper tantrum, Abe, nine years old, strikes out at you.

   a. _____ Pick him up bodily and spank him.

   b. _____ Restrain him from hitting you by holding him, assure him no one will harm him, and take him to his room until you feel sure the tantrum is spent.

23. There has been stealing in the cottage and you can't find out from the group who is responsible.

   a. _____ Serve an ultimatum to the group that unless they expose the culprit(s), you will cancel T.V.-viewing for a month.

   b. _____ Threaten the imposition of fines on the whole group.

   c. _____ Schedule a group meeting to talk about the situation and involve the children in arriving at a solution to the stealing.

   d. _____ Ask the leadership group to put a stop to the thefts.

24. Paul, age fifteen, a physically strong boy, is violent-prone. He is difficult to control, and the other children as well as staff seem afraid of him.

   a. _____ Ask for an increased dose of sedating medication.

   b. _____ Suggest to the other workers on the team that you jointly ask for Paul's removal from your group.

   c. _____ Request an interdisciplinary meeting to evolve more effective ways of dealing with Paul.

   d. _____ At an opportune time, talk with Paul about the effect of his attitude and behavior on others, admitting that he frequently makes you feel afraid of him. Suggest that it might be helpful to both of you if he could talk to you when he feels something is upsetting him.

19 THE CHILD CARE WORKER'S TASKS
Discussion Topics and Practice Review Exercises

DAILY LIVING

Discussion Topics

1. The instructor might use the following technique to get the group involved in discussion of this topic:

   a. Ask group to list on a blackboard the child care worker's tasks.

   b. Get a consensus regarding ranking importance.

   c. Ask the group what do they think are the tasks that workers find most enjoyable? Most problematic? That take up the greater part of workers' time? That workers would like to give more time to, but can't?

2. Ask group to list the obstacles they face in carrying out their tasks. Survey the group's opinion regarding the most severe obstacles.

3. Ask the group to define self-awareness. Ask them to differentiate between "sympathy" and "empathy." To illustrate, a role-playing exercise is suggested.

Role-Play

The group is told that they are going to try an exercise designed to help them perceive a situation from another person's point of view which should increase their ability to empathize. The group is arranged in a circle. Each participant is asked to write down on a piece of paper "I am a child." Beginning with "I am" each one is to write three or four sentences describing a particular problem he (the child) is experiencing. For example: "I am a child. I don't want to be here, I want to be with my family. My brother and sister remained at home. Why do I have to suffer?"

The instructor collects these cards, shuffles them, and then asks each participant to pick a card randomly. He is then to attempt to put himself in that child's shoes, to feel what he is feeling and to think what he is thinking. To involve the group, the leader illustrates as follows:

> I am a child. I am in this cottage but I want to be with my family. I was sent away while my brother and sister remain at home. It is not fair, and I feel unloved and rejected. I feel so angry sometimes that I hate my parents for what they did to me. Sometimes I feel like running away. I often take out my frustrations on other boys and on my counselors, even when I am not mad at them. I do so because I do not know any other way to get rid of my anger. I really know it's not their fault. I really want to be liked by them. But when I act as I do frequently, I can't blame them for not liking me.

After this demonstration, the instructor asks for volunteers to portray the child listed on their cards. After brief presentations, the other participants are asked to supplement the volunteers' statements.

The second exercise deals with a child care worker. Each one is asked to fill out a card. "I am a child care worker . . ." and to describe briefly an emotion-laden situation he is experiencing in his work. As before, the instructor demonstrates a role enactment and then asks for volunteers.

> I am a child care worker, new in this cottage, and I am overwhelmed by all that I have to do. I find it hard to be a constant target of the children's frustrations and hangups, their hates and hostilities. For example, when I ask Jimmy to do something, he resents it. I don't want to threaten him, but I have to, to get the required chores done. Then there is David. Even when I am nice to him, he literally spits in my face and says nasty things. I get angry and depressed. I know that these are sick children, that they may be testing me or displacing their anger on to me. But when there's too much pressure, I tend to lose control and objectivity. I lose my temper and holler and sometimes I have slapped a child. I know it's not right. I don't know what I should do! I'm afraid to discuss this with my supervisor because he may feel that I am not adequate and give me a poor evaluation. I like this work and would like to stay on.

DAY'S BEGINNING

Discussion Topics

1. Describe some of the problems you face each morning in waking the children and getting them to wash and dress.

2. Describe the methods you find most helpful in getting children out of bed, dressed, and ready for breakfast. Give examples.

3. The instructor may suggest the use of a wake-up sheet helpful in establishing a consistent approach to children, which should be available to all the workers in a cottage. The instructor might ask for volunteers to prepare one for their cottage groups. It should include the preferred method of waking each child, designation of any problems regarding waking, dressing, and performing morning chores.

MEALTIME

Discussion Topics

1. The instructor asks the group what they consider their most serious problems at mealtime. He writes them on a blackboard, and then gets concensus for ranking them for degree of severity. He then calls for discussion regarding solution of the problems.

He might ask:

    a. Which can be resolved by the child care workers?

    b. Which are the responsibility of administration?

    c. What should be done, if anything, by child care workers to bring the problem to the administrator's attention?

2. One problem faced by child care workers are children's food fads or idiosyncrasies regarding what food they will or will not eat.

The instructor presents a problem situation:

Three of the six children at your child care worker's table (John, David, Bill, ten-year-olds) refuse to eat the liver that is being served at the evening meal. You have tasted it. Though liver is not your most favored meat dish, the liver is well prepared and tastes good.

A problem-solving exercise is set up by dividing the group into three subgroups to discuss among themselves what action they would take. After five to ten minutes of discussion, a reporter from each group presents a plan of action and the rationale for it. The total group is then asked to consider which of the three solutions (if they differ) they prefer. This is followed by the instructor's summation of the issues involved: for instance, individualization, group consideration, dietary factors, and so on.

3. The instructor reads the following statement made by an imaginary child care worker:

> Giving children responsibilities at meals (serving, helping with snack preparation, cleanup) creates more problems than benefits, so I prefer doing everything myself. For me it is sufficient that the kids eat and don't bother me.

The group is asked to comment whether they agree fully or partly, or disagree with the above and to give their reasons.

4. "Mealtime for the child care worker as well as the children should be a pleasant experience physically as well as socially."

Is this a realistic statement? Reactions from trainees are requested, and discussion encouraged. Issues raised during discussion should be explored further. Among these will inevitably be:

a. Whether child care workers should eat with the children.

b. Should they eat whatever is served, even though they may "hate certain foods?"

c. Should children who misbehave be sent away from the table?

d. During waiting time for food or during cleanup, should the child care worker have the kids sit quietly or should they be involved in talk, story-telling, planning for cottage activities, word games, and so on.

EDUCATION

Discussion Topics

1. How much should child care workers involve themselves in encouraging children to study?

2. How would you try to develop the children's interest in education?

3. In the case example in Part I, what risk, if any, did Mr. Lewis take in being so direct with Albert? Would you have done it differently? How?

4. Should a study hour be enforced for all children in the cottage? If not, why not?

5. Should a child care worker consult teachers about the school adjustment of their children? Should the children be told about it?

WORK

Discussion Topics

1. What are the values, if any, of assigned work responsibilities in group care?

2. Should work assignments be explained to the youngsters? Why or why not?

3. Should youngsters be paid for such tasks? Why or why not? If yes, how should it be done?

4. On what basis should youngsters be selected for particular work assignments (for example; taking turns, skill, reward, punishment)? Why?

5. On what basis should particular jobs be selected to be included in the work program? Why?

6. What are the pros and cons for rewarding the best work done?

7. What are the pros and cons for punishing work poorly done?

8. How would you provide incentives to promote a high standard of cottage cleanup?

Role-Playing

The instructor suggests a role-playing exercise. Two volunteers are requested to act as child care workers. The rest of the group will comprise a peer group.

The scene is a group meeting called by the workers to evaluate this week's performance regarding house chores. There have been problems which the workers enumerate:

a. Some of the bigger boys are not doing their share; in fact, they force the weaker boys to do their assigned chores.

b. Several of the boys are griping about having to clean the bathrooms.

c. Workers do not like to hound the boys to do their work. After all, it is their house, and they should take pride in keeping it clean, tidy, and nice-looking.

d. Additional issues can be added by the actors.

Finally, the "boys" are asked to react to the above.

There will be counterarguments and gripes from some of the boys. Some may say nothing. After about ten minutes of dialogue, "workers" will state that the cottage work *has to be done.* However, the boys' suggestions about making this task more efficient and more pleasant would be welcome. The group continues discussion for about five minutes.

The instructor then asks the group to talk about the feelings they experienced in their role-playing as child care workers and as the boys.

CLOTHING AND GROOMING

Discussion Topics

1. In what way can the child care worker be involved constructively in the children's appearance and in their selection and care of clothing?

2. Is it important to know the (emotional) significance clothing has for a child, especially an adolescent? Elaborate.

SPENDING MONEY

Discussion Topics

1. Discuss some of the problems you experience in relation to money matters in your group.

2. How should you deal with children who use money destructively: flaunt it, buy friends, help others run away?

3. How do you feel about the situation that some children in your group have more money to spend than necessary while others have very little? What do you do about it?

1. Referring to the case discussed in Part I: Should Tom have given money to David since he had used up his allotment for the trip? Why or why not?

2. Are there any circumstances that justify a worker giving his own money to a child?

3. How should the worker deal with Danny about the extra money he had which he should have turned over to his account instead of keeping it?

4. Should children be allowed to carry pocket money?

CHILDREN'S MAIL

Discussion Topics

1. Do you agree or disagree with the following statement? Explain why or why not. "Reading of children's incoming or outgoing mail without their permission is 'censorship' and the abrogation of the individual's right to privacy."

2. What are the advantages or disadvantages of a policy which permits child care workers to open children's mail?

3. How important is such a policy for treatment purposes? For security reasons?

4. Should children be pressured to write to their families? Explain.

PLAY AND RECREATION

Discussion Topics

1. Why is play important to the children?

2. Why is organized play and recreation preferable to unorganized playtime for disturbed children?

3. Should time be set aside daily for free unstructured playtime as well as for privacy? Explain.

4. How does the child care worker contribute to children's development through his involvement in play activities with them?

5. What activities have you found most successful for leisure time?

6. Are there times when workers should *not* be involved in leisure-time activities with the children?

7. Have you encountered problems in planning and carrying out leisure-time activities? If yes, explain.

8. With reference to question 6, have you encountered problems with the children? Co-workers? Administration?

9. Do you believe off-grounds outings such as trips to zoos, parks, museums, concerts, and camping trips (including overnights) are important? What kind of problems have you had in carrying out such activities?

10. Should T.V. time be scheduled? If not, why not?

11. Should child care workers plan T.V.-viewing by consulting the *T.V. Guide*, newspapers, and so on? What is the advantage, if any, of doing so?

12. Should workers control what programs children should view? Explain.

13. How do you deal with disagreements among children regarding choice of T.V. programs?

BEDTIME

Discussion Topics

1. Why is bedtime a difficult period for children? Explain, giving examples.

2. What are some of the reasons children may have difficulty in falling asleep?

3. List a number of objections by children regarding set bedtime and how you have dealt with these situations.

4. Describe the steps which are helpful in preparing children for bedtime.

5. Discuss pros and cons for letting a child or the group stay up beyond the established bedtime.

6. Sending a child to bed early for disciplinary reasons is not an uncommon practice among child care workers. What is your opinion about its effectiveness? What are the pros and cons for doing so?

Case Example

Mrs. C. complained to Bill, her supervisor, that she could no longer tolerate Danny's behavior. "He is bad. I can't stand what he does to me." She explained tearfully that he has been knocking on her door after midnight, complaining he can't fall asleep. The first time, she gave him some warm milk, the next night she became impatient and told him to go to bed, but he persisted, crying at the door until she opened it. The third night she scolded him and the following day told Danny's caseworker about it. Last night she punished him. Nothing seems to work. She's exhausted.

The group is asked to react to the example above in terms of Mrs. C's attitude and actions toward the child, who is ten years old. Are there alternative ways to handle Danny?

After a brief period of the discussion, the instructor informs the group that Bill had additional information about Danny which he shared with Mrs. C. On the basis of this, should Mrs. C. deal differently with Danny. How?

Bill told Mrs. C. the following: Danny is a seriously disturbed child. He is filled with terrifying fantasies, especially at night. When Danny was five years old, his father died suddenly from a severe heart attack. It occurred late at night while Danny was asleep in an adjoining room. His mother is now ill and, according to his case-worker, Danny is fearful she may die like his father.

HEALTH CARE AND MEDICATION

Discussion Topics

1. Johnny complains to his child care worker that he is "sick." What should the child care worker do?
2. Do you believe that a child who is ill with a cold or flu, but not with a serious illness or infectious disease, could be cared for in the cottage instead of the infirmary? What are the advantages and disadvantages of a sick child remaining in the cottage?
3. What is the child care worker's responsibility in relation to the children who are on medication?
4. Is it appropriate for the child care worker who feels that he can no longer manage a child to request that medication be given to calm him down? If not, why not?
5. Would you prefer prescription of medication to transferring out a very difficult child to a hospital? Explain.
6. Are there risks that one may take the "easy way out" in dealing with difficult children by becoming overdependent on medication to control them? What other methods should be tried first?

PRACTICE REVIEW EXERCISES

Daily Living

I. *Waking*

Check the phrase you consider valid for the following:

1. Children who do not get up promptly when their worker wakes them, do so because —
   a. They are lazy.
   b. It is difficult for them to deal with the demands and expectations that face them.
   c. They do it spitefully to give their worker a hard time.

2. Children who take a long time to dress after waking may do so because—
   a. They are poorly coordinated.
   b. They are stalling to delay facing the tasks and demands that await them in school.
   c. They want to aggravate their worker.
   d. They are lazy.

3. Check the *inappropriate* ways of waking a child:
   a. Address him by name with a cheerful "good morning."
   b. Touch him lightly, calling out his name.
   c. Shake him roughly, saying, "Time to get up."
   d. Ring a bell loudly close to his bed.
   e. Push him out of bed if he is slow in getting up.
   f. If he doesn't get up on first call, reenter room and say in a firm tone, "Get up; it's late."

4. Indicate whether you agree or disagree with the following;
   a. Children need the workers' encouragement and guidance to develop good standards of hygiene and growing.

   Agree _____   Disagree _____

   b. To help younger children dress more efficiently and quickly, a worker may first have to teach them how and then encourage them with praise when they progress even if it's at a slow pace.

   Agree _____   Disagree _____

   c. The method suggested in "b" above is unrealistic. Shaming, warning of consequences for stalling, and finally punishment get quicker results.

   Agree _____   Disagree _____

   d. T.V.-viewing before breakfast is not advisable.

   Agree _____   Disagree _____

II. *Mealtime*

   Indicate whether you agree or disagree with the following:

   1. Food has emotional as well as nutritional significance.

   Agree _____   Disagree _____

   2. A child who has food fads should be forced to eat the food he objects to.

   Agree _____   Disagree _____

   3. A food fad may be symptomatic of anxiety associated with an earlier feeding experience.

   Agree _____   Disagree _____

4. Mealtime should be quiet time so that the workers can enjoy their food without trouble from the children.

   Agree _____   Disagree _____

5. Mealtime is a social event in addition to feeding. Conversation should be encouraged.

   Agree _____   Disagree _____

6. If the food served does not meet the worker's tast preference, he should complain about it in the children's presence and not eat it.

   Agree _____   Disagree _____

7. The worker should assume responsibility for serving out the food; assigning children to do so is too much trouble.

   Agree _____   Disagree _____

8. Telling stories, or involving children in discussing the day's activities during the mealtime, is disruptive.

   Agree _____   Disagree _____

9. A child who is disruptive during meals should be removed from the table, but not deprived of the meal.

   Agree _____   Disagree _____

10. Depriving children of food is an appropriate mode of punishment.

    Agrce _____   Disagree _____

Education, Work, and Play

1. How can a child care worker be helpful to children with their schooling?

   _____

   _____

2. Check whether you agree or disagree with the following:

   a. It is advisable for workers to help a child with his homework.

      Agree _____   Disagree _____

   b. Education is the child's responsibility. The worker should not inquite about nor check a child's homework.

      Agree _____   Disagree _____

   c. Children should be paid to do house chores.

      Agree _____   Disagree _____

   d. House chores should not be mandatory or compulsory for all the children in the group.

      Agree _____   Disagree _____

e. Children should be involved in planning and evaluating work responsibilities in the home or cottage.

Agree _____   Disagree _____

f. The strongest boy or girl in the group should be given responsibility to see to it that house chores are done.

Agree _____   Disagree _____

g. It is not advisable for workers to work along with the children.

Agree _____   Disagree _____

h. Regardless of his capabilities, a child should be held responsible for high standards of work performance and should be punished if he does his work poorly.

Agree _____   Disagree _____

3. Check which of the following are the best justification for expecting children to do house chores and work in communal projects:

a. To save money for the agency.

b. Work is instructive—it affords opportunity to develop skills, and assume responsibility.

c. The group home or cottage is the children's "home" during their residence, and they have an obligation to care for it. They are working for themselves.

d. When the children work, they appreciate the effort and energy that is needed to maintain a home.

e. It makes the child care worker's job easier because he doesn't have to do housework.

4. In what ways does a child care worker's involvement with children in play and leisure-time activities help children?

_____

_____

_____

5. Check whether you agree or disagree with the following:

a. Sending children out of the cottage or home to organized recreation programs is preferable to involving them in leisure-time activities within the residence.

Agree _____   Disagree _____

b. Child–worker participation in leisure-time activities serves to strengthen the workers' relationship with the children.

Agree _____   Disagree _____

c. Children should always be scheduled and supervised, otherwise they get into trouble.

Agree _____   Disagree _____

d. Children in group have little privacy. This should be available to them as well as some period of free time during a day, when they do not have to be in supervised activities.

Agree _____   Disagree _____

e. Children should determine what movies or T.V. programs they should see regardless of worker's opinion.

Agree _____   Disagree _____

f. There should be no restrictions about T.V.-viewing.

Agree _____   Disagree _____

Clothing and Grooming; Spending Money

Fill in the missing word:

1. Clothing, like food, has _____ significance.
2. Clothing has special _____ significance for teenagers.
3. Indicate whether you agree or disagree with following:

a. Children in group care should not have choices about quality or style of clothing because they do not pay for it.

Agree _____   Disagree _____

b. Staff should be sensitive about children's clothing preference and approve their purchases as long as it is within the budgetary allowance and not so extremely far out that they are socially unacceptable.

Agree _____   Disagree _____

c. If older children prefer to shop for clothing on their own, it should be approved as long as they bring back a receipt and inform their worker in advance what they intend to purchase.

Agree _____   Disagree _____

d. Child care workers should insist that children wear appropriate clothing in rainy or cold weather.

Agree _____   Disagree _____

e. When a child refuses to accept clothing from the clothing supply room, he should be told that he has no right to complain because he is a public charge and should be grateful for whatever he is given.

Agree _____   Disagree _____

4. Indicate whether you agree or disagree with following:

   a. All children are entitled to a modest amount of spending money.

   Agree _____   Disagree _____

   b. Children should not be permitted to carry money because many of them will misuse it.

   Agree _____   Disagree _____

   c. Parents should be discouraged to give their children excessive amounts of spending money.

   Agree _____   Disagree _____

   d. During visiting, parents should give money to worker for a child's account rather than to the child.

   Agree _____   Disagree _____

   e. When there are great differences in the amount of spending money that the children possess, it creates tensions in the group.

   Agree _____   Disagree _____

   f. It is risky, if not burdensome, for a child care worker to spend his own money on the children.

   Agree _____   Disagree _____

5. List ways children may use their spending money in destructive ways:

   _____

   _____

   _____

Bedtime

1. In what ways do children express anxiety about bedtime?

   _____

   _____

   _____

2. What can a child care worker do to ease pre-bedtime tensions?

3. Under what circumstances should a worker agree to children's request that they stay up later than the scheduled bedtime?

4. Why is it unproductive to use early bedtime as punishment?

20 PROBLEMATIC BEHAVIOR
Discussion Topics and
Practice Review Exercises

TEMPER TANTRUM

Discussion Topics

1. Describe how a genuine temper tantrum differs from a feigned or faked temper tantrum in terms of behavior preceding the actual outburst, behavior during the tantrum, and the aftermath.

2. How should the worker handle the child with the genuine temper tantrum? How should he act with the manipulator?

BEDWETTING AND SOILING

Discussion Topics

1. How can the child care worker be helpful to the enuretic child?

2. How should the bedwetting be handled?

3. How should he deal with those children who ridicule or abuse the bedwetter?

4. Why is shaming the soiler inadvisable?

5. If a child care worker's patience with a soiling child is at the breaking point, what should he do?

LYING

Discussion Topics

1. How should a child care worker convey to children that lying is unacceptable to him?

Role-Playing Exercises

The object of this exercise is to demonstrate the need to react to the child rather than the lying. The instructor asks for four volunteers to reenact the following situations:

Jimmy, nine years old, was an hour late in returning from his session with the caseworker. His child care worker angrily asked him why he was late and what he had been doing for the last hour. Jimmy said, "I'm not late. I came back after my session." The worker knew that this was not true. Jimmy's caseworker had telephoned three-quarters of an hour ago to inform the worker that Jimmy was upset during the session and might act up upon his return to the cottage.

Bill, sixteen years old, returned a half-hour late from his scheduled casework session, explaining to John, his worker, that he had an extended interview because of an "important" problem he had to discuss with Mr. S. "But I called the clinic to check and was told Mr. S. was not in his room." "Oh," said Bill. "It was so nice outside, Mr. S. suggested we talk while walking." While this seemed rather strange to John, the new child care worker, it was still a feasible explanation which he could check the following day with Mr. S. "O.K.," said John, "Next time tell Mr. S. to call me if he sees you beyond the scheduled time."

That night while John was saying good-night to the boys before leaving, he overheard Bill's roommate say "Boy! You must have had some casework session with Jane." Bill laughed, "Yeah, and I got away with it!" John then realized that Bill had lied to him. He was angry, but it was too late to make a fuss. He decided to talk to Mr. S. next morning and then confront Bill. He was even angrier when Mr. S. informed him that Bill had only seen him for a half-hour because he said John needed him in the cottage earlier for a special job.

After the role-playing, the instructor presents a description of each child:

Jimmy is a seriously disturbed child who is frequently disoriented about time. He is so involved in his fantasies that he is literally out of reality, forgets where he is, or what time it is.

Bill is a psychopathic-like youngster who is a pleasure-oriented child and tries to manipulate others to do or get what he wants.

He then asks the volunteers who acted as the child care workers that if this information had been available to them, would they have acted differently with Jimmy and Bill, respectively? If so, why? The other trainees should be encouraged to add their opinions.

STEALING

Discussion Topics

1. List various motives for stealing.
2. Discuss what action, including disciplinary, the child care worker should take in the following situations:

   a. John steals indiscriminately, even things that seem useless to him, and he always manages to get caught.

   b. Bill, a child from a socioeconomically deprived family, tends to take other children's possessions.

   c. Don, a very disturbed (diagnosed as schizophrenic) boy, steals his roommates' toys and clothing.

   d. Bill and Rod stole money from other children prior to running away; when they were returned, they admitted stealing so that they could buy train tickets.

   e. The worker discovers that one of his boys has a lot of money to spend and give to his friends following a break-in of a staff apartment.

   f. During a shopping trip the worker notices that Mary has a new blouse which she did not purchase. Mary later admits she stole it from the store.

   g. Following a city trip, the worker learns that while Jim was on a home visit he stole a car and, while driving, he damaged and then abandoned it.

   h. Money is missing from the cottage account. The worker believes that the boys know who the culprit is. When questioned, they deny such knowledge.

3. How would you, as a child care worker, deal with pervasive stealing in your cottage? You get complaints about it, but no one is able or willing to identify the culprit.

RUNAWAYS

Discussion Topics

1. List reasons why children run away.
2. John threatens that he will run away. What should the worker do?
3. Jim tells the worker that he has something "confidential" to tell him about a planned mass runaway. Should the worker honor such confidentiality? What should he do?
4. Should there be a policy that *all* runaways should be punished? If not, what are the exceptions?
5. What disciplinary action, if any, should be taken in the following runaway situations. If you do not recommend punishment, what else should be done?

   a. Jane, ten years of age, runs away a few hours after her arrival. She is known to have run away from foster homes and another institution.

   b. Billy, age twelve, periodically absconds while living in a residential treatment center located in midtown of New York City. It is relatively easy to do this because the front door cannot be locked from the inside because of fire regulations. He generally visits friends in his former neighborhood and comes back by himself.

   c. Tom's running away has occurred after a return from a home visit.

   d. Mary ran away after an argument with her cottage mother.

   e. Jim ran away following a confrontation with a teacher which ended when he was slapped by the teacher.

   f. Ben ran away because he expected to be beaten up by the leadership group in his cottage; his expecations were correct.

   g. Jane ran away at the invitation of her boyfriend who sent her a letter urging her to do so.

   h. Tim ran away after being severely criticized in the presence of the whole football team for poor performance.

   i. John stole money from the canteen and ran away when he was told he would have to see the director of the institution.

   j. Bill, aged seventeen, ran away when he learned of an evaluation meeting decision that he was not considered ready to leave the institution.

   k. A week before her planned departure, Joan ran away.

l. Billy, age twelve, ran away when he was informed that his mother was hospitalized.

SEXUAL BEHAVIOR

Discussion Topics

1. What should the worker do in the following situations:

a. While watching T.V., Jimmy is masturbating in the presence of other children.

b. The worker notes that Mary masturbates nightly after going to bed.

c. The worker comes upon two boys involved in mutual masturbation.

d. The worker learns that several of the older boys have sexually assaulted one of the younger boys in the cottage.

e. After showering, several of the girls run around in the nude.

f. Bill exposes his genitals to the female worker on duty.

g. David has returned from his home visit with a batch of pornographic magazines and shares them with the other boys.

h. A number of children, individually and as a group, are using profane, sexually provocative language which annoys their worker.

i. During a bed check after lights out, the worker finds two ten-year-olds in bed together.

j. As in "i" above, the girls are sixteen years old.

k. A similar situation occurs with two fourteen-year-old boys.

l. The worker learns that James, age fifteen, solicits sexual contact with other boys.

m. The worker hears of a plan by some girls to have boys visit them at midnight.

2. Is it justifiable to consider a boy homosexual if he displays effeminate mannerisms? Explain. Or a girl who tends to be "tomboyish"?

3. How should child care workers plan coed activities to avoid sexual acting-out?

4. What should a worker do in the following coed situations?

a. Jane asks permission to visit her boyfriend in his cottage.

b. At a coed cottage party, Joan and her boyfriend are sitting on the couch holding hands while the other children dance or play games.

c. Upon leaving the dining hall, Jim kisses Ann, his girlfriend, good-bye.

d. At a coed party, several boys and girls suggest they all watch a T.V. program. Should staff agree? Why not?

e. Having received staff permission to view a T.V. program, Jim, supported by Ann, suggest that all lights be turned off.

f. During a party, Ms. Adams becomes aware that Mary is not in the living room. After a search she locates her in her room with one of the boys, sitting on the floor listening to records, or lying in her bed petting, or having intercourse.

5. Should boys and girls in a coed setting be allowed unrestricted visiting in each other's cottages? If not, why not?

6. What is your opinion regarding coed group residences? What are the advantages? Disadvantages? How, if at all, could the risks of sexual acting-out be avoided?

7. How should workers in an adolescent cottage (boys or girls) convey to the children that they are available for discussion of any questions about sexuality?

8. When youngsters inquire of a worker about his personal life, including sexual matters, how should he or she respond?

9. These discussion questions refer to the case in Part I.

a. Do you think that Mrs. Williams' and Miss James' concern is justified?

b. Does the girls' behavior confirm that they are homosexual?

c. What specific behavior and attitudes on the part of a person would justify labeling him or her as homosexual or lesbian?

d. What are the risks of separating the girls by transfer to separate cottages?

e. Do you believe that the girls' behavior, if it continues, will affect the other girls detrimentally? If yes, how?

DRUG ABUSE

Discussion Topics

1. In your opinion, what are the essentials to be included in the agency drug policy regarding the use of drugs by children?

2. What would your attitude be toward children in the following situations:

a. You learn that last night some of the boys drank beer in the cottage.

b. You learn that last night some of the boys got drunk on hard liquor.

c. You come upon a group of boys smoking marijuana in the cottage.

d. Johnny, who came back from a home visit, was distributing marijuana cigarettes to some of his friends.

e. Jim is caught selling marijuana to others.

f. Substitute barbituates or amphetamines for marijuana in the above instance.

g. The same for LSD or acid.

h. Heroin or cocaine.

1. In considering the case on alcohol abuse brought up in Part I, what is your opinion of Mr. B's interpretations?

2. What is your reaction to the boys' challenge that adults are hypocritical when they tell youngsters not to drink?

3. If you, as a child care worker, are asked whether you indulge in drinking, what would your response be?

   a. Should you involve yourself in explaining matters of your private, personal life? Explain.

   b. If you would have responded in the affirmative, what rationale would you give for occasional or "social" drinking of alcoholic beverages?

Case Situation

A number of incidents of amphetamine highs among the older children have been discovered. There are rumors that boys in cottage 15, the oldest boys' cottage, may have distributed the pills. The child care workers of cottage 15 have been asked to "keep their eyes open."

One evening after lights out, as Andrew, the senior child care worker, left the cottage, he decided to return later on to check out whether the boys had settled down to sleep. A half hour later, he walked in quietly. On his way upstairs he heard voices emanating from Jason's room, which had a light on. He listened attentively and heard phrases about "speed" and "pills." As Andrew opened the door, he saw Jason and Phil sitting on the bed with a quantity of colored pills spread out on the blanket. The boys were startled and Jason hurriedly tried to shove all the pills into a brown paper bag. Phil was cringing in fear. Andrew said firmly, "Give me that bag." As Jason hesitated, Andrew pushed him aside, collected the rest of the pills and put them in the bag. He then ordered the boys to sit down and began to talk with them. Just then a number of boys who had either been awake or awakened by Andrew's entry thronged the hall outside of Jason's room. Andrew told them to go back to their rooms. However, he did not lower his voice as he spoke to Jason and Phil, because he wanted the others to hear what he had to say. He planned to emphasize the serious consequences of violating the institution's rules regarding drugs, the risk to the other children, institutional and legal consequences of possession and sale of drugs on campus, and the risks of drug abuse.

Role-Playing Exercise

Instructor suggests enactment of the above situation, using three volunteers. He gives the following character sketches and suggests that after the role-playing exercise is completed, the group as a whole get involved in evaluating what occurred. Afterwards they should deal with the important question of the child care worker's role in dealing with drug abuse issues, the workers' values regarding drug usage, and their roles in a drug education program.

Character Sketches.   Andrew is an experienced, highly knowledgeable child care worker who feels strongly about drug abuse, especially about drug pushers. He is determined to come down hard on the two boys, especially Jason, who he thinks is the "brains" behind this incident.

Jason is sixteen years old and has a history of delinquent acts including suspected drug experimentation. He resents authority, feels bitter about being in the institution, is manipulative, shrewd, and exploits boys like Phil. In the past, he has called staff "hypocrites" when they talked about drug abuse, alcohol, and smoking. According to him, they have a double standard, namely, loose morals for themselves and puritanical ones for the kids. Andrew can expect a lot of "back talk" from him which will be defensive and accusatory in style and content.

Phil is a fifteen-year-old boy of limited intelligence and who is educationally disadvantaged. He is a close collaborator of Jason and is influenced by him to do his dirty work. Andrew thinks that since Phil was in a home visit last weekend, he might have been influenced by Jason to make contact in their neighborhood to get the drugs for use and sale on campus.

PRACTICE REVIEW EXERCISES

Temper Tantrum

1.   Differentiate between a genuine temper tantrum and a temper outburst.

_____

_____

2. Check true or false for the following:
   a. Temper tantrum behavior is irrational.

   True _____ False _____

   b. The best way to terminate a temper tantrum is to slap the child.

   True _____ False _____

   c. The onset of a temper tantrum is generally preceded by a period of "rumbling and grumbling."

   True _____ False _____

   d. The most effective way of dealing with a child in a state of temper tantrum is to hold him tight and remove him from the group.

   True _____ False _____

   e. A worker might prevent the onset of a temper tantrum if he perceives the building up anxiety and talks to the child.

   True _____ False _____

   f. Some children stage a *feigned* temper tantrum to get their way.

   True _____ False _____

Bedwetting and Soiling

1. a. Bedwetting is a willful habit which can be stopped by punishment.

   True _____ False _____

   b. Shaming is an effective method of putting a stop to soiling.

   True _____ False _____

   c. Enuretic children and children who soil are unhappy children.

   True _____ False _____

   d. Scapegoating of these children should be supported by the child care workers.

   True _____ False _____

Lying

1. a. There are different kinds of lying.

   True _____ False _____

   b. "Fantasy" lying is the most offensive.

   True _____ False _____

   c. There should be no differentiation in punishing a child who lies because of anxiety and one who lies to cover up a delinquent act.

   True _____ False _____

d. If lying doesn't harm anyone, the worker should ignore it.

True _____   False _____

Stealing

1. a. Stealing in group living cannot be tolerated.

True _____   False _____

b. Understanding the causes for stealing is important if we want to help a child stop stealing.

True _____   False _____

c. The young child who appropriates another's toys should be treated the same as a youngster who steals money from his roommates.

True _____   False _____

d. Punishment is generally not effective in stopping compulsive or impulsive stealing.

True _____   False _____

e. Child care workers should take an affirmative stand against stealing and lying.

True _____   False _____

Runaways

1. a. Emphasis should be on prevention rather than punishment of runaways.

True _____   False _____

b. All runaways should be treated similarly in terms of disciplinary action.

True _____   False _____

c. Children who run away expose themselves to danger.

True _____   False _____

2. List reasons why children may run away from a residential setting.

Sexual Behavior

1. Complete the following:
   a. Sexual behavior includes _____

   _____

   b. Adolescents tend to _____ with varied sexual behavior.

   c. Why is it risky as well as unfair to label a boy who shows effeminate characteristics or a girl who is "tomboyish" as "homosexual"? _____

   _____

2. Which of the following merits prompt action?

   a. Before falling asleep, Jimmy, age nine, masturbates occasionally.

   b. Mary, age sixteen, seems to be masturbating occasionally when she is alone in her room.

   c. Dan, age twelve, has been sexually assaulted by Billy, age fifteen.

   d. Mary is kissed by her boyfriend at a coed dance.

   e. Billy uses profane language excessively.

   f. Mary informs her worker that she may be pregnant.

3. State whether you agree or disagree with the following:

   a. Masturbation is sinful and should be punished.

                    Agree _____   Disagree _____

   b. Since profanity among children in group care is prevalent, workers should not make a fuss about it.

                    Agree _____   Disagree _____

   c. Overt homosexual behavior in group care should not be tolerated.

                    Agree _____   Disagree _____

   d. One must guard against hasty labeling of a child as homosexual.

                    Agree _____   `Disagree _____

   e. Unsupervised coed parties in group care are not advisable.

                    Agree _____   Disagree _____

   f. A worker should not hesitate to give sexual information to children.

                    Agree _____   Disagree _____

   g. It is inadvisable for a worker to discuss with children personal intimacies.

                    Agree_____   Disagree _____

4. Check which of the worker's actions are appropriate in the following situations.

   a. At a coed party, Mary and her boyfriend are observed petting. Workers should—

     (1) Ignore it.

     (2) Suggest to them it is not appropriate.

     (3) Suggest that they join in the dancing.

     (4) Expel the boy from the cottage and send Mary to her room.

   b. Jimmy is masturbating while watching T.V. in the presence of other children. The worker should—

     (1) Remove him from the room and talk to him about the inappropriateness of his behavior.

     (2) Ignore him.

c. The worker notes that Mary masturbates nightly after going to bed. The worker should —

    (1) Consult Mary's caseworker.

    (2) Do nothing.

    (3) Punish her.

    (4) Talk with her about it.

d. The worker comes upon two boys involved in mutual masturbation. He should —

    (1) Tell the boys to stop it.

    (2) Lecture them about the evils of such actions.

    (3) Tell them they risk becoming homosexual.

e. The worker learns that several of the older boys have sexually assaulted one of the younger boys in the cottage. The worker should —

    (1) Report the act to administration.

    (2) Talk with the boys, stressing the seriousness of their actions.

    (3) Make sure they are punished severely.

f. After showering, several of the girls run around in the nude. The worker should —

    (1) Ignore it.

    (2) Tell them it is inappropriate and unacceptable behavior.

g. David has returned from his home visit with a batch of pornographic magazines and shares them with the other boys. The worker should —

    (1) Confiscate the magazines.

    (2) Punish David.

    (3) Talk to him about the inappropriateness of such an act.

h. A number of children, individually and as a group, are using profane, sexually provocative language which annoys their worker. He should —

    (1) Complain to the supervisor.

    (2) Punish them.

    (3) Discuss why it is annoying and why it is unacceptable behavior.

i. During a bed check after lights out, the worker finds two ten-year-olds in bed together. He should —

    (1) Tell them to return to their own beds.

    (2) Discuss it with their therapists so that appropriate action, if any, is in order.

    (3) Ignore it.

j. A worker is informed that some of her girls plan to invite boys to visit them after bedtime hours. She should —

    (1) Ignore it since it may not be true.

    (2) Alert the supervisor to have strict night coverage.

    (3) Inform the girls about it and warn them of punishment.

    (4) Call a group meeting to discuss the rumor.

21
THE RELATIONSHIP NETWORK
Discussion Topics and Practice
Review Exercises

RELATIONSHIPS WITH INDIVIDUAL CHILDREN

Discussion Topics

1. What do we mean when we say that we have "established a good relationship with a child"?

2. Why do children avoid establishing a relationship with adults? With peers? How is this expressed in behavioral terms?

3. Why should manipulation be discouraged and dealt with promptly?

4. How would you deal with the following type of manipulators?

    a. Johnny tends to manipulate others to make himself feel big.

    b. Mary manipulated and then watches with satisfaction the consequent dissention she creates among her cottage counselors.

    c. Jimmy seems to be driven by an uncontrollable urge to perpetuate the hostile relationship he witnessed in his home. He tries to cause dissension among the child care workers in his cottage and between his cottage staff and social worker.

    d. Joan manipulates in order to get what she wants.

5. How can a worker know when he is being manipulated or "conned"?

6. What are the consequences for the worker who lets himself be manipulated? For the child who does it? How may it affect the group?

7. Is it important to establish expectations and goals for each of the children in your group? What is the best way of going about it?

    a. Draw up a list based on team conference material, and tell the child that he has to live up to it?

    b. Ask the child to list goals for himself?

    c. Sit down with a child, and together formulate goals for him to work toward?

8. In communicating with children, do you find that frequently nonverbal communication, or even silence, is just as important in understanding what a child is trying to tell you?

Case Analysis

At this point the instructor could discuss nonverbal communication in some detail, beginning with case examples below. The first illustrates a child's *anger* reaction against himself which he projected onto his child care worker. The second is illustrative of a *fear* reaction.

Jim returned to the cottage just before supper from a shopping trip. He immediately became aware there was something bothering Danny. Danny did not respond to his "hello," then he walked about restlessly, a surly look on his face. He seemed irritated, touchy, defensive, and almost got into a fight with one of his friends because of a critical comment regarding his behavior. During dinner he complained about the food, quarreled, and challenged Ben, a much stronger boy, to a fight. He seemed to be looking for a confrontation where he might be hurt. It was at this point that Jim asked Danny, "What's the matter, Danny? Something must be troubling you." Danny burst out in a loud high-pitched voice, "Mind your own business. You're always picking on me. I hate you." With this, he got up and stalked away from the table, holding back tears. Jim shook his head but didn't follow Danny. He decided to talk with him later.

Before completing the description of the incident, the instructor might ask the group about the meaning of Danny's behavior—what emotion is being experienced? What defense mechanisms is Danny using? How should Jim deal with Danny? Would the approach to Danny be different if Danny were seven years old instead of fourteen? (This is asked because in the case of a younger child, the behavior displayed by Danny might be indicative of a pending temper tantrum.) In Danny's case, it was reactive to a real situation which became clear later on.

It seemed to Jim that Danny's anger was covering up something unpleasant, some hurt. The question was, Who had hurt Danny, or was it something to do with himself? Did he get into difficulty with another boy, or did he get a troubling letter from home? After Danny left the table, the other boys told Jim that during the afternoon while Jim was away, Danny participated in a baseball game with a neighboring cottage. He did poorly, made errors, and was struck out with bases loaded. He seemed upset but refused to talk about it.

This information helped Jim prepare for his talk with Danny. Trainees are then asked, "If you were Jim, what would you do?"

Ms. Wilson, Mary's worker, was puzzled by her behavior. The day preceding her visit to her family, Mary's behavior changed dramatically. She was tense, preoccupied, and delayed getting her things ready which she generally took with her. Her face was pale, her brow furrowed, and she did not smile. She did not look directly at others. At times, she perspired, although it was cool. During mealtime, she ate poorly and was fidgety at the table. She avoided her peers and seemed depressed. She complained of not feeling well, but the nurse at the infirmary stated that there was no indication of illness. That night, she avoided participating in the group games and was touchy and tearful when asked what the trouble was. She even got angry at her best friend and almost provoked a fight with another girl. She told her worker in a surly and whining tone, "Leave me alone." Her worker did not pursue the matter further. During the night, Mary ran away and was picked up by a police car while walking on the parkway in a direction away from the city where her mother lived. The administrator on duty who brought her back from the local police station deprived her of her home visit. He asked the child care worker to call her mother early the following morning to inform her that Mary would not be going home because she had run away.

The trainees are then asked: "What does Mary's action suggest? What nonverbal message was she giving her worker? Should her worker have been more active in this case, and have pursued the matter further?"

The facts learned later from the caseworker who talked with Mary and her mother were the following: During her last home visit, Mary was molested sexually by her mother's paramour. Mary had fought him off, but she did not tell her mother about the incident. Nor did she discuss it with her caseworker. When the administrator deprived her of the home visit, she was not upset and the following day was in a better mood.

10. Some children may become very dependent on their workers. They may make endless demands on a worker's time and energy. How should one deal with them without making them feel rejected?

11. Some adults like children to become dependent and encourage it. Is this helpful to a child's (independent) development? Should child care workers be aware of this possibility so that they can control it before overdependency is established?

Practice Review Exercises

1. Fill in the missing words in the following:
   a. A positive _____ between child care worker and each of the children in his group is essential.
   b. Children coming into group care are generally _____ of others.
   c. Understanding a child's verbal and _____ verbal messages and the worker's self- _____ of his reactions to the child is basic to establishing a _____ relationship between the two.
   d. The worker is subject to a testing period by children during which he can expect to be a target of emotions, and _____ .

2. Three basic components of a significant relationship between a child and child care worker consists of:
   a. Ease of _____ between them.
   b. A positive response to the worker's _____ .
   c. Worker becomes a _____ for the child's identification.

3. Define:
   a. Active Listening.
   b. Self-Awareness.
   c. Ambivalence.
   d. Transference.
   e. Counter-transference.

4. Define Gordon's no-lose method of resolving a relationship conflict.

   _____

   _____

5. Check which of the following may be a consequence of the authoritarian approach — in other words, forcing a child to do as the worker wants so that he feels he comes out the winner.
   a. Child has greater respect fot the worker.

   b. The relationship is damaged.

   c. The child may become resentful or hostile to the worker.

   d. He may resort to deviant ways of dealing with the workers and other people such as lying, avoiding responsibility, manipulation.

   e. His distrust of adults will increase.

   f. He will adopt the worker's authoritarian method and may become a bully.

   g. He'll be grateful to the worker for teaching him to obey.

6. Check which of the following may be the consequence of overpermissiveness by the worker because he wants to avoid a confrontation or power struggle with a child.

   a. The child likes the worker because he lets him win.

   b. The child loses respect for the worker.

   c. It spoils the child.

   d. He does not learn to take adult direction.

   e. He learns that if he makes a fuss he can get away with things.

   f. He won't learn self-discipline.

RELATIONSHIP WITH THE GROUP

Discussion Topics

Peer Culture

1. What is meant by the informal peer group culture?

2. What is "pecking order"?

3. How would you cope with destructive leadership from a gang-type leader?

4. Under what circumstances, if at all, should a child care worker enlist the help of natural cottage leaders in managing the group?

5. Can strong-arm tactics be avoided if natural cottage leaders are involved in group management tasks? If so, how?

6. What is meant by a kangaroo court? Why shouldn't they be permitted?

7. Are there any circumstances which justify group punishment? Explain.

Decision-Making

1. Should one involve youngsters in decision-making? Why or why not? If so, in what area and to what extent?

2.   How can a child care worker let youngsters participate in decision-making in a meaningful way without giving up his responsibilities and authority?

Intergroup Relations

1.   A case example is illustrated by the following incident:

While Mary was in the kitchen preparing evening snacks, she heard a commotion in the living room. John, her co-worker, who was on the porch chatting with several boys, also heard it. When they entered the living room, they saw David and Tom in a physical struggle and heard them exchange ethnic and anti-semitic slurs. Several of the boys encircling them egged them on with additional insulting references about Jews and blacks. John stopped the fight and dispersed the group. He and Mary decided to meet with the boys after snacktime to discuss the incidents focusing on the racial and religious slurs. They felt that they should take advantage of this incident to deal with issues of prejudice. It might help the kids face the issue and be helped to greater understanding of ethnic and religious differences, face their prejudices, and learn to become more tolerant of others who differ from them.

The instructor asks the group what points they would stress if they were in Mary's and John's place.

2.   Group is asked about feelings of conflict experiences by white child care workers in control or disciplinary situations involving them with black children. Similarly, black workers expressed their feelings about white children.

3.   What are some of the problems in dealing with a group of children of diverse ethnic, racial, and cultural backgrounds? Give examples if you have experienced any. How did you deal with the individuals involved or the group as a whole? The instructor may wish to deal more extensively with the topic. He should encourage contributions from the trainee group who are knowledgeable about the subject. Supplementary readings from the literature (for example: *Black Child Care, Families of the Slums, Black Families in White America,*[a] and others) should be recommended.

---

[a] Comer, J.P., and A.F. Poussaint. 1975. *Black Child Care.* New York: Simon and Schuster.
Minuchin, S.; B. Montalvo; B.G. Guerney, Jr.; B. Rosman; and F. Schumer. 1967. *Families of the Slums.* New York: Basic Books.
Billingsley, A. 1968. *Black Families in White America.* Englewood Cliffs, N.J.: Prentice-Hall.

The Individual Within the Group

1. How would you go about helping the withdrawn, the socially inept, or the anxious child to become more comfortable in group living?

2. How would you go about making it possible that each child, at one time or another, has an opportunity for privacy.

3. Many youngsters in group living tend to "scapegoat"—to exploit the weak and those who differ from the acceptable group norms.

    a. How can the child care worker protect such a youngster from peer abuse?

    b. How can the worker help such a child gain greater status or recognition in the group?

    c. How should he interpret such a child to the group?

An assignment to construct a sociogram of their groups may be helpful in sensitizing the trainees to status positions in peer groups. One or more of these sociograms could then be used to analyze how the existing status distribution affects the functioning and lifestyle of the group, whether it enhances or is a deterrent to the therapeutic goals of the cottage group and of individual children, and whether an effort should be made to intervene in order to modify the existing status distribution.

4. The following case situation illustrates a worker's dilemma about dealing with a difficult youngster who defies adult authority and bullies other children.

While John was in the kitchen with two of the boys preparing evening snacks, he heard a crashing sound and ran toward the living room. He saw Timmy, one of the younger boys on the floor, next to an overturned game table. Checkers were strewn all over the floor. Wayne, the biggest boy in the cottage, was standing over Timmy, laughing and ordering him to "Pick up those checkers!"

John asked Timmy to get up and, turning to Wayne, demanded, "What happened?"

"Nothing. I didn't do anything. Why do you always pick on me first?" demanded Wayne.

"I'm not blaming you nor am I picking on you. I'm just asking," said John firmly. He then turned to Timmy and asked him about the matter, but the latter tearfully said, "Nothing." He asked the other boys, and their response was silence.

John felt certain that Wayne was responsible and that Timmy and the other boys were afraid to tell the truth. He felt that if Wayne were guilty, as he suspected, he would have to punish him severely. However, he would have to have more proof. He therefore postponed action until he had consulted his co-workers. In the meantime he would have to give Wayne and the other boys a message that he was not being fooled. So he said to Wayne firmly, "Help me pick up the table." At first Wayne hesitated but obeyed in a surly manner. He also asked several of the boys, including Timmy, to pick up the checkers. They did so in silence.

The following morning John reviewed the situation with his two co-workers Richard and Dave. They felt there should be a confrontation with Wayne, but between John and Wayne or with all of them together, could not be decided. They each felt strongly about Wayne's tendency to bully the younger children, about his defensiveness, provocativeness, lack of cooperation, and attempts to manipulate them to his own benefit. John felt discouraged about his inability to reach Wayne. He has tried to be friendly but the youngster has rebuffed his advances. There have been occasions when Wayne has made him so angry that he was on the brink of hitting him. Wayne seemed to know this. On those occasions he would smirk and challenge John, "You can't hit me. I know the rules." The boy was right because there was a rule against striking a child. What constantly infuriated all of them were Wayne's statements such as, "I ain't done nuttin'. What are you picking on me for?"

John pointed out to the others that he was not sure that he could control himself in a face-to-face discussion with Wayne because at this point he was very angry with him. He therefore asked them to decide whether they should see him together or he should handle it himself.

In the meantime, John had learned from some of the other boys that Wayne had accused Timmy of cheating in the game and shoved him hard against the table which was knocked over. The informants had pleaded with John not to divulge to Wayne that they were responsible for this information. Consequently, there were a number of problems to be discussed before seeing Wayne.

In a role-playing exercise, three volunteers are asked to reenact this meeting between John and his co-workers. The conversation should deal with the following questions:

a. What decision should they make about seeing Wayne? Should John see him alone or should they see him together?

b. Since Wayne's pattern of denial will inevitably result in his demand for proof of his guilt, how should they deal with the information they obtained from the other boys?

c. What should they try to accomplish with Wayne?

d. Should they punish him for his action and if so, what should it be?

e. Should there be a group meeting to discuss Wayne's behavior toward the other boys and toward staff?

Following reenactment of this situation, other topics might be discussed:

a. Could John have handled the incident in a different way than he did?

b. Should John have punished Wayne immediately? Why or why not?

Case Analysis

This incident, told by the worker, illustrates the successful handling of a crisis situation instigated by the natural leaders in a group of young children.

On one Monday evening, I was alone in the kitchen cleaning up after supper. The fifteen children and other counselors were settling in the living room to watch the six o'clock news. Seemingly, from out of nowhere, I heard Ann proclaim in no uncertain and rather profane terms that she was not going to obey the directions given by the counselor in the living room. I immediately headed toward the living room to remove Ann from the group. Before taking only a few steps, I heard several voices proclaiming the same decision as Ann. The vocalization was almost in unison, and I, at this point, suspected a planned uprising. I later discovered that my suspicions were correct. As I entered the living room, I made a quick observation of the scene and then seated myself to try to quell the situation at hand. After five minutes of conversation with Ann and her followers, it was apparent that more than conversation was needed to bring an end to this mass rebellion. I sent my co-workers, who was the object of the hostility, to the kitchen. I then singled out the children who were obviously not involved and sent them to the kitchen to continue to watch the news.

As I was removing each child, I spoke with them and assured them of my ability to control the situation. I also told them that they could discuss the situation with the counselor in the kitchen. Tina said she was afraid of Ann. I reassured her that I would protect her. Rose was laughing to herself, occasionally tossing out a profane phrase. I very firmly told her to come with me, and she did so. The next two children to leave were Michelle and Viola. They were both vacillating from withdrawal to rebellion. When asked to, Michelle hesitated and then came with me. Viola looked to Ann and Manda for support after my first request. I then firmly ordered her to follow me. As is usual with Viola, the second command was sufficient. Pat, who always disappears in a crowd, was the next child to leave. She is one of the most obviously disturbed children on the floor and is very adept at emotionally withdrawing. She was waiting to be "rescued" and could not have been more relieved when I told her to come with me. There were now only five children in the living room, all of whom were activists in the rebellion. I first approached Sue who was following the leader for acceptance. Sue likes and respects me, and convincing her to join the others in the kitchen was easy. Patty has virtually no mind of her own and was, like Sue, a follower who was relieved to be removed from the rebellious group.

Remaining were Ann, a leader through her physical prowess and intelligence; Manda, a leader by virtue of her intelligence; and Alice, a small eight-year-old who was serving as Ann's and Manda's support. Through prompting, Alice climbed onto a table and upon her own volition shouted, "Come here, you mother fucker, and I'll punch you in the mouth." Ann and Manda could not resist, and a sigh of relief was echoed by hearty childlike laughter. They had given up the game. Unfortunately, Alice did not have the self-control to stop. I walked to the table and carried her to her room where I spoke to her for a few minutes. She calmed down immediately and shortly joined the group. I returned to Ann and Manda, and after a short discussion, they were sent to their rooms for a half-hour or so to think about the disturbance they had caused. They later returned to participate in the planned group activities.

Some questions for discussion are these:

1. What skills does the worker demonstrate in dealing with this situation?
2. Can you suggest alternate ways of coping with it?
3. If this was an adolescent group, would the worker's method have to be different? how?
4. Should Ann and Manda have been disciplined more severely? If yes, why? What punishment?

Practice Review Exercises

1. Complete the following sentences:
   a. Adaptation to group living presents _____ problems for children.
   b. The worker's relationship with a child evolves and is sustained in _____ _____ living.
   c. The worker has to _____ within the context of group living.
   d. The group should be the medium for each child's _____ .
   e. Adult acceptance, caring, sensitivity of individual needs, and enrichment of group life provides a sense of _____ for all of the children in the group.
2. List four requirements of healthy group living.
   a. _____ b. _____
   c. _____ d. _____

3. Define: Group cohesiveness _____

            Group process _____

4. List the three stages of discussion (or therapy) groups.

        _____

        _____

        _____

5. Complete the following:

    a. The first session of a group meeting should define

       _____ and establish _____

    b. Lack of participation or disruptive behavior during the first meeting may be due to feelings of _____ among the children.

    c. Expression of resistance by group members is inevitable, and the worker should be aware of its various manifestations. This includes _____

      _____ , _____ , _____ , _____ .

    d. _____ by everyone should be encouraged by the group leader.

6. Indicate whether you agree or disagree with the following:

    a. It is very important for a worker to be aware of the friendship pattern in his group.

                       Agree _____   Disagree _____

    b. The informal peer culture, consisting of status relationships, peer leadership, and peer group mores and practices, can be disregarded in group care.

                       Agree _____   Disagree _____

    c. It is risky for a child care workers to turn over authority to the natural leaders in their groups.

                       Agree _____   Disagree _____

    d. Group punishment should not be undertaken lightly; it may backfire or not give the desired results.

                       Agree _____   Disagree _____

    e. Peer courts or kangaroo courts should be encouraged because they are objective.

                       Agree _____   Disagree _____

RELATIONSHIP WITH PARENTS

Discussion Topics

1. "During visits to children, parents may behave in a way which is indicative that they have problems with separating from their children." If you agree with this statement, relate some of your experiences in this respect.

2. Have you been faced with severe problematic behavior on the part of parents, and how did you handle it.

3. What are the most difficult behaviors for you to cope with in terms of parents?

4. Are there any limits placed upon you as a child care worker to talk freely with parents? If so, how do you feel about it?

5. What are the purposes of home visiting by children?

6. Do you find that home visits in general are constructive? In what ways may they be destructive to children? Explain, using examples.

7. What kind of problems, if any, do you have following children's return from home visits?

8. Should the worker be involved in the separation process from his family and community by being introduced to the family before the child's admission? Should he or jointly with his parent(s) bring the child from his home to the residence?

9. How actively should the child care worker be involved with the child's family?

10. What role should he play in helping the child negotiate his relationship with his parents?

11. Should the worker be active in facilitating the child's reintegration into family and community during the discharge process?

Practice Review Exercises

Indicate whether you agree or disagree:

1. There has been a tendency to isolate children from parents after placement.

Agree _____   Disagree _____

2. Parents' feelings about placement should not be given consideration since they don't have significance in the child's treatment.

Agree _____   Disagree _____

3. Children in group care tend to romanticize their families and therefore don't see them objectively.

Agree _____   Disagree _____

4. During visiting hours, parents should be made to feel welcome by child care workers.

Agree _____   Disagree _____

STAFF RELATIONSHIPS

Discussion Topics

1. What are some of the problems in working together as a child care team? (Include orienting new workers, consistency of approaches to the children, sharing responsibilities, working through differences, and so forth.)

2. What are the essential elements in a good working relationship between two child care workers who work together? How can such a relationship be developed and sustained?

3. How do you view your status as a member of the residential treatment team? Do you feel comfortable in expressing your point of view to the "professional" membership? Do you have any criticism on the way the interdisciplinary team functions?

4. The instructor might suggest to trainess a role-playing exercise, demonstrating a typical (to their experience) interdisciplinary meeting on a child. Volunteers are to reenact the roles of psychiatrist, psychologist, caseworker, educator, child care worker, and administrative supervisor. The rest of the group observes the interaction within the team, especially the input by the child care workers and the reaction of the more professional staff to the child care worker's contributions.

5. Should child care workers develop and present to the interdisciplinary treatment conference a *child care treatment plan* for each child in their group? Elaborate on the process involved.

6. Should a cottage treatment plan for the group as a whole be developed? What is involved?

7. What should a child care worker expect of his supervisor?

8. What would be the most difficult kind of experience for you to share with your supervisor? Why?

9. What do you expect to contribute to or to learn from conferences with your supervisor?

Practice Review Exercises

Complete the following sentences:

1. _____ in approach among the child care workers team is essential.

2. Ongoing staff _____ is most in group care.

3. Without a sense of _____ and _____ it is unlikely that supervision will be effective.

4. Treatment planning must include _____ objectives, _____ objectives, and _____ to deal with problem behavior.

5. Successful team work requires staff _____ , _____ , _____ , _____ , _____ .

6. Planning for a group living unit should be based on children's _____ , _____ , _____ , _____ .

COMMUNITY RELATIONSHIPS

Discussion Topics

1. Why is it important (for child care workers) to maintain good relationships with immediate neighbors, local schools, recreation facilities, police and so on, in the immediate community?

2. As a group home worker, what problems do you find most difficult to cope with? Discuss this in relation to the child, residents, administrative supports, staff coverage, management of the house, neighbors, leisure time activities, and visits by the resident's family and friends.

3. You have received a telephone call from a security officer of a local department store that one of the residents has been apprehended for stealing a pair of gloves:

    a. What action, if any, should you take to have the youngster returned to the home?

    b. Should you plan to talk with him in private about this matter? What issues would you discuss?

    c. Should you and your coworker also convene a group meeting to discuss the implications of this incident? What issues would you cover during the session?

Role Play

1. Ask for two volunteers to enact the above conference between worker and child. After 10 minutes of role play, ask the rest of the group to react to the role play.

2. Suggest that the group re-enact the above meeting. Two volunteers are to act as the child care workers who initiate and lead the discussion; with the rest of the group to play the role of the children.

Practice Review Exercises

1. Explain why the responsibilities of the community based group home child care worker are more complex than that of the worker in a large congregate institution or residential treatment center.
2. What special skills are required to manage a group home?

PROGRAM EVALUATION

Discussion Questions

1. Why is an ongoing evaluation of program advisable?
2. How would you feel about a comprehensive evaluation of your cottage (or group home)?
3. Which aspects of group living are most important to evaluate periodically?
4. Why is staff continuity and stability important in group child care settings?
5. What do you consider the major reasons for the high staff turnover among child care workers?
6. What working conditions do you consider to be the major contributions to staff burn-out among child care workers? How could they be minimized or avoided?

Practice Review Exercises

Utilizing the suggested nine areas of study in evaluating the child care component of group child care programs, namely, the quality of child care, adult leadership, degree of consistency, relationships, expectations, quality of group life, recording, team work and staff stability, review your particular group living unit.

Write an evaluation statement indicating to what extent *you feel* the suggested criteria delineated in the text are or are not satisfied. What suggestions do you have for improvement, if any?

APPENDIXES

ANSWERS TO PRACTICE REVIEW EXERCISES

CHILD DEVELOPMENT

1. Physical care, affection, a sense of belonging, adult guidance, and a sense of achievement.

2. 1 — Trust vs. Mistrust (0 – first year); 2 — Autonomy vs. Shame (2nd year); 3 — Initiative vs. Guilt (3 – 5 years); 3 — Industry vs. Authority (6 – 11 years); 5 — Identity vs. Identity Diffusion (12 – 18 years).

3. Sexual identity, vocational choice, and dependence versus independence from parents.

4. *a* — True; *b* — True; *c* — True; *d* — False; *f* — True; *g* — True.

5. *a, d, e, f.*

6. Lack of wholesome family environment; insecurity in forming close and significant relationships with others; hostile (or at least ambivalent) attitudes toward authority; educational disadvantage; delinquent-oriented values.

CONCEPTS

1. *a* and *c.*

2. *a* — False; *b* — True; *c* — True.

3. 1 — *Authoritarian*: dictatorial, gives orders, expects unquestioned obedience.

2—*Laissez-faire*: lack of direction, minimal control.

3—*Democratic*: encourages participation, respect for the individual, cooperation stressed.

4. *a*—Agree; *b*—Agree; *c*—Disagree; *d*—Agree; *e*—Agree; *f*—Agree.

5. *Identification*: The individual strives to pattern himself after a person or persons significant in his life by patterning his characteristics, beliefs, and values.

6. Identification.

7. Physical security is assured for everyone; no one should be abused. Emotional security and atmosphere of acceptance, caring, and respect. Social responsibility.

8. Agree.

9. *a.*

10. Cooperation and collective effort.

11. *a* and *b*.

12. *b* and *c*.

13. *b, c, d, f, g, h, j, k, l.*

14. If the information turns out to involve a risk to life and safety of the child or other persons, or destruction of property, preventive action is essential.

15. *Discipline* may be defined as the degree of established order to facilitate group living.

   Punishment is as action (by adults) to influence (children's) behavior or long-range development by exposing them to unpleasant consequences.

16. To assure ordered living which is essential for the safety, sense of security, and constructive group environment.

17. *a*—False; *b*—False; *c*—True; *d*—True; *e*—True; *f*—False; *g*—False; *h*—False; *i*—False.

18. (1)—It should not be delayed but meted out as soon as possible after the offense.

   (2)—It should not be excessive.

   (3)—The disciplinary action should not be motivated by anger or administered with a sense of hostility toward the child.

19. *a, c, g.*

20. *c* and *d.*

21. *b.*

22. *b.*

23. *c.*

24. *c* and *d.*

THE CHILD CARE WORKER'S TASKS

Waking

1. *b.*

2. *a, b.*

3. *c, d, e.*

4. *a*—Agree; *b*—Agree; *c*—Disagree; *d*—Agree.

Mealtime

1.—Agree; 2.—Disagree; 3.—Agree; 4.—Disagree; 5.—Agree; 6.—Disagree; 7.—Disagree; 8.—Disagree; 9.—Agree; 10.—Disagree.

Education, Work, and Play

1. Gets children ready for school, keeps informed about child's educational progress and behavior in class, help with homework, expresses a positive attitude toward learning.

2. *a*—Agree; *b*—Disagree; *c*—Disagree; *d*—Disagree; *e*—Agree; *f*—Disagree; *g*—Disagree; *h*—Disagree.

3. *b, c, d.*

4. Helps child develop skills in activities and sports, helps him learn to be a cooperative member of a team, strengthens relationship with child because they are doing enjoyable, fun things together.

5. *a*—Disagree; *b*—Agree; *c*—Disagree; *d*—Agree; *e*—Disagree; *f*—Disagree.

Clothing and Grooming; Spending Money

1. Emotional.

2. Social.

3. *a*—Disagree; *b*—Agree; *c*—Agree; *d*—Agree; *e*—Disagree.

4. *a*—Agree; *b*—Disagree; *c*—Agree; *d*—Agree; *e*—Agree; *f*—Agree.

5. To buy friendship; to flaunt their affluence; to buy excessive amounts of candy or drugs, alcohol, and so on; to help finance children who plan on running away.

Bedtime

1. Try to postpone going to bed; cause trouble such as refusing or delaying their shower, or getting into fights or arguments; showing their anxiety in ways that are evident.

2. Remind children in advance to slow down on play activities or T.V.-viewing; get them to shower or put out clothing for the next day; reading to the younger children; tuck them into bed.

PROBLEMATIC BEHAVIOR

Temper Tantrum

1. A temper *tantrum* is characterized by severe, irrational, explosive, uncontrollable behavior which is preceded by a period of tension and restlessness. A temper *outburst* is characterized by extremely angry behavior which may or may not be irrational and is generally of short duration.

2. *a*—True; *b*—False; *c*—True; *d*—True; *e*—True; *f*—True.

Bedwetting and Soiling

a—False; *b*—False; *c*—True; *d*—False.

Lying

a—True; *b*—False; *c*—False; *d*—False.

Stealing

a—True; *b*—True; *c*—False; *d*—True; *e*—True.

Runaways

a—True; *b*—False; *c*—True.

1. Homesickness; disturbing news from home; group conflicts; threat of punishment; peer influence; conflict with staff.

Sexual Behavior

1. *a.* Masturbation, profane language, sexual perversions, homosexuality, heterosexuality.

   b. Experiment.

   c. Because it is not adequate proof of homosexuality.

2. *c, e, f.*

3. *a*—Disagree; *b*—Disagree; *c*—Agree; *d*—Agree; *e*—Agree; *f*—Agree; *g*—Agree.

4. *a*—(2) and (3).

   b—(1).

   c—(1) and (4).

   d—(1).

   e—(1), (2), and (3).

   f—(2).

   g—(3).

   h—(3).

   i—(1) and (2).

   j—(2).

THE RELATIONSHIP NETWORK

Relationship with Individual Children

1. *a.* Relationship.

   b. Distrustful.

   c. Non- _____ , _____ awareness, positive _____ .

   d. displaced _____ , manipulation.

2. *a.* Communication.

2. *b.* Direction (or demands, requests).

2. *c.* Model.

3. *a. Active listening* involves listening to a child's presentation of his problem or what concerns him in a way that that makes him feel the adult is interested, cares, and will help him or support him in working out his own solution.

b. *Self-awareness* implies the capacity to be aware of one's feelings, in relation to one's actions, to other people's actions, and to perceive objectively how one is viewed by others.

c. *Ambivalence* is the coexistence of opposite emotions, attitudes, or wishes toward the same person or situation.

d. *Transference* is the unconscious transfer to others of feelings and attitudes originally associated with significant persons (parents, siblings) in one's early life.

e. *Countertransference* means, in the case of a worker, that he reacts to the child's actions with a degree of anxiety which determines the child's counter-reaction. This will be subjective based on a linkage of the child with a significant person in the worker's earlier life experiences. The reaction is generally emotional; it may be a positive as well as a negative response.

4. The no-lose method of resolving relationship conflicts assures that both parties (adult and youngster) will strive to work out a solsution satisfactory to both of them. No one will lose, both will win, because each other's needs were respected and met.

5. *b, c, d, e, f.*

6. *b, c, d, e, f.*

Relationship Within the Group

1. a. Adjustment.

   b. Group.

   c. Individualize.

   d. Growth (and development).

   e. Cohesiveness.

2. (1) — Open and free communications among the members of the group including staff.

   (2) — Balance between individual and group needs.

   (3) — Children's involvement in planning and decision-making.

   (4) — A sense of group cohesiveness.

3. *Group cohesiveness* is characterized by respect for the individual, a sense of wellbeing about membership in the group, motivation to work together, and a sense of "we-ness." *Group process* is the ongoing character of the interpersonal relationships.

4. Stages of orientation, conflict, and development of cohesiveness.

5. *a.* Objectives _____ ground rules.

    b. Anxiety.

    c. Expression of verbal hostility; diversionary acts such as "horsing around," arguing, causing interruptions, attempts to dominate the group discussion, making demands.

    d. Participation.

6. *a* — Agree; *b* — Disagree; *c* — Agree; *d* — Agree; *e* — Disagree.

Relationship With Parents

1 — Agree; 2 — Disagree; 3. — Agree; 4. — Agree; 5. — Agree.

Staff Relationship

1. Consistency.

2. Communication.

3. Security _____ trust.

4. Long-term _____ , short-term _____ , strategies.

5. Commitment to common goals, consistency of approach, mutual respect, ongoing communication.

6. Needs, developmental level, capabilities, degree of involvement in achieving established goals.

OUTLINE FOR A CHILD CARE SUPERVISION WORKSHOP

This addendum for child care supervisors is a supplement to the section on Child Care Supervision, Part I, which acquaints workers with the supervisory process. It suggests an in-service training format[a] for child care supervisors in the form of a workshop whose objectives are:

1. To serve as a forum for sharing ideas, experiences, and insights regarding supervision of child care staff;
2. To identify basic principles of supervisory practice and to become acquainted with more effective supervisory practice methods.
3. To examine problems confronting supervisors and methods for resolving them.

This addendum does not include either the content of the child care worker's job or the educational methodology, since those subjects comprise this book. It outlines the content of the workshop as follows.

1. OBJECTIVES OF CHILD CARE SUPERVISION

a. What are the basic objectives of supervision, which involves teaching, monitoring, and evaluation?
b. What is the supervisor's role, his tasks, and the responsibilities he has in achieving these objectives?

a. This format was tested during the fall of 1980 at the Jewish Child Care Association of New York. Workshops were led jointly by the author and a group care division director.

2. COMPONENTS OF SUPERVISION

What, if any, are the issues and problems in carrying out the responsibilities related to the administrative, educational, and supportive components of supervision? For example:

a. In the *administrative* component, the tasks include scheduling work assignments, communication and interpretation of agency policy, monitoring of workers' performance, and evaluation.

b. *Educationally*, in the teaching role, what content should be emphasized? What skills taught? Goals? Service plan formulated?

c. The *supportive* component includes advocacy, enabling role, support in dealing with difficult problems and crises.

3. LEADERSHIP AND MOTIVATION

a. How does one get workers to perform at an optimum level? (How do you get workers to work with a sense of commitment?)

b. How does one develop and sustain a sense of cohesiveness among staff? How does one enhance a *consistency* with children, among staff as a whole, among workers who are on different shifts, and on-call workers?

4. MECHANISMS OF SUPERVISION

a. Individual supervisory conference.

(1)—What content should be covered in a supervisory conference?

(2)—What is the ambiance of the conference—frequency and regularity, privacy, protection from interruptions?

(3)—Should workers be expected to submit an agenda prior to the conference? What is supervisor's responsibility in preparing for a conference?

(4)—What supervisory techniques do you find most useful? Which would you want to develop more fully?

b. Group supervision.

(1)—What are the advantages and disadvantages of group supervision? If used, should it be a substitute for individual supervision? How can individual and group supervision serve to enhance a worker's functioning?

c. Peer supervision.

(1)—Should we encourage peer supervision for instance, (by use of senior worker in a leadership role)?

d. Demonstration (in cottage, on floor, or group home).

5. EXPECTATIONS AND VALUES

To what extent should a supervisor make clear to his workers:

a. Agency and his own expectations (of them) related to job performance?

b. Agency values they are required to support and uphold (for example, in relation to substance abuse, sexual behavior (on the job), corporal punishment, and so forth?

c. How do we help workers resolve conflicting values (one's own versus the agency's)?

d. How does the supervisor deal with his own values that may conflict with agency policy and procedures?

6. CRISIS SITUATIONS

a. To what extent should the supervisor involve himself in child-worker conflict situations? Child care team conflicts? Interdisciplinary team conflicts?

b. To what extent should he take over disciplinary action from the workers?

7. DELEGATION OF RESPONSIBILITIES

a. Is it feasible to delegate certain supervisory responsibilities to the more experienced workers in the unit? For example, accountability? Feedback? What others?

b. What, if anything, prevents this from taking place?

8. SELF-AWARENESS

a. Developing self-awareness on part of supervisor in relation to his supervisees.

b. Helping individual workers develop self-awareness regarding their attitudes and reactions to their supervisor, colleagues, and children.

a. A sense of empathy for the child care worker's role is important. How should one go about getting this?

b. Are there risks to one's supervisory role in a personal ("buddy-buddy") relationship?

c. A supervisor is frequently confronted with supervisees who present serious problems to the supervisor, colleagues, and children. They may include irresponsibility, provocation, hostility, destructiveness (to children), resistance to learning, and so on. How do you deal with this? How do you cope with the frustration and anger evoked by such a supervisee?

d. Visualize a situation where a supervisor dislikes a worker. Can he supervise that worker effectively?

9. ROLE OF SUPERVISOR IN THE HIRING-AND-FIRING PROCESS

a. What do you look for in interviewing applicants?

b. What are the frustrations in the process of terminating an unsatisfactory worker?

c. What are the steps in terminating a worker?

10. INTEGRATION

a. What problems do you face in relation to the functioning of the inter-disciplinary team?

b. Are treatment goals, service plans, and strategies developed *with* or *for* child care staff?

c. How do you deal with frustrations stemming from interdisciplinary planning and evaluation?

d. How do you help your workers deal with these frustrations?

11. WORKER EVALUATION

a. Evaluation is viewed as an ongoing process—from hiring to termination. In the written evaluation, what should be included?

b. What difficulties, if any, do you experience when evaluating a "problem" worker?

c. What are the dilemmas facing a supervisor when evaluating the unsatisfactory performance of a worker who, for years, had been given positive evaluations by previous supervisors or no evaluations past the probationary evaluation?

12. UNMET NEEDS

What do you consider your unmet needs as a supervisor?

13. OTHER TOPICS

What other topics or items not covered above do you want discussed?

14. EVALUATION OF THIS WORKSHOP

a. Has the workshop been of value?

b. What topics were most pertinent?

c. What were not of interest to you?

d. What is your evaluation of the style of leadership?

e. The methods of presentation?

f. The quality of participation?

g. What changes would you suggest?

RECOMMENDED BIBLIOGRAPHY

Adler, J. 1976. *The Child Care Worker: Concepts, Tasks and Relationships.* New York: Brunner–Mazel.

Aichorn, A. 1934. *Wayward Youth.* New York: Viking Press.

Allerhand, M.; R. Weber; and M. Haug. 1966. *Adaptation and Adaptability.* New York: Child Welfare League of America.

Alt, H. 1960. *Residential Treatment for the Disturbed Child.* New York: International Universities Press.

American Association for Children's Residential Centers. 1972. *From Chaos to Order: A Collective View of the Residential Treatment of Children.* New York: Child Welfare League of America.

Beker, J.; P.M. Gitleson; P. Kaminstein; and L. Finkel-Adler. 1972. *Critical Incidents in Child Care, A Case Book.* New York: Behavioral Publications.

Bettelheim, B. 1974. *A Home for the Heart.* New York: Knopf.

_____ . 1950. *Love is Not Enough.* Glencoe, Ill.: Free Press.

_____ . 1955. *Truants from Life.* Glencoe, Ill.: Free Press.

Billingsley, A. 1968. *Black Families in White America.* Englewood Cliffs, N.J.: Prentice-Hall.

Birnbach, D. 1971. "The Skill of Child Care." In *The Practice of Group Work,* edited by W. Schwartz and S.R. Zalba. New York: Columbia University Press.

Burmeister, E. 1967. *Tough Times and Tender Moments in Child Care.* New York: Columbia University Press.

_____ . 1960. *The Professional House Parent.* New York: Columbia University Press.

Burns, C. E. 1971. "White Staff, Black Children: Is There a Problem?" *Child Welfare* 50, no. 2: 90–96.

D'Amato, G. 1969. *Residential Treatment for Child Mental Health.* Springfield, Ill.: Charles C. Thomas.

Dinnage, R., and Pringle, M. L. K. 1967. *Residential Child Care: Facts and Fallacies.* London: Longmans.

Erikson, E. H. 1963. *Childhood and Society.* New York: Norton.

Foster, G. W., R. Vanderven, Karen, Dahlberg, Kroner, Eleanor R., N. T. Carbonara; and G. M. Cohen. 1972. *Child Care Work with Emotionally Disturbed Children.* Pittsburgh: University of Pittsburgh Press.

Goldfarb, W.; I. Mintz; and C. W. Stroock. 1969. *A Time to Heal; Corrective Socialization; A Treatment Approach to Childhood Schizophrenia.* New York: International Universities Press.

Hylton, L. F. 1964. *The Residential Treatment Center.* New York: Child Welfare League of America.

Krueger, M. A. 1978. *Intervention Techniques for Child Care Workers.* Milwaukee, Wisc.: Franklin Publishing.

Linton, T. E. 1969. "The European Educateur Program for Disturbed Children." *American Journal of Orthopsychiatry* 39, no. 1: 125–133.

Mayer, F., and A. Blum, eds. 1971. *Healing Through Living.* Springfield, Ill.: Charles C. Thomas.

Mayer, M. F. 1958. *A Guide for Child Care Workers.* New York: Child Welfare League of America.

Mayer, F. M.; L. H. Richman; and E. H. Balcerzak. 1977. *Group Care of Children.* New York: Child Welfare League of America.

Minuchin, S.; B. Montalvo; B. G. Guerney, Jr.; B. Rosman; and F. Schumer. 1967. *Families of the Slums.* New York: Basic Books.

Polsky, H. 1962. *Cottage Six: The Social System of Delinquent Boys in Residential Treatment.* New Tork: Russell Sage Foundation.

Polsky, H., and D. Claster. 1968. *The Dynamics of Residential Treatment: A Social System Analysis.* Chapel Hill: University of North Carolina Press.

Redl, F., and D. Wineman. 1967. *The Aggressive Child.* Glencoe, Ill.: Free Press.

Toigo, A. 1972. "The Dynamics of the Residential Institution: A System Theory Approach." *Child Care Quarterly* 1, no. 3: 252–263.

Treischman, A. E., and J. K. Whittaker. 1972. *Children Away From Home.* Chicago: Aldine.

Treischman, A. E.; J. K. Whittaker; and L. K. Brendtro. 1969. *The Other 23 Hours.* Chicago: Aldine.

Whittaker, J. K. 1979. *Caring for Troubled Children.* San Francisco: Jossey-Bass.

INDEX

ABOUT THE AUTHOR

Dr. Jack Adler, social worker and educator, is currently Director of Staff Training, Jewish Child Care Association of New York and Adjunct Assistant Professor, Columbia University School of Social Work. Most of Dr. Adler's long career in social work in this country and in Europe has been spent in group child care service—as caseworker, child care worker, psychotherapist, supervisor, administrator and educator. He has taught social work and child care courses at Columbia, Hunter, New York University and New York State University, StonyBrook, Schools of Social Work. He has published extensively including "The Child Care Worker: Concepts, Tasks and Relationships." A sculptor by avocation, he has exhibited widely.